UNLOCKING
ISAIAH

OTHER BOOKS AND AUDIO BOOKS

BY REG CHRISTENSEN

Fear Not: Messages of Hope, Healing, and

Peace in the Book of Revelation

UNLOCKING
ISAIAH

LESSONS AND INSIGHTS THAT
DRAW US TO THE SAVIOR

REG CHRISTENSEN

Covenant Communications, Inc.

Without Any Ire by Nancy Glazier-Koehler © Intellectual Reserve, Inc. Courtesy of the Museum of Church History and Art.

Cover design copyright © 2013 by Covenant Communications, Inc.

Published by Covenant Communications, Inc.
American Fork, Utah

Printed in the United States of America
First Printing: October 2013

19 18 17 16 15 14 13   10 9 8 7 6 5 4 3 2 1

ISBN 978-1-62108-502-7

CONTENTS

PREFACE

My target audience for this book is those of the general Church populace who have likely always known that Isaiah is an important book but have perhaps felt somewhat intimidated by it. I hope and pray that this book will be a pleasant introduction to a lifetime study of Isaiah. I invite you to lay aside your fears, open your scriptures, pray for personal revelation, and enjoy your journey through Isaiah's sublime testimony of our Savior. Let his poetry and symbolism speak personally to your heart.

The children of Israel at the time of Isaiah were being threatened and oppressed by Assyria. Domination from Babylon would follow. Their temptation was to join with their idolatrous neighboring nations for protection. Isaiah's resounding charge to them was to trust Jehovah and He would protect them.

We of modern Israel face our own challenges, fight our own battles, and are threatened by enemies perhaps even more treacherous and subtle, in many ways, than the Assyrians. Yet, our "liken unto us" charge is the same: trust Jehovah. President Howard W. Hunter taught, "Please remember this one thing. If our lives and our faith are centered upon Jesus Christ and his restored gospel, nothing can ever go permanently wrong. On the other hand, if our lives are not centered on the Savior and his teachings, no other success can ever be permanently right."[1]

Our Heavenly Father delights in providing the opportunity of eternal life for His children. A scriptural statement of His mission is, "For behold, this is my work and my glory—to bring to pass the immortality and eternal life of man" (Moses 1:39). Our Savior delights in carrying out the will and plan of the Father, and He completed His perfect Atonement in accordance with this plan. Of His own mission, Jesus said, "I can of mine own self do nothing: as I hear, I judge: and my judgment is just; because

I seek not mine own will, but the will of the Father which hath sent me" (John 5:30). As we center our faith and trust in our Savior, we gain proper direction and assistance in our progress toward eternal life.

The writings of Isaiah inspire us to trust our Savior, who said, "Yea, a commandment I give unto you that ye search these things diligently; for great are the words of Isaiah. For surely he spake as touching all things concerning my people which are of the house of Israel" (3 Ne. 23:1–2).[2]

With that background, I offer three main areas of focus that further explain my intent and desire for this book as we come to understand Isaiah. **Come to the Temple—Imagery and Inspiration:** As we come to the temple, we come to Christ. The doctrines and ordinances of the temple point us to Christ and His Atonement. The writing of this book was, in part, prompted by an invitation I received to give some presentations on the theme "What Isaiah teaches us about the temple." As I prepared and presented this topic, I was edified by the opportunity to consider the temple and the purpose thereof as I studied Isaiah. I desire to share some of my thoughts with you in this book.

Let me offer two concepts that guide me in my sharing: temple imagery and temple inspiration. By *temple imagery*, I refer to the specific aspects of temple worship offered by Isaiah. I will highlight and comment on some of these great teachings. By *temple inspiration*, I refer to insights I personally see in the scripture when I read with the perspective of seeking truths related to the temple. I will also share some of these inspirations throughout the book. I believe the doctrine of temple worship is one of the important themes of Isaiah's message. Through temple worship, we more fully learn to trust Jehovah.

The Scholarship of "Liken unto Us": I lay no claim to being a great scholar. I am grateful for the many scholars of the Church and of the world in general. I here recognize two of many sources that have been particularly helpful to me: *Understanding Isaiah*, by Parry, Parry, and Peterson,[3] and *Isaiah: Prophet, Seer, and Poet*, by Victor L. Ludlow.[4] Their dedicated and inspired works have helped me in my understanding.

However, I will lay claim to what I will call the scholarship of "liken unto us." Early in my teaching career, I was inspired by the approach Nephi offered for understanding the writings of Isaiah. He said, "And I did read many things unto them which were written in the books of Moses; but that I might more fully persuade them to believe in the Lord their Redeemer I did read unto them that which was written by the prophet Isaiah; for I did liken all scriptures unto us, that it might be for our profit and learning" (1 Ne. 19:23).

My writing is not intended to be a focused exposition of every verse and teaching of Isaiah—there are helpful commentaries, such as those mentioned above, that do this. My desire is to share insights I've gained from studying Isaiah and how these insights relate to my time and place in the world, with the hope that you will be inspired in your faith by what I say. My writing will be replete with personal applications, anecdotes, and thoughts I've had as I've considered the teachings and truths of Isaiah. These "liken unto us" examples have helped me better visualize and understand the scriptures. I encourage you to do the same—as you consider my illustrations, please think of personal experiences that will help you better understand and relate to the book of Isaiah.

Isaiah in the Book of Mormon and the Context of Isaiah—The House of Israel: I recommend that you take a little time at or near the beginning of your study of this book to read some of the brief comments I share in "Isaiah in the Book of Mormon" and "The Context of Isaiah—The House of Israel." These are found, respectively, in Appendix A and Appendix B. I feel that this information is critical to a proper understanding of the vision and prophecy of Isaiah.

The words of Isaiah have enhanced and strengthened my testimony throughout the years. My simple hope and prayer is that they will do the same for you. I am confident that they will. If my words herein help to enhance your understanding of Isaiah and your testimony of our Savior, my objective will have been met, and I will be grateful.

Sincerely,
Reg Christensen

CHAPTER ONE
WHITE AS SNOW

THE CHILDREN OF ISRAEL OF Isaiah's time were in serious need of repentance—of recommitting to gospel principles.

"But Israel Doth Not Know"

As the book of Isaiah begins, the children of Israel are spiritually sick. Of them the Lord said, "I have nourished and brought up children, and they have rebelled against me. The ox knoweth his owner, and the ass his master's crib: but Israel doth not know, my people doth not consider" (Isa.1:2–3). The Lord, the Bread of Life, had nourished Israel spiritually with truth and physically with manna, but they rejected Him and were now a "sinful nation, a people laden with iniquity, a seed of evildoers, children that are corrupters: they have forsaken the LORD, they have provoked the Holy One of Israel unto anger, they are gone away backward" (Isa. 1:4).[5]

Oxen and asses are domesticated animals, dependent upon the care and keeping of their owners for daily protection and sustenance. If they wander in the wilderness from the watchful care of the master, they put themselves at risk of both attack and destruction from predators. When the attacks come, the ox or the ass may panic and attempt to scurry to safety, but the lion or bear has the advantage in the wild. The only safe haven is at the home manger or crib, where the master can tenderly fold them into his care and keep diligent watch over them. They know and recognize their master and instinctively return to his presence.

Satan tries to get us to go "backward" from the gospel path and away from the protection of our Master. Satan does not have the potential for eternal life and wants to keep this gift from those who do have such potential. He attempts to get us lost in the wilderness of sin.

The Israelite sickness is further described: "The whole head is sick, and the whole heart faint. From the sole of the foot even unto the head there is no soundness in it; but wounds, and bruises, and putrifying sores: they have not been closed, neither bound up, neither mollified with ointment" (Isa.1:5–6).

This analogy of painful sores was strengthened for me on a family vacation with our small children. The morning of our departure, I stepped off the garage step and onto the head of a large finish nail left sticking in a board by one of our sons. I applied ointment and a bandage, and off we went. The first day my foot was fine, the second uncomfortable, the next painful, and the next agonizing, requiring the care of a doctor. He probed the wound and found that the head of the nail had acted as a punch, embedding a piece of shoe leather into my foot. He removed the offending particle, dressed the wound, and it quickly healed. In my denial, I had hoped that I could mostly ignore my condition and that it would get better without intervention.

Israel was sick in the *head* and in the *heart*, symbolizing complete intellectual and spiritual corruption. They were not seeking proper healing but were trying to mask their wounds with the hope that all would be fine. They were thus on a course of destruction. Technically, I could have lived without my foot, but no one lives without head and heart. Israel's only hope of salvation, of healing head and heart, was to seek proper healing by removing the offenses, cleansing the wounds, and then covering them with ointment. They had to apply the healing power of the Atonement.

Another result of Israel's unattended sickness was that they were to be "left as a cottage in a vineyard, as a lodge in a garden of cucumbers, as a besieged city" (Isa.1:8). To eliminate time-consuming travel from home to orchard or vineyard and in order to protect maturing crops from theft or destruction by man or animal, growers would often construct makeshift shelters or "cottages" in the fields where they could stay and watch over the crops night and day until the time of harvest. These shelters covered them and gave them protection from wind, sun, and rain. After the harvest, these temporary shelters were abandoned, left to the elements, and soon deteriorated and collapsed to the point of uselessness. Israel, because of rebellion and hard-heartedness, was becoming as spiritually desolate as an abandoned cottage.

The Hebrew meaning of the word *atonement* is "to cover." Christ desires to shelter us and cover us with His Atonement. To modern Israel, the Lord said, "For behold, I will gather them as a hen gathereth her chickens under her wings, if they will not harden their hearts" (D&C 10:65). If we are humble and submissive, we are fully *covered* by our Savior. If we become rebellious and hard-hearted, we are left *uncovered* from the full power of the Atonement. As consequence for their rebellion, Israel was to be left "as an oak whose leaf fadeth, and as a garden that hath no water" (Isa.1:30). They had refused to trust Jehovah and were thus left to their own corrupt means and methods, which were not working for them.

We as modern Israel may take counsel from these teachings and ask ourselves some searching questions. Do we ever slacken our trust in Jehovah and attempt to live life on our own terms without His guidance? Does the motive of our service ever spring more from social pressure to look good than from a genuine love of the Lord and of His children and from a desire to serve as He would have us serve? Are we seeking to do His will? Or, will He someday ask of us, "When ye come to appear before me, who hath required this at your hand, to tread my courts?" (Isa. 1:12). We are always blessed in seeking to learn how Isaiah's words may teach us and help us deepen our reverence and worship of our Savior and how they ensure us that we are on His errand and not our own.

Cease to Do Evil

What was to be done with rebellious Israel? What are we, of modern Israel, to do? Was it too late for them? Had they gone so far backward that they could no longer go forward? Satan would have them, and many of us, believe such. The Lord beckoned them to return to the true path just as He constantly does with us. The Lord now, through His prophet Isaiah, charts this true path to eternal life and invites His children to follow this path. This path of faith and repentance applies in every dispensation. The language may differ, but the principles are consistent:

Faith: We need to recognize, with gratitude, the Lord's tender admonitions to us. We need to receive of His nourishment and trust in His ability to save us. We need to have faith and trust in Him and not in the arm of flesh. We need to recognize Him as our "owner," as He who purchased us with His blood. We need to follow the counsel the Lord gives to all of His creations: "Hear, O heavens, and give ear, O earth" (Isa. 1:2).

Repentance: We are to humble ourselves and, when necessary, change our direction. We need to go forward in the gospel path and not go "away backward" down dark and strange paths. We are to do whatever is necessary to have our sins remitted by the Lord, changed from scarlet to white. We are to apply the healing balm of our Savior's Atonement: "Put away the evil of your doings from before mine eyes; cease to do evil;

Learn to do well; seek judgment, relieve the oppressed, judge the fatherless, plead for the widow. Come now, and let us reason together, saith the Lord: though your sins be as scarlet, they shall be as white as snow; though they be red like crimson, they shall be as wool. If ye be willing and obedient, ye shall eat the good of the land (Isa. 1:16–19).

Baptism: We must be washed and be made clean through baptism. "Wash you, make you clean" (Isa. 1:16).

Holy Ghost: We strive to "hear the word of the Lord . . . give ear unto the law of our God" (Isa. 1:10).

In making and renewing our baptismal covenants and in participating in the ordinances of the temple, we are set free from the evils and stains of our fallen world. Consider the privilege of receiving baptismal and temple-recommend interviews. Through the guidance of an official priesthood leader, our cleanliness and worthiness are certified. If there is some cleaning and polishing to do, our leaders help us make the needed changes. If there are or have been evils, our spiritual shepherd helps us "cease to do evil" so that we may prepare to receive sacred ordinances. Just as a literal shepherd might groom and cleanse the wool of his sheep, our spiritual shepherds guide us to the Atonement of the Good Shepherd so that our "crimson" deeds may be cleansed through Him and become white "as wool."

In the making and keeping of our baptismal and temple covenants, we "learn to do well." We are taught the great plan of happiness and, through covenants, have our heads and hearts turned from selfishness to selflessness. Our heads are enlightened with pure revelation as to how we can best do as the Lord would have us do. Our hearts are turned to all who suffer and struggle that we might help relieve their burdens and to our fathers in the spirit of Elijah that we may join with them in eternal glory. As we are thus converted, our fallen character is transformed to one of caring for "the oppressed, the fatherless, and the widow." We learn to control our passions and keep them in proper control as the Lord directs. Through the making and keeping of our baptismal and temple covenants, we learn how to live *in* the fallen world and yet not be *of* the fallen world.

White as Snow

In my younger days, I was privileged to enjoy the pristine beauty of the earth in the magnificent mountains near my home. Wintertime was especially inspiring on those occasions when I was deep in the woods with no other person or manmade structure anywhere near. In such a quiet, peaceful, heavenly place, I experienced the beauty of God's creation in one of the most natural and untainted settings on earth. The beauty of the pure white snow, so gently blanketing the forest floor and so beautifully decorating the trees, was awe-inspiring.

Figuratively, our Savior would have us transcend the smog and corruption of the mortal, fallen valley and "come . . . up to the mountain of the Lord" (Isa. 2:3). The path up this mountain is a path of repentance and of His cleansing our crimson sins through the power of His perfect Atonement.

Crimson or red dye is a colorfast dye—it cannot be removed easily, if at all. We learned this firsthand as our young son poured a bottle of red food coloring in the center of our new carpet. All of our attempts to remove the stain did not work. Although we masked it somewhat by our cleaning efforts, we could not absolutely remove it and return it to its pure and natural state. Satan would have us believe our sins are likewise permanent.

Of course, this is false. Through the cleansing power of the Atonement, our stained and fallen lives can be purified and made absolutely clean and natural as pure wool. As we come unto Christ and accept His Atonement, He promises, "And I will turn my hand upon thee, and purely purge away thy dross" (Isa.1:25). He takes us by the hand and leads us through this cleansing process from a darkened world into the light and glory of His kingdom.

White is symbolic of purity and victory. Many aspects of the saving ordinances of the gospel, such as the wearing of white baptismal and temple clothing, remind us of purity and victory over the stain of sin. If we are repentant and humble, our Savior will grant us victory—He will make our stained, fallen, and sinful lives as white as snow!

CHAPTER TWO
THE MOUNTAIN OF THE LORD'S HOUSE

Mountains, in and out of the gospel context, brim with significance and symbolism. Why would one go up a mountain? Some people climb high mountains to push the boundaries of human achievement and gain victory in overcoming tremendous obstacles. Others go there to strive for communion with the divine, perhaps feeling that reaching the top of the highest mountain represents a close connection between heaven and earth. Often, people climb from a desire to test their personal stamina and to challenge their survival skills.

In the scriptures, the Lord's holy purposes are often associated with mountains. Satan's wicked purposes are symbolized by counterfeit mountains in opposition to the Lord's purposes. In Old Testament times, some attempted construction of a "mountain," the Tower of Babel, "whose top may reach unto heaven" (Gen. 11:4) in an attempt to preserve their status and society by the power of their own hands, thus disregarding the plan and purpose of God. The righteous separate themselves from the wicked and "go up to the mountain of the Lord" (Isa. 2:3) while the wicked, "for fear of the Lord," seek protection in mountains of "ragged rocks" (Isa. 2:21).

Isaiah is pleading with his people to come down from the high places and groves of their false worship. He begs them to abandon the artificial great and spacious mountains of man's creation. He invites them to come up to the holy temple, which is full of tremendous potential for both spiritual and physical blessings.

The Mountain of the Lord's House

Isaiah "saw concerning Judah and Jerusalem. And it shall come to pass in the last days, that the mountain of the Lord's house shall be established in the top of the mountains, and shall be exalted above the hills; and all nations shall flow unto it" (Isa. 2:1–2). The mountain of the Lord's house refers to His temple. We often associate Isaiah's house in the mountains with Utah and, specifically, the Salt Lake Temple. The root of *Utah* is a Ute Indian word meaning "hill dwellers."[6] From the perspective of my Utah upbringing, I would describe the Salt Lake Temple as being in the valley, not in the mountains. Yet from my current home in the Midwest or for those who dwell, for example, in Jerusalem, a journey to Utah is definitely a trip "up" to the mountains.

When Church leaders produced the classic film on the construction of the Salt Lake Temple, they appropriately drew from the imagery of Isaiah and entitled it *The Mountain of the Lord*. President Hinckley expanded the imagery of the Lord's mountain when he explained that the Church's new Conference Center in Salt Lake fulfills Isaiah's prophecy of the mountain of the Lord and how "out of Zion shall go forth the law" (Isa. 2:3).[7] From Church headquarters in Salt Lake City, leaders administer the Church and send forth their words. At general conference time, members from all nations flow into Utah to be taught of God's ways. The truth and intent of such teaching is not lessened for those who symbolically go up to the mountain via television, satellite, or Internet communication, or who worship in temples other than the one in Salt Lake.

As we read and ponder the writings of Isaiah, it is helpful to remember that he, like all true prophets, was revealed a portion of God's eternal view of things: a panorama of past, present, and future, all in eternal perspective. Isaiah does not confine his prophecy strictly to a specific dispensation in a particular statement but often blends past, present, and future in an all-encompassing eternal view. Thus, the Salt Lake Temple as the mountain of the Lord's house is a true image as it depicts the day of the early gathering to the Salt Lake Valley, but the mountain of the Lord's house in our current global Church context includes *all* temples throughout the earth. Although temples are often constructed on an elevated topography, such is not required for it to be the mountain of the Lord's house. The temple my wife and I are assigned to, for example, stands majestic, serene, and beautiful in the flatland of Chicago amidst the bustle of a community with not a mountain in sight.

While an elevated temple on a majestic hill or mountainside may beautifully symbolize its purpose, we cannot confuse the symbolic physical proximity to heaven with the more important spiritual communion with God. In the temple, we participate in connecting the purposes of heaven with the purpose of our mortal earth life "to bring to pass the immortality and eternal life of man" (Moses 1:39). As we worthily attend the temple, we are worshipping at the very highest spiritual summit available to man on earth. Through our temple endowment, we are able to more fully view the purpose of our earthly lives as connected with our premortal and postmortal heavenly lives. President Brigham Young taught, "Your endowment is, to receive all those ordinances in the house of the Lord, which are necessary for you, after you have departed this life, to enable you to walk back to the presence of the Father. . . . and gain your eternal exaltation in spite of earth and hell."[8]

Through temple worship, we accept the Lord's invitation given by Isaiah: "O house of Jacob, come ye, and let us walk in the light of the Lord" (Isa. 2:5). As we walk in that light, we lose the desires and tendencies of the natural man for contention and evil. The covenants we make turn our hearts from pride and selfishness to feelings of compassion for our brothers and sisters throughout the world. We learn saving principles and begin to experience the joy of the type of life to be in the pending millennial day: "They shall beat their swords into plowshares, and their spears into pruninghooks: nation shall not lift up sword against nation, neither shall they learn war any more" (Isa. 2:4). This transformation will bring peace, joy, and happiness to all people who remain on the earth.

The Haughtiness of Men Shall Be Made Low

Our temples often face east. In Ezekiel's vision, Christ comes to His temple from the east. "And, behold, the glory of the God of Israel came from the way of the east. . . . And the glory of the Lord came into the house by the way of the gate whose prospect is toward the east" (Ezek. 43:2, 4).

The apostate Israelites looked to the east—not for the Lord but for false gods. They were "replenished from the east, and are soothsayers like the Philistines, and they please themselves in the children of strangers" (Isa. 2:6). True to Satan's constant counterfeiting of spiritual truth, he persuaded wicked Israel to look to the eastern superstition and false influence of witchcraft and sorcery. "In 2:5, the prophet Isaiah commands the house of Israel to 'walk in the light of the Lord,' which comes from the east. Yet the house of Israel attempted to be spiritually revitalized (*replenished*) through apostate, spurious sources from the east (such as the deities and religious systems of the heathen countries), which constituted mockery unto God."[9] The lure of these false gods was material gain and glitter: "Their land is full of silver and gold; . . . they worship the work of their own hands, that which their own fingers have made" (Isa. 2:7–8).

This idolatry manifests itself in many forms in our modern society. Sometimes successful entertainers become obsessed with their image to the point that they go to great expense to strut their fame and wealth to fans that shower them with phony accolades. Some athletes are so drawn in to the pressure to succeed that they succumb to illegal performance-enhancing drugs. Sometimes their fame tempts them into a world of immoral behaviors. Business executives, if not cautious and alert, are often subtly lured along perceived success tracks that take them into the depths of dishonesty and greed.

Universal pride is manifested in those who foolishly seek expensive toys and trophies in a vain attempt to proclaim their superior social status to their neighbors. Satan attempts to persuade people at all economic levels to misuse the God-given resources of the earth for their own pride and self-gratification. In a sense, Satan lures mankind to construct "mountains" of perceived success, be it a mountain of fame, fashion, or fortune. These false and hollow mountains offer no lasting protection or status.

Of the fate of these mountains of the adversary, Isaiah speaks: "The lofty looks of man shall be humbled, and the haughtiness of men shall be bowed down, and the Lord alone shall be exalted in that day . . . And upon all the high mountains, and upon all the hills that are lifted up. . . . the haughtiness of men shall be made low" (Isa. 2:11, 14, 17). Of the fate of false mountains, John the Revelator said, "And every mountain and island were moved out of their places. . . . and the kings of the earth, and the great men. . . . said to the mountains and rocks, Fall on us, and hide us from the face of him that sitteth on the throne, and from the wrath of the Lamb" (Rev. 6:14–16).

At the time of this writing, we are observing a wave of revolution in the Middle East as the citizens of nation after nation are rising up in protest against long-entrenched despots and dictators who have held their citizens in oppressive strangleholds for decades. These tyrants have robbed and plundered their people and have used their ill-gotten mountains of wealth to construct palaces and portfolios for their own presumed protection and self-gratification.

Of course we cannot now predict the specific short-term outcomes of these current events, but the great mountains of wealth so long accumulated and jealously guarded by these wicked rulers are now being— or will someday be—abandoned or wrenched from them as prophesied by Isaiah: "In that day a man shall cast his idols of silver, and his idols of gold, which they made each one for himself to worship, to the moles and to the bats" (Isa. 2:20). This is most appropriate imagery as moles and bats live in darkness and receive no value from the shining glitter of gold—thus all that the wicked thought so precious will become as nothing.

Cease Ye from Man

Isaiah now proclaims his oft-repeated counsel to ancient and modern Israel: "Cease ye from man, whose breath is in his nostrils: for wherein is he to be accounted of?" (Isa. 2:22). Moses was a personal witness to manmade wealth and power in the courts of Egypt. After receiving a great vision of eternity, he proclaimed the same truth taught by Isaiah: "Now, for this cause I know that man is nothing, which thing I never supposed" (Moses 1:10). These are not statements of worthlessness but of humility in the presence of God. Our current power and might pale in comparison to the might, majesty, and power of God, whose desire is to give us all that He has.

To obtain this power, the Lord invites us to come up to His holy mountain—the temple. As we follow this path to the serenity, peace, and beauty of the Lord's house, the wicked in their fear and trembling "go into the clefts of the rocks, and into the tops of the ragged rocks, for fear of the Lord, and for the glory of his majesty, when he ariseth to shake terribly the earth" (Isa. 2:21). They seek to hide from the Lord and His judgments.

Those who choose to seek to make their residence in the Lord's house and kingdom do not live in darkness and fear but rather rejoice in the peace and joy of His holy light.

CHAPTER THREE
THE STAY AND THE STAFF

In chapter 3, we see that the children of Judah persist in putting their trust in the perceived genius of man, "whose breath is in his nostrils" (Isa. 2:22). They are in rebellion and thus in danger of famine and other chastisement. "For, behold, the Lord, the Lord of hosts, doth take away from Jerusalem and from Judah the stay and the staff, the whole stay of bread, and the whole stay of water" (Isa. 3:1).

Stay and *staff* translate from Hebrew words essentially meaning "supply" and "support," and the taking away of such has reference to spiritual and physical famine and destruction. If we do not trust Jehovah, He withholds the full bounty of stay and staff. Those who abandon Christ and His gospel lose His full supply and support, are blinded by the allure of Babylon, and are left to walk forbidden paths of darkness.

Amos, a contemporary of Isaiah, taught, "Behold, the days come, saith the Lord God, that I will send a famine in the land, not a famine of bread, nor a thirst for water, but of hearing the words of the Lord" (Amos 8:11). Such spiritual famine results when we reject Christ and refuse to partake of His life-giving doctrine.

To the Righteous, It Shall Be Well

Isaiah proclaimed, as prophets do in all ages, the principles of stable families and societies. But proud Judah felt they had found a better way as they lusted after their own designs and abandoned the blessings, protection, and guiding inspiration of the Lord. As a result, the respected leaders of their society were to go missing—literally and spiritually—to Babylon: "The mighty man, and the man of war, the judge, and the prophet, and the prudent, and the ancient, The captain of fifty, and the honorable man, and the counsellor, and the cunning artificer, and the eloquent orator" (Isa. 3:2–3). In their place, the younger generation would inherit the burden of leadership without the blessing of righteous role models. "And I will give children to be their princes, and babes shall rule over them. . . . The child shall behave himself proudly against the ancient, and the base against the honourable" (Isa. 3:4–5).

The baseness of our modern world in the form of things like absentee fathers, the rampant sex scandals among elected leaders, and the many forms of bribery and corruption eerily connects us to ancient Israel. When people follow their own lusts and abandon their appointed leadership roles of comforting, empowering, and nourishing those they lead, the consequences of physical and spiritual poverty for families and societies are bitter. "What mean ye that ye beat my people to pieces, and grind the faces of the poor? saith the Lord God of hosts" (Isa. 3:15). The Lord desires to bless us with physical and spiritual abundance. Satan's motive and desire is our spiritual and physical starvation.

In their day of trouble and want, Judah would seek sustenance and not find it—even from their own families. "When a man shall take hold of his brother of the house of his father, saying, Thou hast clothing, be thou our ruler, and let this ruin be under thy hand: In that day shall he swear, saying, I will not be an healer; for in my house is neither bread nor clothing: make me not a ruler of the people" (Isa. 3:6–7). Thus "Jerusalem is ruined, and Judah is fallen: because their tongue and their doings are against the Lord, to provoke the eyes of his glory" (Isa. 3:8).

In his beautiful poetic style, Isaiah offers a correct assessment of the covenant people's misuse of agency and reminds them of the promised blessings of repentance and righteousness: "Woe unto their soul! for they have rewarded evil unto themselves. Say ye to the righteous, that it shall be well with him: for they shall eat the fruit of their doings. Woe unto the wicked! it shall be ill with him: for the reward of his hands shall be given him" (Isa. 3:9–11). Wicked Judah was shirking their family and societal duties. Their children lacked direction and discipline and became "their oppressors" (Isa. 3:12).

In prophetic proclamation, our modern prophets offer us the gospel truth of our family responsibilities: Both husbands and wives are responsible for loving and caring for one another and their children. God has given parents the sacred duty to raise their children in an evironment of love and righteousness. Parents must also provide for their children's physical and spiritual needs, teach them the importance of lovign and serving others, give them a foundation for keeping the commandments fo the Lord, and show them the way to be law-abiding citizens in whatever country they may live in. If parents do not do these things, they will be held accountable before God for these obligations.

Heavenly Father has set forth a pattern, wherein fathers have the duty to lovingly and righteously preside over their families. It is their duty to make sure their families have the necessities of life and that their families are protected at all times. Likewise, mothers must fulfill the duty of nurturing and teaching their children. Together, mothers and fathers must be equal partners in strengthening and building their family unit. [10]

The Daughters of Zion

As an example of how far Israel had fallen, Isaiah now offers a vivid description of their abandoned morals using the example of their women, or "daughters of Zion." He is not singling out women as the only ones with the problem; he is simply demonstrating the seriousness of the plight of the men and women of Israel by using the troubles of the women as his illustration.

I gained some insight of this principle when, as a young soldier on a large military base, I was assigned guard duty at the barracks of the Women's Army Corps (WAC). For sometime thereafter, I commented that the worst language I had ever heard in my life was when I guarded the WAC barracks. Now, in retrospect and with a more mature view, I acknowledge that the WAC language was no different from that of the men in the regular army. My culture and upbringing had simply conditioned me to expect better from women. I could conclude, as perhaps Isaiah did, that when the women get this bad, we know that all of society has a serious problem.

In specific description of the apostate conditions, the Lord proclaimed through Isaiah that the women were "haughty," or vain. They were walking in darkness of sin with "stretched forth necks and wanton eyes, walking and mincing as they go," meaning that they were "walking with short, rapid steps in an affected manner." They wore "changeable suits of apparel" and "glasses, and fine linen, and the hoods and the veils," interpreted as "resplendent garments" and "transparent garments" (Isa. 3:16–23; footnotes).

As consequence of the apostasy of the sons and daughters of Zion, the Lord was to "smite with a scab the crown of the head . . . and discover their secret parts." This meant He would allow the punishment of their actions to fall upon them and "expose: . . . put them to shame." He would "take away the bravery of their tinkling ornaments about their feet," and "instead of sweet smell there [would] be stink . . . instead of well set hair baldness . . . and burning instead of beauty," or "branding (a mark of slavery)" (Isa. 3:17–24; footnotes).

In summary of their plight, because the children of Israel had abandoned the "stay and the staff," or the supply and support of the full power of the gospel in their lives, the Lord removed their spiritual blessings and allowed them the consequence of their own pride. By so doing, they had thus left themselves uncovered from the full protective covering of the Lord's power. They would wander on their own into a fallen and precarious condition.

CHAPTER FOUR
A COVERT FROM STORM

A SIMPLE DEFINITION OF ETERNAL life comes at the conclusion of the longest verse in scripture. After the Lord describes the "new and everlasting covenant" and sealing by the "Holy Spirit of promise," He declares that those who are worthy go "to their exaltation and glory in all things, as hath been sealed upon their heads, which glory shall be a fulness and a continuation of the seeds forever and ever" (D&C 132:19). *Seeds* means children and family. Eternal life is eternal family.

Without the inspired guidance of our living prophets, those who, for no fault or lack of desire of their own, do not marry and have families in this life may be prone to despair and discouragement. Gratefully, our prophets connect our fallen mortal world with the millennial day and the eternities and declare that any perceived loss of blessings from this life will be granted to the faithful in the next life. All worthy people, now or in the future day, come under the glorious promise of the Lord: God's divinely designed plan of happiness makes it possible for family units to continue together after death. In the temple, God's children can perform sacred ordinances that allow them to return to Him and for families to be united forever.[11]

Take Away Our Reproach

The "daughters of Zion," representative of apostate Judah and Jerusalem, are to regret their rebelliousness. The beginning verse of chapter 4—"And her gates shall lament and mourn; and she being desolate shall sit upon the ground" (Isa. 3:26)—would actually be a better fit as the last verse of chapter 3. In fact, it is so arranged in the Hebrew Bible. In their lament, Judah and Jerusalem cry out and proclaim the cause of their sorrow—that they had placed their potential of eternal family at risk. "And in that day seven women shall take hold of one man, saying, We will eat our own bread, and wear our own apparel: only let us be called by thy name, to take away our reproach" (Isa. 4:1).

Reproach by definition means barrenness or lack of posterity and has been the heartache of many throughout history. The sorrow of Sarah and Abraham until the birth of Isaac was that "Sarai was barren; she had no child" (Gen. 11:30). Rachel suffered the same until the birth of Joseph, when she joyously proclaimed, "God hath taken away my reproach" (Gen. 30:23).

The power of procreation, the potential for motherhood and fatherhood now and throughout eternity, is essential to our Heavenly Father's plan for our happiness. It is thus no surprise that Satan, who will never be a father and will never have eternal life, exerts so much influence on the world to try to get people to misuse this sacred procreative power.

Our prophets today have given us a solemn proclamation, warning us that anyone who violates their covenants of chastity, abuse their spouse or offspring, or do not fulfill family responsibilities will be held accountable before God. The prophets also warn that the weakening or failing of the family until will be extremely detrimental to individuals, communities, and nations.[12]

The reproach or barrenness of not having opportunity for marriage or posterity in mortal life, contrary to the despair and doubt caused by Satan, *will* be taken away by the Lord in His due time through His tender mercy and with no loss of blessing or happiness. The reproach or barrenness resulting from sin and rebellion may be taken away by the Lord through the power of His atoning sacrifice to those who will choose to follow the course of humility and repentance. If their repentance is full and complete, they too will experience no loss of blessing or happiness.

In response to a sincere plea of "take away our reproach," the Lord offers the hope of a brighter day "when the Lord shall have washed away the filth of the daughters of Zion, and shall have purged the blood of Jerusalem from the midst thereof by the spirit of judgment, and by the spirit of burning" (Isa. 4:1, 4). During the Millennium, those who have heeded the Lord's beckoning and repented of their sins will remain on the earth, after wickedness has been cleansed from it. This washing and purging is possible through the sweet miracle of the Atonement. This hope of a brighter day and this path of repentance lead God's children toward eternal life where their loved ones may be sealed to them forever.

Shall Be Called Holy

All of God's children who choose to walk this path of humility and repentance shall be called "holy" by the Lord. "And it shall come to pass, that he that is left in Zion, and he that remaineth in Jerusalem, shall be called holy, even every one that is written among the living in Jerusalem" (Isa. 4:3). The word *holy* in Hebrew translation connects to the word *temple*. "The Hebrew term translated as 'holy' has the root meaning of 'temple.' Isaiah is saying, in essence, that those who 'remain in Jerusalem shall be called a temple people,' presumably because they worship in the temple. The group becomes *holy* because of the cleansing/purging process identified by Isaiah as the 'spirit of judgment' and the 'spirit of burning' (4:4). Also, God is called Holy One (41:14; 1 Jn. 2:20); in the last days, those in Zion will be like God in their holiness."[13] When the Lord thus refers to a holy nation or people, He is referring to a temple-worthy people who live and serve in gospel light.

Our prophets and apostles throughout time have taught the doctrine of a holy people as in this declaration of Peter to the New Testament Saints: "But ye are a chosen generation, a royal priesthood, an holy nation, a peculiar people; that ye should shew forth the praises of him who hath called you out of darkness into his marvellous light" (1 Pet. 2:9).

A Cloud by Day and a Fire by Night

As we walk in gospel light and keep our baptismal and temple covenants, we receive the daily protective guidance of the Lord in our homes and families. The Lord would have us prepare our homes to be sacred abodes patterned after the temple. Just as the dark and degrading influences of our fallen world are kept at bay when we enter the holy temple, the same should be with our homes and our personal lives. If we are willing, the Lord will help us: "And the Lord will create upon every dwelling place of mount Zion, and upon her assemblies, a cloud and smoke by day, and the shining of a flaming fire by night: for upon all the glory shall be a defence" (Isa. 4:5).

The Hebrew word translated "defence" means "canopy" or "protective covering."[14] Those who abandon sacred covenants are left uncovered. In the temple, we receive the ordinances and covenants that bring the *covering* of the Atonement into the full protective force in our lives. In the temple in our day, we don protective, sacred clothing that reminds us daily of the covenants we have made. As we go about our lives doing our best to keep our promises to the Lord, He promises us the protective covering spoken of by Joseph Smith in the dedication of a holy temple: "And we ask thee, Holy Father, that thy servants may go forth from this house armed with thy power, and that thy name may be upon them, and thy glory be round about them, and thine angels have charge over them" (D&C 109:22).

I considered the protective covering of the temple years ago when our children were small and we would return to our home after the activities of the day. We often had a clear and prolonged view of our temple on the horizon. In the daylight, the dominant feature seemed to be the main body of the temple standing like white and billowing clouds against the backdrop of majestic mountains and blue sky. In the darkness, the tall spire with its golden illumination was the focus of my attention. When I saw it I often thought of the ancient tabernacle: "And on the day that the tabernacle was reared up the cloud covered the tabernacle, namely, the tent of the testimony: and at even there was upon the tabernacle as it were the appearance of fire, until the morning. So it was alway: the cloud covered it by day, and the appearance of fire by night" (Num. 9:15–16).

Often, my soul was filled with peace from the knowledge that the protective care of the Lord is always upon His children as "a cloud and smoke by day, and the shining of a flaming fire by night" (Isa. 4:5). At the end of our family's daily journey, we would arrive home hopeful that we could keep the world at bay and bring the spirit of the temple into our home, that it might be "a tabernacle for a shadow in the daytime from the heat, and for a place of refuge, and for a covert from storm and from rain" (Isa. 4:6).

During these years, my wife once had an insightful dream. As she stood at our back door, she witnessed a horrifying circle of vicious demons surrounding our home, gnashing and clawing to gain entrance. After a time of apprehension and terror, she realized that the demons were being held at bay from doing us harm. The message was clear that if we would stand firm in the holiness of our home and the temple, Satan could not harm us. We were reminded in sweet assurance of the protective "covert from storm" the temple offers. In speaking of the temple, Joseph Smith declared "that no combination of wickedness shall have power to rise up and prevail over thy people upon whom thy name shall be put in this house" (D&C 109:26).

CHAPTER FIVE
AN ENSIGN TO THE NATIONS

THE LORD SEEKS TO LOVINGLY gather and guide His children to the gospel path. The prophet Hosea tenderly teaches how the Lord seeks to reclaim apostate Israel. "Therefore, behold, I will allure her . . . and speak comfortably unto her. . . . And it shall be at that day, saith the Lord, that thou shalt call me Ishi; and shalt call me no more Baali." *Ishi* translates as "my husband," and *Baali* as "my master" (Hosea 2:14, 16, footnotes). The Lord, in the ongoing marriage metaphor, is not a stern master but a tender husband who nurtures, protects, and strengthens his bride.

Isaiah, in the same spirit as Hosea, now presents a parable to remind us that the Lord, in His tender love and compassion for His children, will simply not let go of them no matter how far they wander. True, because of their agency He lets them stray for a while—as with the Assyrian and Babylonian captivities of Israel—but He stands ready to bring them back to His love and nurturing. The relationship of the Bridegroom to His bride is a love story of highest devotion.

To My Wellbeloved

Drawing from the same imagery as the prophet Zenos's allegory of the olive tree, Isaiah proclaims, "Now will I sing to my wellbeloved a song of my beloved touching his vineyard. My wellbeloved hath a vineyard in a very fruitful hill" (Isa. 5:1). Israel, the Lord's vineyard, had every opportunity to produce good fruit with their secure fence of stones, "the choicest vine," a fine winepress, and even a watchtower for protection, but "it brought forth wild grapes" (Isa. 5:2).

The Lord cries out the lament of any worthy husband of a dishonorable spouse or of a righteous parent of wandering children: "What could have been done more to my vineyard, that I have not done in it?" (Isa. 5:4). The rebellious child might acknowledge, "Oh, you did all you could do, and you need not do more. Just leave me alone!" But such response would ring hollow with the Lord, who knows there is yet more that He must and will do to reclaim His wayward children. In His divine love for them and with His eternal perspective of what they can become, He chastens and allows them the tutoring trial of experiencing the ill effects of their poor choices. He will "take away the hedge thereof . . . and break down the wall" and allow "briers and thorns" to afflict them and "also command the clouds that they rain no rain upon it" (Isa. 5:5–6).

If they persist in wandering on strange paths in lieu of walking in the light of the "strait and narrow path which leads to eternal life" (2 Ne. 31:18), then wander on strange paths they must until they arrive at the weigh station of sorrow, mourning, and humility. When they do arrive at this juncture, the Lord will be there with His arms open, ready to guide them, as with an ensign,[15] back to the strait and narrow path.

Iniquity with Cords of Vanity

The road of the rebellious is a thorny path that yields inequality for individuals, families, and communities, especially where money is concerned. "Woe unto them that join house to house, that lay field to field, till there be no place, that they may be placed alone in the midst of the earth!" (Isa. 5:8). The sinful and rebellious create a society of greed, where the wealthy usurp the lands of the poor and where all who are greedy seek temporal gain at the expense of others.

As people seek out their idol gods of wealth and power, these false gods soon cloud over their testimonies and knowledge of the only true God. "They regard not the work of the Lord, neither consider the operation of his hands" (Isa. 5:12). These idol gods do not save but enslave: "Therefore my people are gone into captivity, because they have no knowledge: and their honourable men are famished, and their multitude dried up with thirst" (Isa. 5:13). The wicked chart for themselves a crash course to destruction where "hell hath enlarged herself, and opened her mouth without measure: and their glory, and their multitude, and their pomp, and he that rejoiceth, shall descend into it." Then hell achieves its purpose with them: "And the mean man shall be brought down, and the mighty man shall be humbled, and the eyes of the lofty shall be humbled" (Isa. 5:14–15).

The devil uses the universal pride and vanity of people to bring them under oppression. Satan is as subtle as a snake—he "whispereth in their ears, until he grasps them with his awful chains, from whence there is no deliverance" (2 Ne. 28:22). If not watchful, we may find ourselves bound to an awful burden we did not intend and do not desire.

I have often related an analogy from my youth to being bound with unwanted burdens. My father and I worked to install an underground, pressurized sprinkler irrigation system throughout the hills and valleys of our small farm. We buried a mainline pipe from the top to the bottom of the property and then connected portable aluminum sprinkler pipes to this mainline. We constructed a long wagon to use in moving the sprinkler pipes from field to field and had the bright idea that we would use our horse to pull this wagon to lessen the damage to the crops caused from the heavy tires of our tractor. All was fine for a few days as we test drove the horse and empty wagon. We did not anticipate what effect the loading of the actual pipes onto the wagon would have on our horse.

All went well as we loaded the first set of pipes and moved forward. On the second move, one of the wagon wheels bounced over a rock, causing the pipes to clang together with an awful sound. I still feel empathy for our poor horse, and in my mind's eye I can see it running in terror through the fields and trees as it was "chased" by what it must have thought to be a ferocious monster. As it ran between two trees and turned sharply, the hitch broke, freeing it from its burden of the pipe wagon. We eventually caught and calmed the horse. We repaired the wagon and installed a different hitch so we could use our tractor from that time forward.

Humans, unlike animals, possess moral agency. Horses, as with the oxen of Isaiah's day, do not choose to be bound to their burdens. As children of God, we can exercise moral agency, and although in our limited eternal perspective we may not desire the consequences of our poor choices, such consequences will be ours as make wrong choices. Sorrow is the sure reward of the rebellious who, in their vanity, chart paths of wickedness. Of the prideful, Isaiah said, "Woe unto them that draw iniquity with cords of vanity, and sin as it were with a cart rope" (Isa. 5:18). Just as our poor horse was bound to an unwanted burden, if we persist in sin, we bind ourselves with tightening cords that become ever more difficult to unloose.

Vanity, or selfish, unrighteous pride, is our universal burden. We all suffer from it to one degree or another. As we choose to follow a course of vanity, we wander from the course of peace and salvation and bring sorrow upon ourselves and others. The Lord warns:

> Woe unto them that call evil good, and good evil; that put darkness for light, and light for darkness; that put bitter for sweet, and sweet for bitter!

Woe unto them that are wise in their own eyes, and prudent in their own sight!

Woe unto them that are mighty to drink wine, and men of strength to mingle strong drink:

Which justify the wicked for reward, and take away the righteousness of the righteous from him!

Therefore as the fire devoureth the stubble, and the flame consumeth the chaff, so their root shall be as rottenness, and their blossom shall go up as dust: because they have cast away the law of the Lord of hosts, and despised the word of the Holy One of Israel. (Isa. 5:20–24)

In the Lord's divine love for us, He allows us to be buffeted by the consequences of our poor choices: "Therefore is the anger of the Lord kindled against his people, and he hath stretched forth his hand against them, and hath smitten them." But though He chastens us, "His hand is stretched out still" (Isa. 5:25). With that hand, He chastens as needed but also waves a banner of salvation to beckon us back into His fold: "And he will lift up an ensign to the nations from far, and will hiss unto them from the end of the earth: and, behold, they shall come with speed swiftly" (Isa. 5:26).

An Ensign to the Nations

The vanguard company of the Mormon pioneers, led by President Brigham Young, entered the Salt Lake Valley on Saturday, July 24, 1847. Before entering the valley, President Young had seen the Salt Lake Valley and the designated temple site in prophetic vision. In the vision, he saw an angel standing on a cone-shaped hill pointing to where the temple was to be built. On Sunday, the small pioneer company worshipped and kept the Sabbath. On Monday, July 26, President Young and other leaders climbed this conical hill overlooking the valley and, in a symbolic gesture of gathering Israel, waved a banner in fulfillment of Isaiah's prophecy.

From the hill known to us today as Ensign Peak, President Young viewed the valley and envisioned how the city was to be laid out and where the temple was to be built. Some days later, he thrust his cane into the ground and designated the specific site for the temple.

Sister Elaine Dalton, as Young Women general president of the Church, gave us additional understanding of the value and significance of the ensign to the nations. In April of 2008, she and her counselors held their first presidency meeting by hiking Ensign Peak and unfurling their own banner in a symbolic gesture of the need for a return to virtue. Of this experience, Sister Dalton said, "We hiked to the top of Ensign Peak, and as we looked on the valley below, we saw the temple with the angel Moroni shining in the sun. For each of us, it was clear. The vision of our presidency was the temple. . . . The temple is the reason for everything we do in the Church. The temple was the reason our pioneer ancestors left their established home and came west."[16] And of course, the reason for the temple is in fulfillment of God's desire to grant immortality and eternal life to His children. We gather to the temple to receive what we need to continue our course to eternal life, through the Atonement of Jesus Christ. As we gather to the temple, we gather to our Savior and to His purpose for us.

In likening Isaiah's message to our day, ancient Israel and we of modern Israel have gone astray to varying degrees. The Lord's chastening hand is over us to help us repent and return to Him. As we do so, that same hand remains stretched out to us to guide us to the temple. Many are accepting the beckoning call and are gathering in great numbers to the restored gospel and are receiving their saving ordinances in the holy temple.

Through the miracle of modern communication and transportation, our message goes forth to the world. Leaders and missionaries travel from place to place so "swiftly" that they do not even get "weary nor stumble," and they arrive at their destination hardly before the "girdle of their loins be loosed, nor the latchet of their shoes be broken." Modern planes and trains speed along with "wheels like a whirlwind," and young missionaries "roar like young lions" in their bold proclamation of gospel truth (Isa. 5:27–29).

To a spiritually darkened world bound to its sins as an ox to a cart, the gospel message roars "against them like the roaring of the sea" (Isa. 5:30). If we are willing to heed the message, accept the outstretched hand of the Lord, and answer favorably to His beckoning banner, He will manifest His power and blessing unto us. Through this power and blessing, we may enter the holy temple and receive the necessary ordinances to help us along our path to "eternal life, which gift is the greatest of all the gifts of God" (D&C 14:7).

CHAPTER SIX
CALLED TO SERVE

ISAIAH RECEIVED A TREMENDOUS CALLING from the Lord to teach and nurture rebellious Israel. He expressed his feelings of inadequacy with this expression: "Woe is me!" (Isa. 6:5).

Calls to serve in the Church are calls to learn and grow. Many years ago, I was called to serve as a counselor in a branch presidency and subsequently as a branch president at the Missionary Training Center in Provo, Utah. I felt inadequate and unqualified. My first experience in my calling was the weekly devotional where the twenty-five hundred or so missionaries sang their special hymn, "Called to Serve."[17] The spirit and power of this hymn and the individual and combined faith of the missionaries buoyed me up and helped inspire my courage to go forth in my calling.

Isaiah learned, as we all have opportunity to learn in our callings, that when the Lord calls someone to serve, He qualifies them for the service. This chapter is an inspiring account of the calling of Isaiah, the Lord's prophet.

His Train Filled the Temple

Isaiah probably received his call to serve in 740 B.C., "in the year that king Uzziah died." The Lord brings Isaiah, in vision, to His holy temple to issue to him his prophetic call. "I saw also the Lord sitting upon a throne, high and lifted up, and his train filled the temple" (Isa. 6:1).

The heavenly setting of Isaiah's call to serve is consistent with the spiritual pattern of ancient times. When Lehi was called, "he was carried away in a vision, even that he saw the heavens open, and he thought he saw God sitting upon his throne" (1 Ne. 1:8). John the Revelator records, "And immediately I was in the spirit: and, behold, a throne was set in heaven, and one sat on the throne" (Rev. 4:2).

If we are attentive to the accounts of the callings of our modern prophets and apostles, we learn that their charge and ordination is completed in the temple. In the sanctity of the Lord's house, He commissions them to take the gospel message to the world and, as special witnesses, to bear testimony of Him.[18]

What is meant by the prhase, the Lord's "train filled the temple"? *Train* as here used invokes the image of the part on a bridal gown that trails on the ground behind the bride. We may consider this symbolic of a train of people obediently following a worthy leader. The train of the Lord that filled the temple may also represent His brilliance and glory being spread throughout the earth. Those who accept the invitation to walk in His holy light put themselves in step as His true followers.

The "seraphims," or heavenly beings, mentioned in the second verse of this chapter express their joy in glorious praise: "Holy, holy, holy, is the Lord of hosts: the whole earth is full of his glory" (Isa. 6:2–3). To speak the word *holy* in triple repetition as they do is to emphasize the superlative or exceptional nature of the phrase. Why do these heavenly beings worship the Lord in superlative praise? It is because they have so much to be grateful for. They recognize Him as the divine Son of God and as the Savior of the world. They, like all true disciples, reverence His atoning sacrifice and accept and worship Him as the Father of their salvation, under the guiding hand of their Heavenly Father.

Thy Sin Is Purged

Isaiah's reaction to his call to serve was an expression of his feelings of unworthiness and inadequacy as he may have compared his own fallen and mortal life to the perfection of the Lord: "Then said I, Woe is me! For I am undone; because I am a man of unclean lips, and I dwell in the midst of a people of unclean lips: for mine eyes have seen the King, the Lord of hosts" (Isa. 6:5). What mortal man would not feel imperfect in the presence of a perfect being? Though the Lord invites and even commands us, "Be ye therefore perfect" (Matt. 5:48), the leaders He calls are not and, in fact, cannot be perfect until after devoted service in a fallen and imperfect world and continued growth and progress until the time of their resurrection when the Atonement takes full effect in their lives.

Since Isaiah speaks of the uncleanness of his lips, the Lord symbolically cleanses his lips with a burning coal, representing the cleansing by the power of the Holy Ghost: "Then flew one of the seraphims unto me, having a live coal in his hand, which he had taken with the tongs from off the altar: And he laid it upon my mouth, and said, Lo, this hath touched thy lips; and thine iniquity is taken away, and thy sin purged" (Isa. 6:6–7).

From Moroni we learn of those who had been baptized who "were wrought upon and cleansed by the power of the Holy Ghost" (Moro. 6:4).

As Isaiah's mouth and soul are cleansed by the Lord, he is now ready to be filled with the Lord's message of redemption to fallen Israel and Judah. The Lord endows his prophets with the necessary utterance to fulfill their appointed missions. To Enoch, who also felt woefully inadequate, the Lord said, "Go forth and do as I have commanded thee, and no man shall pierce thee. Open thy mouth, and it shall be filled, and I will give thee utterance, for all flesh is in my hands, and I will do as seemeth me good. Say unto this people: Choose ye this day, to serve the Lord God who made you" (Moses 6:32–33). In the tradition of Enoch and other prophets who have spoken the message of salvation to the world, Isaiah is now ready for his call to carry on.

Convert and Be Healed

Our Heavenly Father, in the premortal council, designated the Savior for His plan with the inquiry, "Whom shall I send?" Jesus answered the call: "Here am I, send me. And another answered and said: Here am I, send me. And the Lord said: I will send the first" (Abr. 3:27). Isaiah typified the Savior in his response to his call to serve: "Also I heard the voice of the Lord, saying, Whom shall I send, and who will go for us?" Isaiah, buoyed up and cleansed from his sins, replied, "Here am I; send me" (Isa. 6:8). The Lord then charged Isaiah to go forth and gave him an intimation of the difficult task ahead: "And he said: Go and tell this people—Hear ye indeed, but they understood not; and see ye indeed, but they perceived not" (2 Ne. 16:9).

Happily, the message of redemption and salvation is available to all the people of all the earth; sadly, not all will choose to accept these glorious truths. The message is pure, sweet, and simple, but there is a price to be paid in order to understand. It takes effort. Isaiah was told, "Make the heart of this people fat, and make their ears heavy, and shut their eyes; lest they see with their eyes, and hear with their ears, and understand with their heart and convert, and be healed" (Isa. 6:10). Of course the Lord wants all to "convert and be healed," but humility and righteous use of agency are requisite to understanding. The people Isaiah would teach had hardened their hearts and become deaf and blind to the word of the Lord. Isaiah was to speak in such a manner that would require them to pay the price of opening their eyes and ears that they might find truth.

Lord, How Long?

Now that Isaiah has received his calling, he desires to know the length of his mission. "Then said I, Lord, how long?" The Lord basically answers that he is to teach as long as there are people to teach: "Until the cities be wasted without inhabitant, and the houses without man, and the land be utterly desolate" (Isa. 6:11). This desolation ultimately occurred with the Babylonian captivity of Judah, over one hundred years after the end of Isaiah's forty-year term of service (about 700 B.C.). Essentially, Isaiah was to prophesy for the rest of his mortal lifetime.

Our modern prophets and apostles are called to lifetime service. Although we of the general membership of the Church are not given lifetime callings in the organizations of the Church, we *are* called to keep our covenants for a lifetime. As Alma baptized Helam, he taught, "Ye have entered into a covenant to serve him until you are dead as to the mortal body; and may the Spirit of the Lord be poured out upon you; and may he grant unto you eternal life, through the redemption of Christ, whom he has prepared from the foundation of the world" (Mosiah 18:13). We covenant with God to love and serve Him forever. As we covenant to serve the Lord forever, He promises us "forever," or eternal life, with Him in His kingdom.

CHAPTER SEVEN
IMMANUEL

THIS CHAPTER BEGINS WITH SOME rather confusing interactions between countries and peoples. Let us try to simplify it. The first line of the chapter heading explains: "Ephraim and Syria wage war against Judah" (Isa. 7). Remember that Isaiah's time was during that of a divided Israel. *Ephraim* refers to basically the ten northern tribes of Israel who were neighbors to Syria while *Judah*, also a tribe of the house of Israel, resided mostly in the south near Jerusalem. Isaiah lived in Jerusalem, or Judah, and prophesied to them. He was also the last great prophet to prophesy unto the entire house of Israel before the scattering of the ten northern tribes.

We now ask, why would Ephraim, the Northern Kingdom, fight against Judah, the Southern Kingdom? Assyria was the threatening menace of the time and by now had a reputation of brutality and plunder, having already conquered several nations. Ephraim and Syria united in an attempt to force Judah to join them in fighting against Assyria. It would not work. In fact, in not too many years, Assyria would conquer the northern tribes of Israel and carry them away into captivity. Assyria would then conquer much of Judah before a small remnant of Judah finally trusted the Lord and received His protection.

Fear Not These Smoking Firebrands

Any time people are faced with "wars and rumors of wars" and the world is "in commotion," it is natural that "men's hearts shall fail them" (D&C 45:26). When Judah, "the house of David," heard that Ephraim and Syria had conspired against them for refusing to join their coalition, their hearts failed them, causing them to shake with fear as a tree in the wind. "And his heart was moved, and the heart of his people, as the trees of the wood were moved with the wind" (Isa. 7:2).

As a fearful Ahaz, king of Judah, hid in the fuller's field, where the women gathered to wash their clothes, the Lord sent him a message of peace and assurance through Isaiah about the proposed alliance. "Take heed, and be quiet; fear not, neither be fainthearted for the two tails of these smoking firebrands [Ephraim and Syria]. . . . Thus saith the Lord God, It shall not stand, neither shall it come to pass. . . . and within threescore and five years shall Ephraim be broken, that it be not a people" (Isa. 7:4, 7–8). As the fearsome Assyrians continued their conquering march, the Lord, through Isaiah, petitioned Judah not to enter an alliance but to trust in Him. As mentioned, they eventually did put their trust in the Lord and received His promised protection.

God with Us

King Ahaz was a wicked king who would not welcome a message from the Lord—but he got one anyway. "Moreover the Lord spake again unto Ahaz, saying, Ask thee a sign of the Lord thy God; ask it either in the depth, or in the height above. But Ahaz said, I will not ask, neither will I tempt the Lord" (Isa. 7:10–12).

Regardless, the Lord communicated His great sign to Ahaz: "Behold, a virgin shall conceive, and bear a son, and shall call his name Immanuel. Butter and honey shall he eat, that he may know to refuse the evil, and choose the good. For before the child shall know to refuse the evil, and choose the good, the land that thou abhorest shall be forsaken of both her kings" (Isa. 7:14–16).

Isaiah often speaks in dualistic prophecy—dual meanings from one expression. The birth of Isaiah's own son (see Isaiah 8:3), along with the birth of the Savior, serves as an example of this dual meaning.[19] The birth of our Savior into mortality certainly meets the conditions of the prophecy. Mary met the conditions of being a virgin—she was completely chaste and, although not perfect, she was spiritually undefiled by the sins and pollutions of the world. Christ was born into humble circumstances, with "butter and honey," common foods of the humble people, being the staples of His diet. The clarification of our inspired chapter headings illuminates the meaning of this as Messianic prophesy: "Christ will be born of a virgin" (Isa. 7). The Gospel of Matthew also validates this interpretation of the prophecy: "Now all this was done, that it might be fulfilled which was spoken of the Lord by the prophet, saying, Behold, a virgin shall be with child, and shall bring forth a son, and they shall call his name Emmanuel, which being interpreted is, God with us" (Matt. 1:22–23).

In the midst of fear and threatening war, we thus have this wonderful and eternal reassuring promise of "God with us." As we liken this prophecy to our day and to our perspective of ancient Judah, we are assured that Jesus Christ, the divine Son of God, came and accomplished the Atonement. If Judah and Israel would make the Savior the central focus of their faith, in Him they would have protection from the Assyrians and from all enemies.

Where There Were a Thousand Vines

The Immanuel prophecy was lost on Israel for the present. As a result of their continuing rebellion, "the Lord shall hiss for the fly," meaning the Lord would allow or call for plagues and troubles to come upon them. He would "shave with a razor that is hired, namely, by them beyond the river, by the king of Assyria," meaning that Assyria would yet play a major role in the conquering and humiliation of rebellious Israel. The Lord allows the wicked to punish the wicked. The Assyrians would be the "razor" of His chastisement. So many people would be killed or taken that the few left could be sustained with minimal resources, even "that a man shall nourish a young cow, and two sheep" (Isa. 7:18, 20–21). As a result of their war and rebellion, their land would be left desolate, and "where there were a thousand vines at a thousand silverlings, it shall even be for briers and thorns" (Isa. 7:23). Steep is the price of rebellion.

CHAPTER EIGHT
THE WATERS OF SHILOAH

OUR SAVIOR IS *THE* MASTER Teacher. He often puts Himself into the imagery He teaches, as in the Bridegroom and "fountain of living waters" metaphors (Jer. 17:13). Through imagery of treasures and tombs, lost sheep and lilies, and seeds and sackcloth, He helps us visualize His gospel and personalize the principles thereof deep in our hearts.

In like manner, Isaiah is a master teacher. He instructs through imagery of cottages and cords, lambs and lions, and fire and famine. He uses his own name and the names of his sons to teach the scattering and gathering of Israel: "Behold, I and the children whom the Lord hath given me are for signs and for wonders in Israel" (Isa. 8:18).

For Signs and for Wonders

What are the signs and wonders of the names of Isaiah and his sons? Isaiah's wife conceived a son, and the Lord instructed him to "call his name Maher-shalal-hash-baz," which name means "to speed to the spoil, he hasteneth the prey" (Isa. 8:1, 3, footnote d). Israel is on a fast-track to destruction. Because of rebellion, they are soon to be *spoil* and *prey* of the Assyrians. "For before the child shall have knowledge to cry, My father, and my mother, the riches of Damascus and the spoil of Samaria shall be taken away before the king of Assyria" (8:4). Israel would be captured and then scattered.

The name of Isaiah's other son reminds us of the Lord's promise to gather Israel. "Shear-jashub" means "the remnant shall return" (See Isaiah 7:3, footnote a). Thus Isaiah's two sons remind us of two of the major themes of his ministry: the scattering and gathering of Israel.

The key to the gathering, or saving, of scattered Israel is taught by Isaiah's own name, which means "the Lord is salvation." Central to the ministry of Isaiah is his focus on Christ and His power to gather and save.

In this chapter, "Isaiah presents three images of Jesus Christ that have special meaning for us today—water, temple, and light. First, Jesus is as essential to our spiritual salvation as water is to our physical salvation. . . . Second, we will find peace and comfort in Jesus Christ if we permit him to be our temple (the focus of our worship). . . . Third, as we walk through mortality, which is like passing in the shadow or in darkness, we receive great hope, comfort, and joy when we accept Jesus as our 'great light'" (Isa. 9:2).[20]

The Waters of Shiloah

Isaiah warned, "Forasmuch as this people refuseth the waters of Shiloah that go softly. . . . Now therefore, behold, the Lord bringeth up upon them the waters of the river, strong and many, even the king of Assyria, and all his glory: and he shall come up over all his channels, and go over all his banks" (Isa. 8:6–7). All who reject the Savior's invitation receive the hard waters of His justice, as with the flood of destruction upon those who rejected Noah's warning or the destroying waters of the Red Sea upon the arrogant Egyptians. If Israel and Judah would not accept the soft waters of Christ's beckoning—His tender, gentle invitation to come unto Him—they would be punished by the hard waters—the heavy chastening hand—of His justice administered through the Assyrians. Specific to the warning and prophesy of Isaiah, those who would reject "the waters of Shiloah" would "be broken in pieces" (Isa. 8:9) by the Assyrians. Assyria, like an overflowing river, would surge destructively across the Northern Kingdom of Israel and also across the Southern Kingdom right up to Jerusalem, where it would at last be stopped.

Shiloah is a name for Christ. "*Waters of Shiloah*. . . . refers to Jesus Christ, who is the 'fountain of all righteousness' (Ether 12:28; 8:26; 1 Ne. 2:9) and 'the fountain of living waters' (Jer. 2:13; 17:13; Ps. 36:8–9). The image of waters is symbolic of Jesus because he cleanses the righteous who enter the waters of baptism; he also invites us to drink from the waters of salvation, which forever quench the thirst of those who partake."[21]

The imagery taught by the waters of Shiloah became etched in my mind many years ago through the experience I had of wading underground through the ancient tunnel constructed by King Hezekiah in about 701 B.C. to bring the life-giving waters of the Gihon spring in the Kidron valley from outside of the wall of Jerusalem into what was to later be known as the pool of Siloam on the inside of the city wall. It was an awe-inspiring experience for me to traverse something so ancient and so essential to the temporal salvation of Judah at this time of defense against the Assyrians. This water supply, despite the ebb and flow of the seasons, has remained constant throughout the centuries.

Interestingly, the name Siloam is the Greek transliteration of the Hebrew name Shiloah. It is instructive to associate the life-giving sustenance and healings of the waters of Siloam, or Shiloah, with Christ, the Waters of Shiloah. His love and mercy are constantly flowing in our lives. Just as water gave life and security to besieged Jerusalem, Christ gives life and security to all of God's children through all ages. To the man born blind, the Savior said, "Go, wash in the pool of Siloam, (which is by interpretation, Sent.) He went his way therefore, and washed, and came seeing" (John 9:7). As physical blindness was cured at the waters of Siloam, spiritual blindness may be cured at the waters of Shiloah, or through Christ, the Source and Giver of living water.

At the time of Isaiah, the water here mentioned from Gihon was the main source of water for Jerusalem. We are reminded in the Book of Mormon that Christ, or Shiloah, is the only source of our salvation: "And now, behold, my beloved brethren, this is the way; and there is none other way nor name given under heaven whereby man can be saved in the kingdom of God" (2 Ne. 31:21).

With gratitude, we recognize the ever-flowing and life-giving sustenance of our Savior. As He taught the woman of Samaria, "But whosoever drinketh of the water that I shall give him shall never thirst; but the water that I shall give him shall be in him a well of water springing up into everlasting life" (John 4:14).

He Shall Be for a Sanctuary

Continuing the protective theme of the great Immanuel prophecy of the previous chapter, Isaiah reminds Israel that "God is with us." "And he shall pass through Judah; he shall overflow and go over, he shall reach even to the neck; and the stretching out of his wings shall fill the breadth of thy land, O Immanuel. Associate yourselves, O ye people, and ye shall be broken in pieces; and give ear, all ye of far countries: gird yourselves, and ye shall be broken in pieces; gird yourselves, and ye shall be broken in pieces. Take counsel together, and it shall come to nought; speak the word, and it shall not stand: for God is with us" (Isa. 8:8–10).

Isaiah counsels Israel not to seek protection from anyone except the Lord. "Say ye not, A confederacy, to all them to whom this people shall say, A confederacy; neither fear ye their fear, nor be afraid" (Isa. 8:12). Rather, they are to "sanctify the Lord of hosts himself; and let him be your fear, and let him be your dread" (Isa. 8:13). If they accept Christ, "He shall be for a sanctuary," but if they reject Him, He shall be "a stone of stumbling and for a rock of offence" (Isa. 8:14).

Sanctify the Lord is literally translated from Hebrew as "make him a temple, the Lord of Hosts." "He shall be for a sanctuary" has the same meaning.[22] We are to come unto Christ and find our protection and sanctuary in Him. Our faith in our Savior is the reason for our hope in the future and for our courage in the face of our temporal and spiritual enemies. As we make and keep sacred temple covenants, we gain inner strength and peace to see us through our mortal tests and trials. As we come to the temple, we come to Christ—the temple helps us on our way to Christ, in whom we have sanctuary and salvation.

Seek unto Their God

Isaiah's repeated and resounding plea for Israel is that they not succumb to the lure of Satan by making coalition with their idolatrous neighbors who dwell in spiritual darkness and seek their counsel from "familiar spirits, and unto wizards that peep, and that mutter" (Isa. 8:19). Isaiah warns Israel that the reward of their apostasy will be that "they shall look unto the earth; and behold trouble and darkness, dimness of anguish; and they shall be driven to darkness" (Isa. 8:22).

Lucifer means "The Shining One," "Lightbringer," or "Son of the Morning."[23] *Perdition* means "to lose, ruin, . . . irreparable loss."[24] Lucifer, the name of Satan before his premortal rebellion and fall, fought against the great plan of our Heavenly Father and thus became Perdition; his actions brought him irreparable loss. In his misery, he works to ruin the eternal life of all of Father's children. His works are couched in darkness and deceit. He impresses the faithless with the allure of his magic.

Isaiah invites the people to seek out light and follow the Lord's revealed course of seeking true communion with the dead. "Should not a people seek unto their God? for the living to the dead? To the law and to the testimony: if they speak not according to this word, it is because there is no light in them" (Isa. 8:19–20).

Isaiah's mission, like our mission today, is to gather Israel to the brightness and glory of gospel truth. We are to be a light unto the world: "Ye are my disciples; and ye are a light unto this people, who are a remnant of the house of Joseph" (3 Ne. 15:12). In all we do, we are to bring people to Christ, who is *the* Light of the world: "Behold, I am the law, and the light. Look unto me, and endure to the end, and ye shall live; for unto him that endureth to the end will I give eternal life" (3 Ne. 15:9).

CHAPTER NINE
FOR UNTO US A CHILD IS BORN

THE GREATNESS OF ISAIAH'S PROPHETIC ministry centers in the greatness of his Messianic prophecy—his testimony of Christ, the Great Light. Shining brightly throughout this glorious testament to an oppressed people in dark trials is the guiding light of the Atonement that gleams true and eternal.

A Great Light

I have experienced the stark contrast of light and darkness on multiple occasions with my family as we have visited Timpanogos Cave, accessed from the trailhead in American Fork Canyon in Utah. As we were deep in the cave and well away from any sliver of natural light, our guide would turn off all the artificial lights and leave us momentarily in total darkness. I was always relieved when the light was turned on again and further reassured as we emerged from the dark cave into the welcome natural light of day.

In the despairing darkness of trial and oppression, we may fully appreciate gospel light and turn our vision to the Creator of natural light. From the confines of the Liberty Jail in one of his darkest trials, the Prophet Joseph called out, "O Lord God Almighty, maker of heaven, earth, and seas, and of all things that in them are, and who controllest and subjectest the devil, and the dark and benighted dominion of Sheol—stretch forth thy hand; let thine eye pierce; let thy pavilion be taken up" (D&C 121:4).

Rebellious Israel, even in their dark apostasy, was offered the hope of a brighter day: "The people that walked in darkness have seen a great light: they that dwell in the land of the shadow of death, upon them hath the light shined" (Isa. 9:2). The great light that would bring them out of darkness would be the Savior of the world, who would be born into mortality and affect the Atonement of all mankind that all may be redeemed from sin and death.

This prospect of redemption through the life and mission of our Savior is the most glorious cause of rejoicing in all time and eternity. We all join, likely with the music of George Frideric Handel stirring in our souls, in the blessed acclamation, "For unto us a child is born, unto us a son is given: and the government shall be upon his shoulder: and his name shall be called Wonderful, Counsellor, The mighty God, The everlasting Father, The Prince of Peace" (Isa. 9:6).

Wonderful, Counsellor

Imagine being accused of a serious crime with much evidence mounted against our cause and a tenacious prosecutor whose sole intent is our condemnation and destruction. Now imagine the joyous relief that would be ours at the appointment of a competent legal counselor whose sole motive is our salvation and who has within his grasp the power and knowledge to accomplish such. In the spiritual sense, this is our mortal condition. We are subject to the justice of the law. We are granted the mercy of the Lawgiver. Christ counsels us in wisdom and truth. He charts a true path for our deliverance. He is our blessed Mediator, our Advocate with the Father.

In His role as our Advocate, He extends us empathy and love. He reminds us of the desire of our Heavenly Father to save all of His children. He does not judge us harshly for some slight oversight or misunderstanding. He sees that we get the very best outcome we can possibly receive. He upholds, lifts, and guides us into the enduring path of gospel light. Through His mercy and tender love, we come to more fully recognize that He represents perfect light and perfect love and that we may come into the fullness of His love and redemption. Our Messiah is most certainly a "Wonderful Counsellor."

The Mighty God

Our Savior is a God of miracles. At His word, the elements move, matter is organized, and worlds are created. By His design, planets orbit perfectly stars light the sky, rivers flow, the sun shines with proper, life-giving intensity, rains nurture the earth, and seeds sprout and grow to sustain life. All of these miraculous happenings teach us of Him. "And behold, all things have their likeness, and all things are created and made to bear record of me" (Moses 6:63). At His charge, the sea parts to protect His chosen, despots and tyrants encounter the limits of their power, and Satan and his forces are kept in check. According to His word, doors of nations are opened to the proclaiming of the gospel, temples are built, saving ordinances are performed, and the sons and daughters of the Father are sealed up unto eternal life.

Central to the plan and purpose of Christ's mission is that He is one with His Father in His "work and glory—to bring to pass the immortality and eternal life of man" (Moses 1:39). The greatest of all of Christ's miracles is the change He brings to the human soul. Through His power, broken hearts are healed, the sorrowful are comforted, tears are wiped away, pride gives way to humility, selfishness to selflessness. A mighty change is wrought in the human heart. We owe all of our spiritual renewal and progress, now and future, to Him. As Nephi has reminded us, "And now, my beloved brethren, after ye have gotten into this strait and narrow path, I would ask if all is done? Behold, I say unto you, Nay; for ye have not come thus far save it were by the word of Christ with unshaken faith in him, relying wholly upon the merits of him who is mighty to save" (2 Ne. 31:19). Our Messiah is truly a Mighty God.

The Everlasting Father

Our Heavenly Father and His Son Jesus Christ, although one in purpose, each have distinctive roles as fathers. Heavenly Father is the father of our spirits, the father of Christ's spirit, and the father of Christ's body. Christ is the Firstborn and the Only Begotten Son of the Father, the father of creation, and the father of our salvation. King Benjamin taught, "And now, because of the covenant which ye have made ye shall be called the children of Christ, his sons, and his daughters; for behold, this day he hath spiritually begotten you; for ye say that your hearts are changed through faith on his name; therefore, ye are born of him and have become his sons and his daughters" (Mosiah 5:7).

The prophet Abinadi expounds the fatherly role of Christ: "I would that ye should understand that God himself shall come down among the children of men, and shall redeem his people. And because he dwelleth in the flesh he shall be called the Son of God, and having subjected the flesh to the will of the Father, being the Father and the Son—The Father, because he was conceived by the power of God; and the Son, because of the flesh; thus becoming the Father and Son—And they are one God, yea, the very Eternal Father of heaven and earth" (Mosiah 15:1–4).

Abinadi is teaching of the two offices of Christ—of His roles as the divine Son of God and as the father of our salvation. Abinadi continues in helping us understand how Christ, under direction of our Heavenly Father, serves as the father of our salvation:

> Yea, even so he shall be led, crucified, and slain, the flesh becoming subject even unto death, the will of the Son being swallowed up in the will of the Father. And thus God breaketh the bands of death, having gained the victory over death; giving the Son power to make intercession for the children of men. . . . that all those who have hearkened unto their words, and believed that the Lord would redeem his people, and have looked forward to that day for a remission of their sins, I say unto you, that these are his seed, or they are the heirs of the kingdom of God. For these are they whose sins he has borne; these are they for whom he has died, to redeem them from their transgressions. And now, are they not his seed? (Mosiah 15:7–8; 11–12)

What joy we have in the knowledge that we may qualify to be spiritual sons and daughters of Christ and thereby gain eternal life. How grateful we are that He is our Everlasting Father!

The Prince of Peace

Christ is the Prince of Peace. The rulers of the nations of the world often display futile attempts at peace negotiation through unwise political union, intimidation, coercion, threats, bribery, bullying, oppression, and false promises. Near the end of His mortal ministry, Christ declared to his Apostles, "Peace I leave with you, my peace I give unto you: not as the world giveth, give I unto you. Let not your heart be troubled, neither let it be afraid" (John 14:27).

In His ministry of peace, the Prince of Peace invites all people to trust in Him and not join with those of impure motive. He works by invitation rather than by coercion. He is perfectly faithful and true to His Father and to principles of eternal truth. The key to finding peace and joy is to center our lives on Christ and His Atonement. Those who rebel at His word and warning have as their reward a fleeting pseudopeace that melts away at the first sign of darkness. In the great vision of the redemption of the dead, we learn about the wicked that "where these were, darkness reigned, but among the righteous there was peace" (D&C 138:22).

Righteousness brings peace to a troubled world, generally and individually. How glorious and blessed is our Savior, the Prince of Peace.

His Hand is Stretched Out Still

There is a saying, "If you feel distant from God, guess who moved?" The answer and implication is that He is constant but we sometimes waver in our commitments to Him. His steady commitment to us is taught by some beautiful repetitions of His response to the sins of Israel.

Israel vainly proclaimed their own strength: "The bricks are fallen down, but we will build with hewn stones: the sycomores are cut down, but we will change them into cedars" (Isa. 9:10). In response, the Lord's perfect and calculated blend of justice and mercy is thus expressed: "For all this his anger is not turned away, but his hand is stretched out still" (Isa. 9:12). To the rebellious, the Lord's hand is a hand of chastening justice—to the repentant it is a beckoning hand of tender mercy.

Those who should have been the shepherds of Israel had apostatized and were leading the flock to destruction. "For the leaders of this people cause them to err; and they that are led of them are destroyed" (Isa. 9:16). The Lord would allow His justice to work on them: "Therefore the Lord shall have no joy in their young men, neither shall have mercy on their fatherless and widows: for every one is an hypocrite and an evildoer, and every mouth speaketh folly. For all this his anger is not turned away." But true to His character of mercy and abounding love, "His hand is stretched out still" (Isa. 9:17).

Israel would descend to the depths of evil and receive the scorching rebuke of the Lord's justice, "for wickedness burneth as the fire." They would even lose familial love, for "no man [would] spare his brother" and "Ephraim, Manasseh: and they together shall be against Judah." Nevertheless, the Lord waits for the day of their repentance: "For all this his anger is not turned away, but his hand is stretched out still" (Isa. 9:18–21).

Israel would lose compassion and charity for those in need. They would "turn aside the needy from judgment, and . . . take away the right from the poor of my people, that widows may be their prey, and that they may rob the fatherless!" Nevertheless, through all of their strange wanderings, the Lord reiterates in chapter 10 that He stands firm and consistent in His justice and mercy. "For all this his anger is not turned away, but his hand is stretched out still" (vv. 2, 4).

Many years ago, I gazed in awe at the ceiling of the Sistine Chapel wherein Michelangelo portrayed the creation of Adam by God, whose right arm is stretched out to touch the hand of Adam. The two hands do not quite touch. I do not know what was in the heart and mind of Michelangelo in this depiction, but in my heart and mind is the message that *we* have the responsibility to reach out and take the outstretched hand of our Heavenly Father. Jacob taught,

> And how merciful is our God unto us, for he remembereth the house of Israel, both roots and branches; and he stretches forth his hands unto them all the day long; and they are a stiffnecked and a gainsaying people; but as many as will not harden their hearts shall be saved in the kingdom of God. Wherefore, my beloved brethren, I beseech of you in words of soberness that ye would repent, and come with full purpose of heart, and cleave unto God as he cleaveth unto you. And while his arm of mercy is extended towards you in the light of the day, harden not your hearts. (Jacob 6:4–5)

We answer the outstretched hand of the Lord's beckoning through our commitment to His gospel in the keeping of our sacred baptismal and temple covenants. As we do so, He lovingly grasps our hand and leads us to eternal life. He encourages us, "be of good cheer, for I will lead you along. The kingdom is yours . . . and the riches of eternity are yours" (D&C 78:18).

How blessed we are for the "perfect atonement" (D&C 76:69) of our Savior, the "Wonderful, Counsellor, The mighty God, The everlasting Father, The Prince of Peace" (Isa. 9:6).

CHAPTER TEN
WHOLE WORK ON MOUNT ZION

UNFORTUNATELY, MANY PEOPLE TEND TO brush off the Old Testament, thinking it is too old or too difficult to understand or too irrelevant for our modern times. I have often told my students that the Old Testament is "as relevant as tomorrow for our lives, but there is a price of study and pondering to pay for understanding."

The tenth chapter of Isaiah is relevant to our day. It speaks of the destruction of Assyria and the gathering of the righteous in such a way as to give us a pattern for the destruction of the wicked and the salvation of the righteous in our day. As the chapter heading states, the "destruction of Assyria is a type of destruction of the wicked at the Second Coming" (Isa. 10).

The fulfillment of the parable of the wheat and tares seems appropriate to our study of this chapter. The Bible teaches of the Savior's approach to the wheat and tares in this parable: "Let both grow together until the harvest: and in the time of harvest I will say to the reapers, Gather ye together first the tares, and bind them in bundles to burn them: but gather the wheat into my barn" (Matt. 13:30). Joseph Smith, in his inspired translation, corrects the order of the harvest: "Gather ye together first the *wheat* into my barn; *and the tares are bound* in bundles *to be burned*" (JST, Matt. 13:29). We will follow this pattern in our discussion of this chapter: first the wheat and then the tares.

The Wheat: Whole Work on Mount Zion

In the midst of the prophecy of the destruction of the Assyrians, the Lord reminds us of the "whole work" of His mission. "Wherefore it shall come to pass, that when the Lord hath performed his whole work upon mount Zion and on Jerusalem, I will punish the fruit of the stout heart of the king of Assyria, and the glory of his high looks" (Isa. 10:12).

What is the Lord's "whole work," and where is it performed? His work is to bring us to eternal life. He performs this work in our daily lives as we show faith, give service, practice obedience, and worship Him through our actions. Our course of worship in seeking eternal life leads us to the temple, for there we receive the covenants and ordinances needed to help us receive eternal life. The temple of Jerusalem was on "mount Zion." The temples of today are scattered throughout the world on many of the Lord's "mountains."

As the Assyrians were soon to be punished at the time of this prophecy, so in modern times will the Lord perform His work and then punish the wicked. He will first gather the wheat and then burn the tares. Granted, some punishment will always befall the wicked, and the work of gospel conversion will continue through the millennial day, but the mission of the current modern Church is to gather "the wheat" to Christ and His gospel.

As the righteous are gathered from among the wicked, they will "stay upon the Lord, the Holy One of Israel, in truth. The remnant shall return, even the remnant of Jacob, unto the mighty God" (Isa. 10:20–21). We recall from chapter 7 that the name of Isaiah's son, Shear-jashub, means "the remnant shall return" (see Isaiah 7:3, footnote a). To "return" is to repent. To "stay upon the Lord" is to always remember Him and keep our covenants with Him—to rely on Him throughout our entire life.

Those who stay committed to the Lord need not fear the Assyrians or any other oppressors, ancient or modern. "Therefore thus saith the Lord God of hosts, O my people that dwellest in Zion, be not afraid of the Assyrian: he shall smite thee with a rod, and shall lift up his staff against thee. . . . For yet a very little while, and the indignation shall cease" (Isa. 10:24–25). Yes, there will be times of trial, but the righteous will endure and be preserved. Though in the last days the Saints of Zion will suffer persecution, the Lord's compensatory blessings are found in Zion, wherein we learn of and receive the power of the Atonement of Jesus Christ. To dwell in Zion is to enjoy a pure life. To be pure is to "stay upon the Lord in truth."

As we work to live pure lives, the burden of our sins is lifted through the Atonement of Christ and by the power of the Holy Ghost: "And it shall come to pass in that day, that his burden shall be taken away from off thy shoulder, and his yoke from off thy neck, and the yoke shall be destroyed because of the anointing" (Isa. 10:27). *Anointing* refers to our Messiah, the Anointed One. Through Him, we gain purity and receive redemption from sin.

The Tares: The Rod of Mine Anger

Once the righteous are safely garnered, *"the tares are bound* in bundles to be burned" (JST, Matt. 13:29). In our modern society, we have many members and rulers of organizations and of nations who follow a lustful and greedy binge-type diet, acquiring an ostentatious portfolio of the things of the world. In their evil pursuits, they "turn aside the needy . . . take away the right from the poor of my people, that widows may be their prey, and that they may rob the fatherless!" (Isa. 10:2).

In response to these sins, the Lord's "anger is not turned away, but his hand is stretched out still. O Assyrian, the rod of mine anger, and the staff in their hand is mine indignation. I will send him against an hypocritical nation, and against the people of my wrath will I give him a charge, to take the spoil, and to take the prey, and to tread them down like the mire of the streets" (Isa. 10:4–6). The Lord generally serves justice upon the wicked by the hand of others who are wicked: "It is by the wicked that the wicked are punished; for it is the wicked that stir up the hearts of the children of men unto bloodshed" (Morm. 4:5). In the case of rebellious Israel, the Assyrians were the "rod" of the Lord's anger; He allowed wicked Assyria to punish wicked Israel.

The ancient and modern plagues of idolatry are destroyed in the Lord's due time and by His hand and methods: "As my hand hath found the kingdoms of the idols, and whose graven images did excel them of Jerusalem and of Samaria; Shall I not, as I have done unto Samaria and her idols, so do to Jerusalem and her idols?" (Isa. 10:10–11).

We may gain some perspective of the Lord's destruction upon the wicked as we contemplate the great forest fire of 1988, a fire that burned for most of the summer in Yellowstone National Park, affecting about one-third of the area of the park. We took our children to the park the next summer and were saddened by the sight of thousands of blackened acres that were once green and beautiful. We did, however, notice sprigs of green sprouting up through the ashes. Several years later, we visited once again and saw tremendous new growth and renewal, validating that nature's cleansing course had been the right course, just as God's plan of cleansing and renewal for His children is always proper.

Prior to His Second Coming, the Lord will cleanse the earth: "Therefore shall the Lord, the Lord of hosts, send among his fat ones leanness; and under his glory he shall kindle a burning like the burning of a fire. And the light of Israel shall be for a fire, and his Holy One for a flame: and it shall burn and devour his thorns and his briers in one day; And shall consume the glory of his forest, and of his fruitful field, both soul and body: and they shall be as when a standardbearer fainteth" (Isa. 10:16–18).

Those who refuse the beckoning hand of the Lord and who persist in their lustful greed will be pruned away: "Behold, the Lord, the Lord of hosts, shall lop the bough with terror: and the high ones of stature shall be hewn down, and the haughty shall be humbled. And he shall cut down the thickets of the forest with iron, and Lebanon shall fall by a mighty one" (Isa. 10:33–34).

His Hand Is Stretched Out Still

These prophecies of the burning of the tares remind me of what has been a curious scripture for me: "Behold, now it is called today until the coming of the Son of Man, and verily it is a day of sacrifice and a day for the tithing of my people; for he that is tithed shall not be burned at his coming" (D&C 64:23). We might ask, "So, if someone just sends in their tithing money, will they be saved no matter what?" Mormon answers this question: "For behold, God hath said a man being evil cannot do that which is good; for if he offereth a gift, or prayeth unto God, except he shall do it with real intent it profiteth him nothing" (Moro. 7:6). We must pay our tithing with an eye single to God's glory.

And while some may pay it for the wrong reasons, there are some who find it difficult to pay at all. It has been my observation over the years that the nonpayment of tithes and offerings is one of the more prevalent roadblocks for people who wish to hold a current temple recommend. We often speak a truism that we pay tithing with faith and not with money. Payment of tithing is a great barometer of faith. Exercising faith in the payment of tithes constitutes the antidote for both those who pay tithing without real intent and those who withhold because they don't understand that paying tithes is really a blessing from the Lord. Those who exercise consistent faith, to include the consistent and long-term payment of tithing, will experience a purifying and refining of the soul and thus be protected from the destructive plagues and burnings brought forth upon the wicked, burnings and destruction that will indeed come to cleanse the earth in preparation for the new life that is to follow.

Roots of renewal are always present in the souls of God's children as long as they have not passed the point of no return and become sons of perdition. From the dark ashes of destruction, new life will spring up. The wicked, even in their mortal destruction, continue to be under the protective and watchful care of the Messiah, whose "hand is stretched out still" (Isa. 10:4). The righteous will go forth to inherit an eternal life more glorious than ever imagined. This redemption from sin and death comes through the Atonement of Jesus Christ, the "stem of Jesse": "And there shall come forth a rod out of the stem of Jesse, and a Branch shall grow out of his roots" (Isa. 11:1).

CHAPTER ELEVEN
THE STEM OF JESSE

ONE OF THE MANY GREAT blessings of the Restoration of the gospel in the latter days is our ever-expanding canon of scripture. We are fortunate beyond measure to have all of the standard works combined with the words of our modern prophets to guide us and give us prophetic interpretations. Of particular importance is what our past and present prophets teach us about the Atonement and mission of Christ. One specific instance is the help we receive in understanding the Stem of Jesse.

The Stem of Jesse

There is some scholarly confusion about the identity of the stem of Jesse discussed in the eleventh chapter of Isaiah. Joseph Smith took this question in direct appeal to the Lord: "Who is the Stem of Jesse spoken of in the 1st, 2d, 3d, 4th, and 5th verses of the 11th chapter of Isaiah?" He received a simple answer: "Verily thus saith the Lord: It is Christ" (D&C 113:1–2).

Nephi, after quoting the largest portion of Isaiah prophecies contained in the Book of Mormon, gives us his prophetic commentary. In describing Christ, Nephi uses the very language of Isaiah 11:4, which describes the attributes of the stem of Jesse (see v. 1): "And with righteousness shall the Lord God judge the poor, and reprove with equity for the meek of the earth. And he shall smite the earth with the rod of his mouth; and with the breath of his lips shall he slay the wicked" (2 Ne. 30:9).

Christ, this stem of Jesse who would yet come forth, would grow in great wisdom and understanding in emulation of His Father: "And I, John, saw that he received not of the fulness at the first, but received grace for grace; And he received not of the fulness at first, but continued from grace to grace, until he received a fulness; And thus he was called the Son of God, because he received not of the fulness at the first" (D&C 93:12–14).

He would receive "the spirit of wisdom and understanding, the spirit of counsel and might, the spirit of knowledge and of the fear of the Lord" (Isa. 11:2). As previously discussed, He would be known as "Wonderful, Counsellor, The mighty God" (Isa. 9:6). He would be a perfect judge.

A sad characteristic of our fallen world is that we often pass judgment upon each other based on such things as our physiques, our mental capacities, our skin color, and the hearsay of others. The Stem of Jesse, who has sprung forth from roots of perfection, passes perfect judgment. He does "not judge after the sight of his eyes, neither reprove after the hearing of his ears: But with righteousness shall he judge the poor, and reprove with equity for the meek of the earth" (Isa. 11:3–4). We can trust Him to deal with us in perfect truth and righteousness.

In this same perfect and precise judgment, He will perfectly and precisely bring justice to the wicked. Their lifetime of struggle to launder their money securely in secret hiding places or shelter themselves in impenetrable bunkers will be no contest for the Lord, who will simply "smite the earth with the rod of his mouth, and with the breath of his lips shall he slay the wicked" (Isa. 11:4). No physical scheme or barrier can shield them from His perfect justice.

Our protection and salvation come from striving to follow the Lord in all things. He does not just tell us the path—He shows us the path by His example. "And righteousness shall be the girdle of his loins, and faithfulness the girdle of his reins" (Isa. 11:5).

In All My Holy Mountain

Perhaps we have all fantasized, as I occasionally have, how pleasant and peaceful it would be to live in a temple-like environment. As we come to understand the great plan of happiness of our Heavenly Father and the end result of the atoning sacrifice of our Savior, we realize that such a permanent life in a peaceful and holy realm is not mere fantasy—it is a reality. Such life is our divine inheritance.

As John the Revelator saw the celestial kingdom in glorious vision, he "saw no temple therein: for the Lord God Almighty and the Lamb are the temple of it. And the city had no need of the sun, neither of the moon, to shine in it: for the glory of God did lighten it, and the Lamb is the light thereof" (Rev. 21:22–23). As the wicked are removed from the earth and the earth receives renewal and paradisiacal glory in the Millennium and then goes on to become celestial, there is no need for a designated building or mountaintop to serve the purposes of the temple. The purposes of the temple will have been achieved as the whole earth becomes as the temple.

In our temporal, fallen world, the ferocious and the terrible pursue and prey upon the domesticated and the peaceful. Wolves, leopards, and lions destroy lambs, kids, and calves. Despots, tyrants, and warmongers abuse and destroy the weak, the poor, and the peace seekers. In the holy realm of the Millennium and of the celestial kingdom "the wolf also shall dwell with the lamb, and the leopard shall lie down with the kid; and the calf and the young lion and the fatling together; and a little child shall lead them. And the cow and the bear shall feed; their young ones shall lie down together: and the lion shall eat straw like the ox" (Isa. 11:6–7). In this glorious day, the feuds of families, peoples, and countries will merely be topics of historical study, not accounts of the current news cycle. "The envy also of Ephraim shall depart, and the adversaries of Judah shall be cut off: Ephraim shall not envy Judah, and Judah shall not vex Ephraim" (Isa.11:13).

In our fallen realm, we must constantly guard our children from snake pits of evil wherein cunning predators seek to exploit and abuse them. In the paradisiacal realm, "the sucking child shall play on the hole of the asp, and the weaned child shall put his hand on the cockatrice' den" (Isa. 11:8).

Of this future time when the whole earth becomes as the temple, the Lord said, "They shall not hurt nor destroy in all my holy mountain: for the earth shall be full of the knowledge of the Lord, as the waters cover the sea" (Isa. 11:9). The glory of the temple, His holy mountain, will expand and shroud the whole earth in peace and joy.

The Root of Jesse—An Ensign of the People

"And in that day there shall be a root of Jesse, which shall stand for an ensign of the people; to it shall the Gentiles seek: and his rest shall be glorious" (Isa. 11:10). "Latter-day Saint scholars generally agree that the *root of Jesse* refers to the Prophet Joseph Smith. He is a descendant of both Jesse and Joseph; he held the priesthood; he possessed the keys of the kingdom; he played a primary role in the lifting of the ensign upon the tops of the mountains; and the keys of the gathering of Israel were committed into his hands (D&C 110:11).[25] Joseph's life and ministry certainly fit the descriptions given here and, as such, are intertwined with the prophecy of Isaiah.

When Moroni visited Joseph Smith, "he quoted the eleventh chapter of Isaiah, saying that it was about to be fulfilled" (JS—H 1:40). Joseph was to be the leading prophet of the Restoration. He would receive the authority and give leadership to the second gathering of Israel: "And it shall come to pass in that day, that the Lord shall set his hand again the second time to recover the remnant of his people, which shall be left, from Assyria, and from Egypt . . . and from the islands of the sea" (Isa. 11:11).

The first gathering of Israel was under the hand of Moses as they were brought out of Egyptian bondage and into the land of promise. The second gathering of Israel was to be under the hand of Joseph Smith, who would bring them, figuratively, out of spiritual Egypt, or out of apostasy and darkness. Of this gathering, the Prophet Joseph Smith said, "The time has at last arrived when the God of Abraham, of Isaac, and of Jacob, has set his hand again the second time to recover the remnants of his people . . . from the islands of the sea . . . and establish that covenant with them, which was promised when their sins should be taken away."[26]

In proclaiming the restored gospel to the world, Joseph fulfilled the prophecy that the Lord would "set up an ensign for the nations, and . . . assemble the outcasts of Israel, and gather together the dispersed of Judah from the four corners of the earth" (Isa. 11:12). This gathering would bring Israel to the Lord and His temple and to the eternal covenants offered therein. "And even so I have sent mine everlasting covenant into the world, to be a light to the world, and to be a standard for my people" (D&C 45:9).

Significantly, Joseph received the priesthood keys of gathering Israel to Christ and the temple while in the temple at Kirtland and from one who held the ancient keys of gathering: "After this vision closed, the heavens were again opened unto us; and Moses appeared before us, and committed unto us the keys of the gathering of Israel from the four parts of the earth, and the leading of the ten tribes from the land of the north" (D&C 110:11).

This great gathering of latter-day Israel is truly a "marvellous work and a wonder" (Isa. 29:14). Dispersed and lost souls from all parts of the world are traveling the road home to gospel light and truth. Isaiah spoke of "an highway for the remnant of his people, which shall be left, from Assyria; like as it was to Israel in the day that he came up out of the land of Egypt" (Isa. 11:16). This highway is a path of faith, repentance, baptism, and guidance of the Holy Ghost, who leads the gathered souls to their Savior.

CHAPTER TWELVE
TRUST JEHOVAH

AT THE DAWN OF THE Restoration, the Lord told Martin Harris to "speak freely to all; yea, preach, exhort, declare the truth, even with a loud voice, with a sound of rejoicing, crying—Hosanna, hosanna, blessed be the name of the Lord God!" (D&C 19:37).

Hosanna means "save now" or "grant us salvation." Jesus Christ, the Great Jehovah, is the granter of our salvation and "the author and finisher of our faith" (Hebrews 12:2). We praise Him forever for His grace and mercy to us. We honor Him by remembering His sacrifice and by keeping His commandments. We revere Him as the focus of our faith and the source of our salvation.

Jehovah Is My Strength and My Song

Occasionally, in teaching the Old Testament to my young seminary students, I have given them a preassessment in the form of a multiple-choice quiz. I ask such questions as, "Who created the earth?" "Who gave the ten commandments to Moses?" and "Who spoke to and guided the prophets?" I am often amazed that some do not recognize Jehovah, the God of the Old Testament and of our salvation, as our Savior. Some have not yet discovered the beauty of continuing revelation and how ancient passages are clarified by modern prophets.

The Bible, standing alone, is sometimes a bit confusing. To Moses, the Lord said, "And I appeared unto Abraham, unto Isaac, and unto Jacob, by the name of God Almighty, but by my name JEHOVAH was I not known to them" (Ex. 6:3). Joseph Smith in his inspired translation clarifies the verse: "I am the Lord God Almighty; the Lord JEHOVAH. And was not my name known unto them?" (JST, Ex. 6:3).

To Abraham, the Lord spoke, "Abraham, Abraham, behold, my name is Jehovah, and I have heard thee, and have come down to deliver thee"

(Abr.1:16), and on another occasion, "My name is Jehovah, and I know the end from the beginning; therefore my hand shall be over thee" (Abr. 2:8).

Isaiah clearly understood the identity and saving role of Jehovah and joyfully proclaimed his praise of Him. "And in that day thou shalt say, O Lord, I will praise thee: though thou wast angry with me, thine anger is turned away, and thou comfortedst me. Behold, God is my salvation; I will trust, and not be afraid: for the Lord JEHOVAH is my strength and my song; he also is become my salvation" (Isa. 12:1–2). *Trust* is the Old Testament equivalent of *faith*. "Trusting Jehovah" or "Faith in the Lord Jesus Christ" (A of F 1:4) is the first principle of the gospel.

The Wells of Salvation

Isaiah was a gifted poet. In English, our poetry often consists of rhymes. A common characteristic of Hebrew poetry is parallelism—the repetition of words or phrases to accentuate the thoughts and feelings of the poet. As a simple example, I invite you to ponder these words and phrases of parallel praise of the Lord: (As you do so, match all of the parallel italicized words. Also match together all of the **bold** titles) "*Praise* **the Lord,** *call upon* **his name,** *declare* **his doings** . . . *make mention* . . . **his name.** . . . *Sing unto* **the Lord.** . . . *Cry out and shout* . . . **for great is the Holy One**" (Isa. 12:4–6; emphasis added).

Also notice the repetition of a major theme of the chapter: salvation. "God is my *salvation*; . . . he also is become my *salvation*. . . . draw water out of the wells of *salvation*" (Isa.12:2–3; emphasis added). Joseph Smith defined salvation: "Salvation consists in the glory, authority, majesty, power and dominion which Jehovah possesses and in nothing else; and no being can possess it but himself or one like him."[27] The key to becoming like Christ is the Atonement. Related to the Atonement is the temple endowment, for therein we receive the ordinances and covenants that lead us to salvation.

I was once taught that we give thanks unto God for what He gives us; we praise Him for who He is. In this small chapter, we have grand praise for Jehovah, who is the Father of our salvation. He is the "fountain of living waters" (1 Ne. 11:25). In Him, we have "a well of water springing up into everlasting life" (John 4:14). Isaiah proclaims a sweet and hopeful promise: "Therefore with joy shall ye draw water out of the wells of salvation" (Isa. 12:3). It is no wonder that we praise Him with our whole souls!

Sing unto the Lord

At the time of Passover and the conclusion of His ministry, Jesus entered Jerusalem in triumph. Although within days He would suffer and atone for the sins of the world and be crucified at the hands of the wicked rulers of the Jews, He would triumph over death and hell and, by so doing, enable the salvation of mankind.

As He entered Jerusalem, His grateful disciples honored Him with palm branches and shouts of praise, "saying, Hosanna to the Son of David: Blessed is he that cometh in the name of the Lord; Hosanna in the highest" (Matt. 21:9).

At the temple, His disciples again praised Him with shouts of "Hosanna to the Son of David." Next, He "cast out all [those] that sold and bought in the temple" (Matt. 21:12). The reaction of the wicked chief priests and scribes was that "they were sore displeased" (Matt. 21:15), and they now hastened their plans for His destruction. They were more concerned with the loss of their status and profession than with the loss of their salvation. They had lost the testimony and blessing of their Messiah and the spirit of true temple worship. They had perverted this sacred place into a marketplace for their apostate practices of administering the law for their own gain. Sadly, the significance of the shouts of "Hosanna" in regard to the saving power of the temple was lost on them.

With the gospel restored in latter days, the Lord hastened the work of building His temple so He could provide the ordinances of salvation to His beloved followers. As the Kirtland Saints, in their hardship, delayed the work, He chastened them: "I gave unto you a commandment that you should build a house, in the which house I design to endow those whom I have chosen with power from on high" (D&C 95:8). He chastened them so He could hasten their salvation. As the temple was completed, shouts and songs of hosanna and praise were offered: "Hosanna, hosanna to God and the Lamb!"[28]

Today, as we hasten to build temples throughout the earth, we pause to give thanks and praise and proclaim hosanna to our Lord and Savior. This work of salvation will continue through the duration of the great millennial day. Through this extended time of peace and prosperity, we may blend our words with the sweet poetry of Isaiah: "And in that day shall ye say, Praise the Lord, call upon his name, declare his doings among the people, make mention that his name is exalted. Sing unto the Lord; for he hath done excellent things: this is known in all the earth. Cry out and shout, thou inhabitant of Zion: for great is the Holy One of Israel in the midst of thee" (Isa. 12:4–6).

CHAPTER THIRTEEN
FAREWELL TO BABYLON

SINCE OUR PREMORTAL LIFE, THE followers of evil have battled the disciples of good: "And there was war in heaven; Michael and his angels fought against the dragon; and the dragon and his angels fought against Michael" (JST, Rev. 12:6). As the fight continues toward its conclusion at the millennial day, those who seek goodness will walk the path toward Christ and His temple. Those who give their allegiance to evil chart a path away from the holy temple and toward the unholy temples of lust and greed. These paths diverge in stark contrast one to another.

Go into the Gates of the Nobles

Church leaders and missionaries are to be "endowed with power from on high" (D&C 105:11) as requisite for their mission of gathering Israel. In a sense, the Lord, *from* the temple—representing His celestial abode— gathers the righteous of all nations *to* the temple—or to His glory: "Lift ye up a banner upon the high mountain, exalt the voice unto them, shake the hand, that they may go into the gates of the nobles" (Isa. 13:2). The "banner" that is lifted up is the message of the restored gospel as it is proclaimed to the world. The "high mountain" may symbolize the temple.

One way to look at the phrase "go into the gates of the nobles" is to join in unity with the "noble and great ones" of all ages in furthering the Lord's work of salvation. The nobles who kept their "first estate" are now tested and tried in their "second estate" and, if faithful, "shall have glory added upon their heads for ever and ever" (Abr. 3:22–26). Opportunity for this glory or eternal life is granted to those who recognize the waving banner of the gospel message and come unto Christ, through the temple, to receive their endowment, or gift, of potential salvation. Having done so, we are to faithfully endure the latter-day battle against evil.

If we are willing to humble ourselves and forsake the world, we will be protected from the plagues and destructions that befall the wicked in the last days. The righteous, through their faith and goodness, place themselves on the right side of the great battle and are spared the Lord's wrath: "I have commanded my sanctified ones, I have also called my mighty ones . . . even them that rejoice in my highness. The noise of a multitude in the mountains, like as of a great people; a tumultuous noise of the kingdoms of nations gathered together: the Lord of hosts mustereth the host of the battle. They come from a far country, from the end of heaven, even the Lord, and the weapons of his indignation, to destroy the whole land" (Isa. 13:3–5).

As the Chased Roe

The wicked who forfeit the sure and peaceful path of the gospel plan in exchange for the allure of the forbidden and damning paths of the world soon find themselves lost in "the mists of darkness . . . the temptations of the devil, which blindeth the eyes, and hardeneth the hearts of the children of men, and leadeth them away into broad roads, that they perish and are lost" (1 Ne. 12:17).

I live in a state with a large deer population. During most of the year, the deer live in relative calm as they saunter through the woods and fields in search of their forage. Then, in the fall during the annual hunting season, the deer become agitated and unsettled. As the horde of hunters takes to the field, the deer run and hide in fear and panic, sometimes fleeing the pursuit of one hunter only to encounter a deadly assault from another.

Those who follow Satan become "as the chased roe, and as a sheep that no man taketh up: they shall every man turn to his own people, and flee every one into his own land" (Isa. 13:14). The "destruction of Babylon is a type of the destruction at the Second Coming—It will be a day of wrath and vengeance" (Isa. 13 chapter heading). In that day, the righteous will be protected from destruction, and the wicked will be brought to the Lord's justice: "Howl ye; for the day of the Lord is at hand; it shall come as a destruction from the Almighty" (Isa. 13:6).

As the rebellious wander their strange paths, they become confused and anxious: "Therefore shall all hands be faint, and every man's heart shall melt" (Isa. 13:7). Consider how, in contrast, those with their faith centered in Christ have surety and confidence on their forward path to eternal life. Those with full faith in Christ stand firm and secure, assured of the truth of the great plan of happiness, and grateful in their understanding of and reliance on the Atonement of Jesus Christ.

The wicked, however, "shall be afraid: pangs of sorrow shall take hold of them; they shall be in pain as a woman that travaileth" (Isa. 13:8).

This birth metaphor is descriptive of the fears and uncertainties that will come upon the wicked at the time of the Lord's judgments. A mother in childbirth may fearfully wonder if she will live. Will her baby live? Will her baby be healthy and whole? How long will these waves of pain endure? All—particularly the spiritually unprepared—may ask similar questions related to their spiritual well-being: Will I live? Will my loved ones live? How long must I suffer?

The person with Christ-centered faith, although tried and tested by life, is not debilitated by fear but moves forward with trust in living prophets who hold and exercise the keys of the priesthood in blessing and guiding all who will follow their counsel. Those with faith centered on Christ are not tossed about by speculative winds of false doctrine but, by heeding the prophets, are continually anchored on the true and sure path to eternal life.

Consider all of the heartache that comes from breaking the law of chastity. Mutual trust is diminished, true love wanes, and the hearts of families and friends are wrenched in sorrow. Although the unrepentant may try to mask the seriousness of the sin, nevertheless, "the day of the Lord cometh, cruel both with wrath and fierce anger, to lay the land desolate: and he shall destroy the sinners thereof out of it" (Isa. 13:9).

In contrast, those who live the law of chastity and are honest in their relationships with the Lord and with others are blessed with an inner peace and assurance that they will be protected and comforted and will escape the serious consequences brought upon the rebellious.

The wicked that boast in their own strength and abandon the counsel of the Lord and His servants will face the terrible day when the Lord "will punish the world for their evil, and the wicked for their iniquity; and I will cause the arrogancy of the proud to cease, and will lay low the haughtiness of the terrible" (Isa. 13:11).

Those who strive to keep in remembrance the gospel covenants they have made and who make a conscious and consistent effort to keep those covenants are humbled and prompted to live a repentant life. As they pursue this true and sure course, they are enabled by the Lord's grace to overcome the trials of the flesh and leave behind the dross of the fallen world. They take comfort in the Lord's promise: "I will make a man more precious than fine gold; even a man than the golden wedge of Ophir" (Isa. 13:12).

Babylon: Her Days Shall Not Be Prolonged

We may learn guiding truths from Isaiah's foretelling of the destruction of ancient Babylon and presenting such as a type for the destruction of spiritual Babylon in our day. Some of the events of our time—such as

World War II—may serve as a tutorial for the final demise of Babylon. Much of the world's population feared the rise of Hitler's Third Reich. Masses of well-equipped, goose-stepping troops, a fast-expanding arsenal of modern weaponry, and eloquently shouted propaganda of misguided leaders created an aura of invincibility. "They are unstoppable," seemed to be the lament of multitudes of terrified citizens.

However, God rules over Satan. Satan has his bounds. Christ holds "the keys of hell and of death" (Rev. 1:18). The Lord in His mercy inspired valiant men and women to oppose the evil empire threatening the world. At first, skeptics had no hope and perceived these defenders of freedom to be mad, but time turned the battle, and the Third Reich fell in defeat, its principals scurrying to escape justice.

In the early days of Isaiah's prophesying, the Assyrians and later the Babylonians, who grew ever stronger, seemed invincible. Anyone who would suggest the demise of these great empires must have seemed mad. But prophets, ancient and modern, do not speak to please man or to be in harmony with social trend or philosophy. Isaiah spoke boldly of the pending fate of Babylon: "And Babylon, the glory of kingdoms, the beauty of the Chaldees' excellency, shall be as when God overthrew Sodom and Gomorrah. . . . And the wild beasts of the islands shall cry in their desolate houses, and dragons in their pleasant palaces: and her time is near to come, and her days shall not be prolonged" (Isa. 13:19, 22).

As we walk through mortality with the gospel of Jesus Christ as our guiding light, we have a clearer view of the world and of the great and spacious buildings of pride, arrogance, and sin (see Isa. 13:11). The allure of such enticements is powerful, but our charge is to live in this world but not be of it. We seek a higher life. As we pursue a higher, eternal life, we will be observers, not fatalities, of the fall of modern Babylon, "whose image is in the likeness of the world, and whose substance is that of an idol, which waxeth old and shall perish in Babylon, even Babylon the great, which shall fall" (D&C 1:16). Our gospel covenants, when kept, protect us from the damning influences of Babylon.

CHAPTER FOURTEEN
HIS PEOPLE SHALL TRUST IN ZION

SATAN, IN THE DUE TIME of the Lord, will be stripped of all power and will fall into oblivion, much as happened in the premortal life: "How art thou fallen from heaven, O Lucifer, son of the morning!" (Isa. 14:12).

In the previous chapter, we used the demise of Third Reich as an example of the pending fall of spiritual Babylon. Just as the architect of the Holocaust ended his reign cowering in his bunker in fear and infamy, Satan, the king of Babylon, will be unseated from his throne and sink into such insignificance that the nations of the earth will wonder at how this lowly tormenter could have ever wielded such great power over the nations.

One of the more profound emotional experiences of my life occurred in Jerusalem when I toured *Yad Vashem,* a memorial to the Jewish victims of the Holocaust. Upon viewing the actual artifacts of the atrocities committed against the Jews, I felt a deep sorrow for the innocent sufferers and frustration and sadness for the perpetrators. Part of the display is the *Garden of the Righteous among the Nations,* dedicated to non-Jews who risked their own lives to save the innocent. This garden is a beautiful and hopeful reminder drawn from an ugly and hopeless time.

For me, the dual message of this experience was a contrast between the terrible destruction of innocent life and the hope in the resurrection and renewal provided by the Atonement of our Savior. The reverent setting of *Yad Vashem* created in my mind and heart a yearning for the day when the whole earth will be at peace and rest and Babylon, along with her king, will be gone forever.

How Hath the Oppressor Ceased

Isaiah speaks of the fall of Lucifer in the premortal world and tells of the coming day when his power over the earth will be revoked: "That thou shalt take up this proverb against the king of Babylon, and say, How hath the oppressor ceased! the golden city ceased! The Lord hath broken the staff of the wicked, and the scepter of the rulers. He who smote the people in wrath with a continual stroke, he that ruled the nations in anger, is persecuted, and none hindereth" (Isa. 14:4–6).

Satan receives the just reward of his evil and is greeted by his followers, who share his dark fate and are amazed at the loss of his power: "Hell from beneath is moved for thee to meet thee at thy coming: it stirreth up the dead for thee, even all the chief ones of the earth; it hath raised up from their thrones all the kings of the nations. . . . Art thou also become weak as we? art thou become like unto us? . . . Thy pomp is brought down to the grave. . . . how art thou cut down to the ground, which didst weaken the nations!" (Isa. 14:9–12).

Perhaps you have observed the downfall, capture, humiliation, and death of evil rulers in our day and wondered, as I have done, how such a seemingly weak and dark person could have ever been the source of so much trouble. In the Book of Mormon, regarding the life and reign of evil Amalickiah, we are told, "Yea, and we also see the great wickedness one very wicked man can cause to take place among the children of men" (Alma 46:9).

Perhaps you have been fascinated, as I have been, by how the wicked rulers of the earth insist on the celebration of their own lives and their perceived greatness as they organize lavish parties in their own remembrance and insist that their subjects display and honor countless photos and images of themselves. They learn this self-centered adulation from Satan, their master, who proclaimed in the premortal realm, "I will ascend into heaven, I will exalt my throne above the stars of God: I will sit also upon the mount of the congregation, in the sides of the north: I will ascend above the heights of the clouds; I will be like the most High" (Isa. 14:13–14).

As we someday see Satan for what he really is, our wonderment will be, "Is this the man that made the earth to tremble, that did shake kingdoms; That made the world as a wilderness, and destroyed the cities thereof; that opened not the house of his prisoners?" (Isa. 14:16–17). As we see the true and ultimate fate of Satan and his subjects, we will more fully realize the truth "that the devil will not support his children at the last day" (Alma 30:60). What a happy day it will be when Satan, his work, and his evil followers fade away into oblivion. As the Lord promised, "The seed of evildoers shall never be renowned" (Isa. 14:20).

Rest from Thy Sorrow

Although we joyfully anticipate the day when Satan, the king of Babylon, will be deposed, we sorrow at the evil grasp of Satan in our current world and, to varying degrees, on our own hearts and the hearts of those we love.

He imprisons people to the extent that he can with his evil lies and damning seductions. Once he grasps us, he doesn't easily let go. His method is to make "the world as a wilderness" and not open "the house of his prisoners" (Isa. 14:17).

In the life of Moses we have a great example of how we may promptly dismiss Satan from our lives. In "an exceedingly high mountain," God taught Moses of his royal heritage: "And I have a work for thee, Moses, my son; and thou are in the similitude of mine Only Begotten." As Satan came tempting Moses, saying, "Moses, son of man, worship me," Moses remembered the lesson of his divine creation and destiny and replied to Satan, "Who art thou? For behold, I am a son of God, in the similitude of his Only Begotten; where is thy glory that I should worship thee? . . . Get thee hence, Satan; deceive me not" (Moses 1:1, 6, 12–13, 16).

As we follow the example of Moses, remembering who we are, where we are headed, and as we keep our covenants, the Lord protects and blesses us with His mercy and redemption: "For the Lord will have mercy on Jacob, and will yet choose Israel, and set them in their own land" (Isa. 14:1). As we endure the trials of mortality and do our best to serve and worship the Lord, we have the promise that "the Lord shall give thee rest from thy sorrow, and from thy fear, and from the hard bondage wherein thou wast made to serve" (Isa. 14:3). The day will come when Satan will be bound and gone from our world, and "the whole earth [will be] at rest, and is quiet: they [will] break forth into singing" (Isa. 14:7).

We find our hope for deliverance in Christ, who comes to free us from death and hell. Through His Atonement, the prison doors may be flung open and the prisoners set free. He was even to bring spiritual freedom to all who "were assembled awaiting the advent of the Son of God into the spirit world, to declare their redemption from the bands of death. Their sleeping dust was to be restored unto its perfect frame, bone to his bone, and the sinews and the flesh upon them, the spirit and the body to be united never again to be divided, that they might receive a fulness of joy" (D&C 138:16–17).

The Lord Hath Founded Zion

While doing our daily battle with Satan and driving him from our lives and into the wilderness prepared for him, we keep our hope bright as we rejoice in the future day when our battles will be over. We joyfully anticipate a time when heaven and earth are joined. Although we must go about our business of life in mortality, we may rightly hope for the day when the whole earth will be cleansed and be at rest.

What will be our feeling at this future day? "What shall one then answer the messengers of the nation? That the Lord hath founded Zion, and the poor of his people shall trust in it" (Isa. 14:32). As we trust Jehovah, we gain the strength and courage needed to properly dismiss Satan from our lives without discussion, hesitation, or argument.

CHAPTER FIFTEEN
MY HEART SHALL CRY OUT

Isaiah was called to deliver "burdens," or messages of doom, to wicked nations such as Moab: "The burden of Moab. Because in the night Ar of Moab is laid waste, and brought to silence; because in the night Kir of Moab is laid waste, and brought to silence" (Isa. 15:1; see also footnote a).

As we consider the wicked nation of Moab of ancient days, we may struggle to find the good—but there was good in Ruth, a Moabitess. The story of Ruth is one of the great stories of devotion, faith, and courage in the Bible. She descended from Moab, the eldest son of Lot, who was Abraham's nephew. Naomi, her husband, and their two sons had come to Moab to escape famine. One of her sons married Ruth, and upon his death and the death of his brother and father, Naomi prepared to return to her homeland. Naomi counseled Ruth to remain in Moab with her own people, where it was supposed she would be more comfortable. To this counsel, Ruth replied, "Intreat me not to leave thee, or to return from following after thee: for whither thou goest, I will go; and where thou lodgest, I will lodge: thy people shall be my people, and thy God my God" (Ruth 1:16).

"And thy God my God"—Ruth had the faith and courage to leave behind the false traditions of her people and convert to following the one true God. Unfortunately, her people would not abandon their false idolatry and continued to wallow in unbelief from one generation to the next. Later, during Isaiah's ministry, he called them to repentance and imposed upon them the Lord's burden, or message of warning, if they would not heed his call.

The High Places

Truly converted souls, like Ruth and Naomi, seek to partake of the saving blessings and ordinances of the Lord. The Moabites established their "worship" rituals in their "high places" to pay homage to their wicked idol-god, Chemosh. They traded reverence of the true and living sacrifice of Jesus Christ for immoral human sacrifice to their dumb idols.

Just as belief in Christ nurtures harmony and peace, idolatry breeds contention, warfare, and perversion. On one occasion when the Moabites were being beaten by the Israelites, "the king of Moab saw that the battle was too sore for him. . . . He took his eldest son that should have reigned in his stead, and offered him for a burnt offering upon the wall (2 Kings 3:26–27). Such evil demands a testimony against their wickedness from the Lord's prophet.

Moab Shall Howl

Isaiah's message of doom for Moab is one of sudden and complete destruction for their rebellion. Their destruction will come "in the night" and strike them at the heart in the central cities of Ar and Kir. In their distress, they go "up to Bajith, and to Dibon, the high places, to weep: Moab shall howl over Nebo, and over Medeba: . . . every one shall howl, weeping abundantly" (Isa. 15:2–3).

While the righteous speak prayers of praise and weep tears of gratitude, the abundant weeping of Moab is of anguish and fear. In consequence of their wickedness, "on all their heads shall be baldness, and every beard cut off" (Isa. 15:2), meaning their lives would be fraught with shame and mourning over their destruction. "Therefore the armed soldiers of Moab shall cry out; his life shall be grievous unto him. . . . For the waters of Nimrim shall be desolate: for the hay is withered away, the grass faileth, there is no green thing. Therefore the abundance they have gotten, and that which they have laid up, shall they carry away to the brook of the willows" (Isa. 15:4, 6–7). These rebellious souls who shed the blood of their own innocents would have blood as their reward: "For the waters of Dimon shall be full of blood: for I will bring more upon Dimon, lions upon him that escapeth of Moab, and upon the remnant of the land" (Isa. 15:9).

My Heart Shall Cry Out for Moab

Isaiah's life mission was not an easy ministry. His lament was, "My heart shall cry out for Moab" (Isa. 15:5). As he prophesied against such terrible apostasy manifest in the horrific practice of human sacrifice, he undoubtedly wept for God's children. As he delivered his burden upon Moab and other idolatrous societies, he himself was greatly burdened. Tradition informs us that Isaiah himself eventually became a victim of apostate murder, being "sawn asunder." Yet he remained true to his faith and his mission. Why would Moab not hear the voice of the Lord unto them through Isaiah and other prophets and come unto true peace and salvation? Why did Israel and Judah continue to seek union with Moab and like societies rather than putting their trust in the true Savior? Once Satan binds a people with his awful chains, they are not easily unloosed (see 2 Ne. 1:13; 28:22).

In the eternal realm where all things are made known, we may better understand how people can go so far astray and will also see more clearly how the divine spark of testimony spans generations and fans to a burning flame in the hearts of those who are humble and willing to believe, such as Ruth and others. We remember that God loved Ruth and the Moabites, just as He loves all of His children of all nations. In His love, He sends His prophets upon the earth to teach and testify. They courageously break down the high places of idolatry and diligently build up temples of true worship throughout the earth.

Ruth followed Naomi in worship of the true and living God. In process, she married Boaz and became the mother of the lineage of Christ. As we follow the example of Ruth by following Christ, we become of His lineage, for He is the Father of our salvation, and we are "his seed . . . heirs of the kingdom of God" (Mosiah 15:11).

CHAPTER SIXTEEN
AS A WANDERING BIRD CAST OUT OF THE NEST

ONE OF MY EARLIEST CHILDHOOD memories is of a day when I found an old bird cage and announced to my family that I was going out to hunt for a bird to put in it. I was not deterred from my quest by their teasing of me for my foolishness. By strange luck, I had not gone far into our horse pasture when sure enough, I found my bird—a young sparrow that had apparently been displaced from its nest and had wandered until it had fallen into a hoof print in the soft mud. The bird, not knowing that I just wanted to protect it, nervously squawked and fluttered as I quickly secured and covered it in my cage and took it back to my family, who were as surprised as I was delighted. Together we cared for the bird and protected it from weather and predators until it could be set free once again.

The Lord would have all people set free from the bonds of sin if only they would listen. When they do not, they wander as lost birds displaced from their nests.

As a Wandering Bird

Chapter 15 was Isaiah's prophecy of, or "burden" to, Moab and the ill that would befall them if they continued in their idolatry. Chapter 16 now tells us how Moab reacts to this burden.

Under threat from the Assyrians, the Moabites had been paying a handsome price for union and protection to the northern tribes of Israel: "And Mesha king of Moab was a sheepmaster, and rendered unto the king of Israel an hundred thousand lambs, and an hundred thousand rams, with the wool" (2 Kings 3:4). As these northern tribes fell into the grasp of Assyria, Moab did the unfathomable and sought coalition with Judah, their long-time enemy: "Send ye the lamb to the ruler of the land from Sela to the wilderness, unto the mount of the daughter of Zion" (Isa. 16:1). In their desperate plight, Moab was described "as a wandering bird cast out of the nest" (Isa. 16:2). They were fearful and desperate and were scurrying from one nation to another seeking for someone to protect them. They had missed the lesson that rather than sending tributes of lambs to similarly weak nations, if they would seek out and follow the Lamb of God, He would protect them.

Their plea was, "Make thy shadow as the night in the midst of the noonday; hide the outcasts; bewray not him that wandereth" (Isa. 16:3). In essence, they were asking to be made invisible from the Assyrians. But their plea for protection would not serve them well. By now they were well conditioned in the exercise of their unrighteous pride: "We have heard of the pride of Moab; he is very proud: even of his haughtiness, and his pride, and his wrath: but his lies shall not be so" (Isa. 16:6).

The Moabites would feel the Lord's chastening hand upon them. Gladness would give way to lamentation. "Therefore shall Moab howl for Moab, everyone shall howl. . . . And gladness is taken away, and joy out of the plentiful field; and in the vineyards there shall be no singing, neither shall there be shouting: the treaders shall tread out no wine in their presses; I have made their vintage shouting to cease" (Isa. 16:7,10).

In their desperate circumstance, Moab continued in vain to plead to their idol gods for protection. "And it shall come to pass, when it is seen that Moab is weary on the high place, that he shall come to his sanctuary to pray; but he shall not prevail" (Isa. 16:12). They had constructed gods of their own hands and displayed them in their groves and high places. Of course, they never intended that these manmade gods would chastise them and speak correction to them. They wanted gods that would silently ignore their sins. Now that they were in a desperate circumstance and so much in need of true guidance and direction, their idol gods did just what idol gods do—absolutely nothing.

A Covert from the Face of the Spoiler

In a sense, the rebellious Jews of Jesus's day also worshipped idol gods of their own making. They professed belief in a coming Messiah but desired one of their own imagining who would defend them against the Romans. Through many generations, the law of Moses had been fashioned into an elaborate façade designed to cover them in their profession.

The Moabites of Isaiah's day likewise looked to anyone they thought would protect and shield them from their enemies: They would have welcomed a general to drive the Assyrians far away. But they missed the Messianic message that Christ would be "a covert . . . from the face of the spoiler . . . And in mercy shall the throne be established: and he shall sit upon it in truth in the tabernacle of David, judging . . . and hasting righteousness" (Isa. 16:4–5). The tabernacle of David may have symbolic reference and connection to temples of all ages. From the temple, Christ bestows His mercy and judgment upon the nations. Those who accept of His invitation to come to the temple receive His protection from all enemies, physical and spiritual.

This message of Christ as our protective covering was lost on the Moabites but certainly should not be lost on us. If we show our faith by our willingness to be obedient, the Lord will become our "shadow as the night in the midst of noonday" (Isa. 16:3), just as He protected ancient Israel: "And the Lord went before them by day in a pillar of a cloud, to lead them the way; and by night in a pillar of fire, to give them light; to go by day and night" (Exodus 13:21).

Just as I sought to rescue, cover, and protect my little bird, Christ seeks to shelter and deliver us. We may tend to squawk and flutter about in the midst of our trials, but if we will calm down and come to understand and rely on the protective and redemptive power of His Atonement, He will cover us, lead us safely along, and deliver us to the glorious eternal life promised us by our Heavenly Father.

CHAPTER SEVENTEEN
SHALL A MAN LOOK TO HIS MAKER

LEGEND AND TRUTH BLEND TOGETHER to give us a perception of the antics of "confidence men" or "con men." The phrase *con man* typically refers to an individual who travels from place to place seeking to gain the confidence of the people and then use that confidence to defraud them of money and property. Our modern instant communications have enabled them to be more subtle than ever as they use tools such as the Internet to market their wares. But their motivations remain the same: greed, pride, arrogance, lust, and deceit. They and Satan, their master, have become more subtle and clever in perpetrating their stunts upon masses of people throughout the world. They are expert in selling "crowns like gold" (Rev. 9:7) in exchange for true crowns of eternal life.

In the previous chapters, we have discussed the burden of Moab. Satan had successfully conned Moab into abandoning the true God in exchange for the lustful pursuit of their idol gods. We now go to the north and observe how Damascus, or Syria, also falls into the pit of Satan's damning lies. They also become as wandering birds displaced from the nest or as tumbleweeds aimlessly rolling through the desert.

The Burden of Damascus

Isaiah now speaks "a message of doom 'lifted up' against Damascus": "The burden of Damascus. Behold, Damascus is taken away from being a city, and it shall be a ruinous heap" (Isa. 17:1; footnote 1a)

Damascus, or Syria, had been a relatively powerful force in Isaiah's day, although not nearly so powerful as their threatening enemy, Assyria. Syria had been an enemy to Judah but had sought unity with the northern tribes of Israel. Once Syria was captured by the Assyrians, Israel was left standing weak and alone with only their adopted idol gods to protect them: "The fortress also shall cease from Ephraim, and the kingdom from Damascus" (Isa. 17:3).

Strange Slips

Isaiah had warned Israel and Syria of the damning effects of their idolatry: "Because thou hast forgotten the God of thy salvation, and has not been mindful of the rock of thy strength, therefore shalt thou plant pleasant plants, and shall set it with strange slips: In the day shalt thou make thy plant to grow, and in the morning shalt thou make thy seed to flourish: but the harvest shall be a heap in the day of grief and of desperate sorrow" (Isa. 17:10–11).

"Strange slips" are scions, or small shoots or buds, cut from one tree or plant to graft into another.[29] Israel had a history of and potential for true worship of the true God. But, in yielding to their lust and greed, they had grafted strange slips of idolatry into their knowledge of God. These strange slips soon grew to smother and overcome the truth. The "pleasant plants" of their faith were soon choked out by the effects of the grafting in of false worship. Through their idolatry, they lost the protection of the true God and became "as the chaff of the mountains before the wind, and like a rolling thing before the whirlwind" (Isa. 17:13). The pleasant plants of their faith had become as dry, lifeless tumbleweeds rolling in the wilderness in whatever direction the winds of whim and lust might blow them.

The plan of salvation is a plan of joy. "Adam fell that men might be; and men are, that they might have joy" (2 Ne. 2:25). The intent and desire of Heavenly Father is that we enjoy happy families and friendships, think pure and uplifting thoughts, live in pleasant and clean surroundings, consume good and nourishing food and drink, and dress in comfortable, modest, and appealing clothing. Heavenly Father desires that we have the contentment of living in safe and trustful relationships wherein we help one another in the actualization of our divine potential. He wants us to experience the peace and happiness of seeing our loved ones grow up in truth and virtue.

Satan, the master con man and crown prince of counterfeit, has forfeited his opportunity for eternal life and family. He is a destroyer of the grandest skill. In his misery, he desires to entice others to become like him. Through long years of experience, he and his myriad helpers hurriedly scurry around inserting strange slips of evil and grafting buds of untruth wherever and whenever they can, as if they sense that the time of harvest and gleaning is nigh.

For those prone to anger "shall he rage in the hearts of the children of men, and stir them up to anger against that which is good" (2 Ne. 28:20).

He persuades people to take offense, even when none is intended. He stirs up segments of society to violently protest in opposition to marriage and family values. He cleverly persuades a spouse to find fault with his or her mate and then fans this flame into bitterness and perceived irreconcilable differences.

For those who have a propensity for apathy, Satan seeks to "pacify, and lull them away into carnal security, that they will say: All is well in Zion; yea, Zion prospereth, all is well—and thus the devil cheateth their souls, and leadeth them away carefully down to hell" (2 Ne. 28:21). Satan inserts the strange slip of disregard for violence or immorality in entertainment. "Oh, it is not *that* bad," or "Well, it has great social value," he persuades them to exclaim. "An occasional drink is all right," or, "Well, I know so-and-so who did such-and-such, and he was a faithful Church member."

For the vain "he flattereth away, and telleth them there is no hell; and he saith unto them: I am no devil, for there is none—and thus he whispereth in their ears until he grasps them with his awful chains, from whence there is no deliverance" (2 Ne. 28:22). Satan carefully implants the bud of invincibility—"I am strong. I can handle it," they proclaim as they sell their soul to the gods of glitz and glitter. "It's okay, we live in the enlightened age," they say as they engage in immorality that is clearly not okay and never was or ever will be in the eyes of the true God.

Gleaning Grapes: Shall a Man Look to His Maker

The gospel is a message of hope. All human souls are God's children, and His plan is sufficient to redeem all who look to Him and hear His voice. He is mindful of each one of His children.

The Assyrians did not capture or destroy all of the ten northern tribes of Israel; some escaped and were allowed to remain in the land: "Yet gleaning grapes shall be left in it, as the shaking of an olive tree, two or three berries in the top of the uppermost bough, four or five in the outmost fruitful branches thereof, saith the Lord God of Israel" (Isa. 17:6). And even though the tribes of Israel were mostly scattered to the four winds, they were not lost to Heavenly Father. Both those who remain in the land and those scattered have a place and purpose in the work of the Lord as He seeks to gather all back to His fold.

Several years ago, as I was enrolled in a military training program, I met a man whose lost soul eventually returned to his Heavenly Father. My assigned bunk mate was a Latter-day Saint, but he was not actively involved in gospel worship or practice. Over many years, he had acquired the addictive habits of the fallen world. He had a serious drinking problem. His language was sometimes profane. Yet he was personable and kind. I liked him. I connected with him, and our friendship continued during the term of our service experiences. After a few years, my military commitment ended, and I did not see him again for many years.

As I was on business in the area of his residence some time later, I had a free evening and decided to attend the temple. As I sat in the chapel before our session, I casually glanced around and, to my astonishment, saw my military friend dressed in white and awaiting our session. After our session, I joyfully greeted him with my indiscreet but playful question: "What are you doing here?" He likewise countered, "I have been coming here for years—where have you been?" I left the temple feeling joy for the wonderful saving grace and redeeming love of our Savior. I was so happy that my friend had been gathered safely home to his spiritual destiny.

After seasons of trial and chastisement, Israel would be gathered home to their true destiny: "At that day shall a man look to his Maker, and his eyes shall have respect to the Holy One of Israel. And he shall not look to the altars, the work of his hands, neither shall respect that which his fingers have made, either the groves, or the images" (Isa. 17:7–8). The "strange slips" of worldly vanity and idolatry would be pruned away and destroyed.

When we as God's children look to Him and heed His call, we are naturally drawn away from the altars of the world and toward the true altars of the temple where we find direction, peace, joy, and eternal happiness. As we are true and faithful, we receive redemption and relief from our trials. Those evil con men that have tormented us will be gone in a day: "And behold at eveningtide trouble; and before the morning he is not" (Isa. 17:14). Joseph's prayer in the Kirtland temple will have fulfillment with all Saints in all temples: "Thou wilt fight for thy people as thou didst in the day of battle, that they may be delivered from the hands of all their enemies" (D&C 109:28).

CHAPTER EIGHTEEN
A PRESENT UNTO THE LORD OF HOSTS

SOMETIMES WITH MY STUDENTS, I have half jokingly said that I could imagine meeting Isaiah someday and asking, "Did you mean this or this about that?" and having him reply, "Yes, and also, this, this, and this." A teacher of mine sometimes commented that he supposed Isaiah's philosophy was, "Why waste words on only one meaning?" As we have already witnessed, Isaiah often offers messages that have application to more than one people and time period, messages that have a dualistic property. The specific meanings and applications of his words may be as varied in specific personal applications as are his readers. Furthermore, he seems generally untroubled by bounds of chronology and often blends together events of the past, present, and future.

I am certainly not suggesting that "anything goes" in interpreting Isaiah. I am suggesting that truth is presented at many levels and with many illustrations. Nephi gives us a grand key for understanding the words of Isaiah. After quoting the largest portion of Isaiah passages contained in the Book of Mormon, he said:

> Wherefore, hearken, O my people, which are of the house of Israel, and give ear unto my words; for because the words of Isaiah are not plain unto you, *nevertheless they are plain unto all those that are filled with the spirit of prophecy.* But I give unto you a prophecy, according to the spirit which is in me; wherefore I shall prophesy according to the plainness which hath been with me from the time that I came out from Jerusalem with my father; for behold, my soul delighteth in plainness unto my people, that they may learn. Yea, and my soul delighteth in the words of Isaiah. (2 Ne. 25:4–5; emphasis added)

The Spirit has the capacity to convey to us, collectively and individually, the myriad sweet messages of hope and peace written by the prophet Isaiah, "for great are the words of Isaiah" (3 Ne. 23:1). Elder Dallin H. Oaks taught, "The idea that scripture reading can lead to inspiration and revelation opens the door to the truth that a scripture is not limited to what it meant when it was written but may also include what that scripture means to a reader today. Even more, scripture reading may also lead to current revelation on whatever else the Lord wishes to communicate to the reader at that time. We do not overstate the point when we say that the scriptures can be a Urim and Thummim to assist each of us to receive personal revelation."[30]

The Land Shadowing with Wings

This chapter begins with a concept that evokes curiosity: "Woe to the land shadowing with wings, which is beyond the rivers of Ethiopia: That sendeth ambassadors by the sea, even in vessels of bulrushes upon the waters, saying, Go, ye swift messengers, to a nation scattered and peeled, to a people terrible from their beginning hitherto; a nation meted out and trodden down, whose land the rivers have spoiled!" (Isa. 18:1–2). Why "Woe"? What is meant by "the land shadowing with wings"?

"Woe" as "sorrow" is likely a mistranslation. From the footnote we learn of a better word—*Hoy*, meaning "greeting." Greeting is a pleasant word of gratitude for the protection and *covering* offered by "the land shadowing with wings." The Savior used the imagery of covering with wings as He lamented for the Jews and taught that He would have gathered and protected them "even as a hen gathereth her chickens under her wings, and ye would not" (Matt. 23:37).

Using our imagination, we can envision the relatively small geography of Judah and Israel in the center, bordered by the great "wings" of Egypt on the one side and Assyria on the other. From the land of the "bulrushes" or "papyrus"—that is, from Egypt—we see imagery of protection to Judah and Israel. Egypt had sought protective alliance with Israel and Judah against the Assyrian threat. If we focus our attention only on the time of Isaiah, we recall that he is trying to get Israel to look to the Lord rather than to Egypt for their protection. However, if we broaden our view, we recall the protection from famine offered in Egypt to Abraham and later to the families of Jacob or Israel. The newborn Savior Himself was protected in Egypt from the murderous decree of Herod.

Now we take another view of the dualistic prophecy of the land shadowing with wings. President Spencer W. Kimball taught, "In that southern world of Zion we reminded them that Zion was all of North and South America, like the wide, spreading wings of a great eagle, the one being North and the other South America."[31] Let us imagine the land of the Americas. Consider the relatively narrow neck of Central America, connected on either side by the two great wings of North and South America. Israel was to be scattered throughout the world, including throughout the Americas. From the Americas, the Lord "sendeth ambassadors by the sea" and by air and land, who would "go . . . swift" to "a nation meted out and trodden down." From the Americas, the Lord would declare, "All ye inhabitants of the world, and dwellers on the earth, see ye, when he lifteth up an ensign on the mountains; and when he bloweth a trumpet, hear ye" (Isa. 18:2–3). Scattered Israel was to be brought under the wings of the gospel restored in America, and then spread throughout the earth.

Symbols of the Wings

The gathering of Israel hinges on the Atonement of Christ and the saving ordinances of the gospel, including the temple and the purposes thereof. Patriarch Hyrum Smith taught at a conference in Nauvoo, "The gathering will continue here until the Temple is so far finished that the Elders can get their endowments; and after that the gathering will be from the nations to North and South America which is the land of Zion. North and South America are the symbols of the wings."[32]

Consider the enthusiasm of the prophets for building temples. Joseph sought the blessings of the temple for the people and exerted his energy to accomplish this purpose in Kirtland, Independence, Far West, and Nauvoo. As the mantle of leadership next fell on President Brigham Young, he tirelessly worked to complete the Nauvoo temple and even stayed, under threat of the mobs, longer than he felt was prudent in order to share the endowment with those preparing for the trek west to give them the protection, the vision, and the courage to accomplish their prophetic destiny. As they left Nauvoo, President Young envisioned the Lord's temple standing majestically in the desert at the trail's end. One of his first acts in the new land of the Salt Lake Valley was to ascend a mountain peak and fulfill Isaiah's prophecy by erecting a banner in symbolic representation of an ensign to the entire world, inviting all to come to Christ and the temple. Shortly after he descended Ensign Peak, he thrust his cane into the desert soil and proclaimed, "Here we will build the Temple of our God!"[33]

Our modern prophets continue this grand mission with their own passion and commitment. We as Saints rejoice at the announcement of each new temple. For example, those gathered in the Nauvoo stake center at the announcement of the rebuilding of their temple were completely overcome with joy for the goodness of the Lord to them. This beautiful temple now stands in splendor as a symbol to all nations that the "puny arm" of man was unable "to hinder the Almighty from pouring down knowledge from heaven upon the heads of the Latter-day Saints" (D&C 121:33).

A Present unto the Lord of Hosts

As President Howard W. Hunter was introduced at a news conference as the fourteenth President of the Church, he said, "I also invite the members of the Church to establish the temple of the Lord as the great symbol of their membership and the supernal setting for their most sacred covenants. It would be the deepest desire of my heart to have every member of the Church be temple worthy."[34]

Why would the deepest desire of the heart of the prophet be to have the Saints be worthy to come to the temple? The prophet speaks the mind and will of the Lord, who wants to give us the greatest "gift," or "present," possible to give—even "eternal life, which gift is the greatest of all the gifts of God" (D&C 14:7). The purpose of the temple endowment, or gift, prepares us to eventually receive eternal life.

John the Revelator saw in vision the faithful elders who had attained eternal life, symbolized by crowns of gold. These faithful souls present themselves to Heavenly Father: "The four and twenty elders fall down before him that sat on the throne, and worship him that liveth for ever and ever, and cast their crowns before the throne, saying, Thou art worthy, O Lord, to receive glory and honour and power: for thou hast created all things, and for thy pleasure they are and were created" (Rev. 4:10–11). The greatest gift our Heavenly Father gives us is the opportunity for eternal life—the greatest gift we can give Him is to present to Him our lives worthy of His gift.

Isaiah now speaks of the gift, or present, to be brought by gathered Israel. "In that time shall the *present* be brought unto the Lord of hosts of a people scattered and peeled, and from a people terrible from their beginning hitherto; a nation meted out and trodden under foot, whose land the rivers have spoiled, to the place of the name of the Lord of hosts, the mount Zion" (Isa. 18:7; emphasis added).

In the Lord's due time, scattered Israel will accept the power of the Atonement in their lives, be gathered to Christ, be endowed on mount Zion with the potential for eternal life, and progress forward to the day when they may in turn present their crowns of eternal life to our Heavenly Father. After many years of trial and wandering, Israel will heed the beckoning call of the ensign on the mountain and come to "mount Zion," or to the temple, where they will be taught and will receive their endowment. They will then return this present of being worthy of eternal life to our Heavenly Father with abounding joy and eternal gratitude for His plan and for the Atonement of His Son. They will continue in joy as their children likewise prepare themselves for eternal life and offer this gift to Heavenly Father.

How sweet are the blessings of the Atonement and the temple, "the great symbol of our membership" in the Lord's kingdom!

CHAPTER NINETEEN
FINE LINEN

THE NATURAL ELEMENTS OF OUR world can serve as a metaphor for the agency of man. Uranium, for example, is not inherently good or evil, but at the choice of those who process it, it may be applied to diverse purposes, such as the production of energy, defensive shields, or destructive weaponry. In the same vein, flax is not inherently good or evil and may be used for food products, linen, or ill purposes of lust or glutteny; in a figurative sense, it can be processed into the "fine flax of the wicked" or into the "fine linen of righteousness."

As Latter-day Saints, we reject the false and damning notion of original sin. We are not born sinful but are rather born into a sinful and fallen world where we may choose to follow a course of good or evil. We are taught in modern revelation that "every spirit of man was innocent in the beginning; and God having redeemed man from the fall, men became again, in their infant state, innocent before God" (D&C 93:38). Our birth into mortality is as though we were given a wealth of natural resources and the power to choose what we would make from them. All people have agency and may choose to work the fine flax of the wicked or weave the fine linen of righteousness. We are "free to choose liberty and eternal life, through the great Mediator of all men, or to choose captivity and death, according to the captivity and power of the devil" (2 Ne. 2:27).

They That Work in Fine Flax

In the continuing prophecies of doom to the nations that rely on their own strength and do not trust in the Lord, we now come to Egypt: "The burden of Egypt. Behold, the Lord rideth upon a swift cloud, and shall come into Egypt: and the idols of Egypt shall be moved at his presence, and the heart of Egypt shall melt in the midst of it" (Isa. 19:1).

The Lord seeks to seal and preserve families and have them live in love and unity. Satan seeks to dismantle and destroy communities and families, driving wedges of jealousy and pride between friends, neighbors, and brothers. At times the Lord allows the tactics of the adversary to be used to chasten His people: "And I will set the Egyptians against the Egyptians: and they shall fight everyone against his brother, and every one against his neighbour; city against city, and kingdom against kingdom" (Isa. 19:2).

Rather than seeking out the Lord for guidance, the Egyptians turn to idolatry: "They shall seek to the idols, and to the charmers, and to them that have familiar spirits, and to the wizards" (Isa. 19:3). As a consequence of their faithlessness, they suffer, among other things, disruption to their natural environment: "The waters shall fail from the sea, and the river shall be wasted and dried up. . . . the reeds and flags shall wither. . . . and every thing sown by the brooks, shall wither, be driven away, and be no more. . . . The fishers also shall mourn" (Isa. 19:5–8).[35]

Because the Lord's just harvest is often delayed for His own purposes, it can look like the wicked are prevailing, getting rich and becoming famous, while the opposite seems true for the righteous. The wicked may delude themselves into thinking that it is their genius that has brought their measured success, while the righteous know they must rely on Christ because they cannot make it on their own. They chart a steady forward course with the Lord, but in seeing that they do not always have the blessing they expect, they may be tempted to cry, "Unfair!" But eventually, truth prevails and justice is rendered. A course of pride and vanity ultimately causes the traveler to wander "as a drunken man staggereth in his vomit" (Isa. 19:14).

As stated earlier, the flax we weave determines how we will be rewarded. The Egyptian people were chastened for their choices: "Moreover they that work in fine flax, and they that weave networks, shall be confounded" (Isa. 19:9).

The Fine Linen of Righteousness

The Lord would have us use the resources He gives for the blessing of all of His children. "Yea, all things which come of the earth, in the season thereof, are made for the benefit and the use of man, both to please the eye and to gladden the heart; Yea, for food and for raiment, for taste and for smell, to strengthen the body and to enliven the soul. And it pleaseth God that he hath given all these things unto man" (DC 59:18–20).

John the Revelator, in expounding the doctrine of the marriage metaphor of Christ as the Bridegroom and the Church as the bride, taught, "Let us be glad and rejoice, and give honour to him: for the marriage of the Lamb is come, and his wife hath made herself ready. And to her was granted that she should be arrayed in fine linen, clean and white: for the fine linen is the righteousness of the saints" (Rev. 19:7–8). All people of the world may choose to wear the fine linen of righteousness, even if their physical garments are patched and repaired or handed down from one to another. Wealth and power do not equate with righteousness.

After the day of chastening and tribulation, Egypt would begin to accept the Lord's invitation to put on the fine linen of righteousness. With this new wardrobe, they would be prepared for the blessings of the temple that would one day come to them. In the temple, they would have opportunity to covenant with the Lord and learn of and prepare for eternal life. "In that day there shall be an altar to the Lord in the midst of the land of Egypt, and a pillar at the border thereof to the Lord. . . . and he shall send them a saviour, and a great one, and he shall deliver them. And the Lord shall be known to Egypt, and the Egyptians shall know the Lord in that day, and shall do sacrifice and oblation; yea, they shall vow a vow unto the Lord, and perform it" (Isa. 19:19–21). The "altar" references the "temple that will be built and dedicated to Jehovah in the land of Egypt," and the "sacrifices, oblations, and vows pertain to temple worship and also to Sabbath worship."[36]

We may marvel at but must not doubt the manifestation of divine love of our Savior for the people of Egypt. If we wonder at the thought of a temple in such an unlikely country as Egypt, we need merely look at the progress of the Lord's work in other nations and places. Consider temples in Japan or Hong Kong. Did that seem possible at the time they battled in world war? Could past generations have imagined that there would be a temple in former East Germany, a temple in the Ukraine, or a reconstructed temple in Nauvoo? All things are possible as the Lord rolls forth His purposes and gathers His people. He chastens and He heals as He invites all to seek to be clothed in the fine linen of righteousness. "The Lord shall smite Egypt: he shall smite and heal it: and they shall return even to the Lord, and he shall be entreated of them, and shall heal them" (Isa. 19:22).

Blessed Be Egypt, Assyria, and Israel

Through our temple dress and worship, we are taught our true nature as God's children and of His desire for us. We dress modestly to travel to the temple. When we arrive, we lay aside the clothing of the world in exchange for the white clothing of the temple, thus symbolizing purity and the fine linen of righteousness. All are equal in the temple. In the temple, as we strive for righteousness, we break down the barriers of prejudice and oppression that so plague our world. Through acceptance and application of the gospel of Jesus Christ and the making and keeping of temple covenants, the Egyptians and the Israelites and the Assyrians begin to lose their venom for one another: "In that day shall there be a highway out of Egypt to Assyria, and the Assyrian shall come into Egypt, and the Egyptian into Assyria, and the Egyptians shall serve with the Assyrians" (Isa. 19:23).

The "highway out of Egypt" seems to refer to the highway of righteousness—the same path all of God's children must follow to be united with Him. This highway, as with all roads in the Church, leads us to our Savior. In traveling this highway, we receive the cleansing and sanctifying power of the Atonement in our lives: "Yea, come unto Christ, and be perfected in him, and deny yourselves of all ungodliness; and if ye shall deny yourselves of all ungodliness, and love God with all your might, mind and strength. . . . then are ye sanctified in Christ by the grace of God, through the shedding of the blood of Christ, which is in the covenant of the Father unto the remission of your sins, that ye become holy, without spot" (Moro. 10:32–33).

In the day of the Lord's healing of the nations, there will be no more pride, arrogance, or idolatry. We will not war one with another. "In that day shall Israel be the third with Egypt and with Assyria, even a blessing in the midst of the land: Whom the Lord of hosts shall bless, saying, Blessed be Egypt my people, and Assyria the work of my hands, and Israel mine inheritance" (Isa. 19:24–25).

Think of it—Egypt, Assyria, and Israel united in righteousness and living in peace and harmony one with another. All things are possible as we clothe ourselves in the fine linen of righteousness and, in so doing, come unto Christ and accept of His Atonement.

CHAPTER TWENTY
HOW SHALL WE ESCAPE?

As an object lesson to the rebellious Egyptians, the Lord directed Isaiah to walk naked and barefoot for three years: "At the same time spake the Lord by Isaiah the son of Amoz, saying, Go and loose the sackcloth from off thy loins, and put off thy shoe from thy foot. And he did so, walking naked and barefoot" (Isa. 20:2).

Our Savior, always the master teacher, loved object lessons. He instructed Peter to "take up the fish that first cometh up; and when thou hast opened his mouth, thou shalt find a piece of money" (Matt. 17:27), with which he was to pay the tribute. With the man born blind, He "spat on the ground, and made clay of the spittle, and he anointed the eyes of the blind man with the clay" (John 9:6). To disgruntled Jonah, who was upset that the Lord would spare the rebellious Ninevites, the Lord "prepared a gourd, and made it to come up over Jonah, that it might be a shadow over his head, to deliver him from his grief. So Jonah was exceeding glad of the gourd. But God prepared a worm when the morning rose the next day, and it smote the gourd that it withered" (Jonah 4:6–7).

Walking Naked and Barefoot

The charge to walk "naked" was likely interpreted to walk "without an upper garment, like a slave or exile" (Isa. 20:2, footnote a). It was customary for slaves to be shaved bald and stripped of clothing as a sign of their slavery and as prevention of the concealing of a weapon.

A person walking naked through the harsh climate of Isaiah's world would be exposed to the vicious hazards of extreme sun and wind, along with the shame of being uncovered and seen by all of the people. Through their idolatry and rebellion, the Egyptians were exposing themselves to the harsh elements of the chastening hand of the Lord. As discussed in the previous chapter, they would experience the loss of their crops and of their economy. Their gods would not protect them. Their sinful ways would bring suffering upon them. They would, in due time, be conquered by Assyria: "So shall the king of Assyria lead away the Egyptians prisoners, and the Ethiopians captives, young and old, naked and barefoot, even with their buttocks uncovered, to the shame of Egypt" (Isa. 20:4). In the day of their sorrow, their pleading cry was to be, "And how shall we escape?" (Isa. 20:6).

How Shall We Escape?

The answer to the question "And how shall we escape?" is easy; the challenge is in applying that answer. The Savior taught, "For my yoke is easy, and my burden is light" (Matt. 11:30). When we choose to allow the Savior to cover us with the power of His atoning sacrifice, we do not gain exemption from trial, but we do gain proper direction and redemption.

We can be instructed on how to escape the Lord's punishment from the book of Jonah, which is written in chiastic form, where the focal point of the writing is given at the center of the entire passage.[37] Here, the focal point of this passage falls in verse 8 of chapter 2: "They that observe lying vanities forsake their own mercy" (Jonah 2:8).[38] Jonah, in his pride, was grateful that the Lord spared him but exercised "lying vanity" in not wanting the Ninevites to be spared. The Lord's Atonement is intended to cover all of God's children. If Jonah was to be covered, as may be illustrated by the growing gourd, then the Ninevites should be covered. If he thought the Ninevites should be excluded from the Lord's mercy and Atonement, then it would only be fair that he be left uncovered, as was illustrated by the withered gourd.

The gourd of Jonah was prepared to be "a shadow over his head" (Jonah 4:6). The ancient tabernacle was covered by a cloud "by day, and the appearance of fire by night" (Num. 9:16). We recall that we began our study of Isaiah with his prophecy proclaiming that, through apostasy, the people were exposing themselves as an abandoned "cottage in a vineyard" (Isa. 1:8). We, like Adam and Eve, are left uncovered by the effects of the Fall and the natural conditions of our fallen world. Faith and repentance lead us to Christ and to the "tabernacle," or temple, where we come under the safe and protective canopy of the Lord's Atonement.

Let us consider some of the ways we may be covered by the Lord's Atonement, using the dedicatory prayer of the Kirtland Temple as our guide:

> Thanks be to thy name, O Lord God of Israel, who keepest
> covenant and showest mercy unto thy servants who walk

uprightly before thee, with all their hearts—
That thy *glory may rest down upon* thy people.

And when thy people transgress, any of them, they may speedily repent and return unto thee, and find favor in thy sight, and be restored to the *blessings* which thou hast ordained to be *poured out upon those* who shall reverence thee in thy house.

That thy servants may go forth from this house *armed with thy power*, and that thy *name may be upon them*, and thy *glory be round about them,* and thine *angels have charge over them.*

That no combination of wickedness shall have power to rise up and prevail over thy people *upon whom thy name shall be put* in this house.

Let the anointing of thy ministers *be sealed upon them* with power from on high.

Put upon thy servants the testimony of the covenant . . . that thy people may not faint in the day of trouble. (D&C 109:1, 12, 21, 22, 26, 35, 38; emphasis added)

Israel was not to look to Egypt for protection—Egypt was to be taken captive and could offer nothing to Israel. The continuing message of Isaiah is that we are to look to the Lord for protection. We are to trust Jehovah! How grateful we are to have the guidance of prophets to help us escape the effects of our fallen world. We are not to wander "naked and barefoot" through the land but are to come unto Christ and accept His protective promises and the covering of His Atonement.

CHAPTER TWENTY-ONE
WATCHMAN, WHAT OF THE NIGHT?

IN THIS CHAPTER, ISAIAH CONTINUES to teach the folly of trusting in the arm of flesh—of seeking the mirage of worldliness.

Early in my life, our family took a road trip to California. In crossing the desert, I was fascinated as I looked far ahead at the highway and saw that it was covered by varying-sized pools of water. I anticipated that we would be able to break the boredom of our journey by stopping to cool off and splash about. I was perplexed that we never seemed to get to the water, as it mysteriously kept moving just beyond our reach. I suppose my parents tried to tell me the water was not real, but I persisted and kept believing in this mirage for a while.

Adulthood has brought recognition to me, as it undoubtedly has to all of us, that many things about our fallen world of Babylon are illusions and are simply not what they often seem to be. Alma taught his disobedient son Corianton about one of the greatest mirages of all: "Behold, I say unto you, wickedness never was happiness" (Alma 41:10).

The Desert of the Sea

Isaiah now delivers one of many "burdens," or messages of doom, to Babylon: "The burden of the desert of the sea. As whirlwinds in the south pass through; so it cometh from the desert, from a terrible land" (Isa. 21:1). Babylon was mostly a land-locked desert and could figuratively be described as a "sea of sand." The Euphrates River, during the annual flood season, would overflow its banks and create a large, shallow sea, in essence a mirage of an abiding, deep sea. In the heat of the sun, the watery sea would soon give way once again to the sand sea.

We know of the terribleness of ancient Babylon. At the time of their greatest might, they certainly must have given the illusion to surrounding nations that they were invincible. And yet the day of their destruction was inevitable. Of this Isaiah said, "A grievous vision is declared unto me; the treacherous dealer dealeth treacherously, and the spoiler spoileth. Go up, O Elam: besiege, O Media; all the sighing thereof have I made to cease" (Isa. 21:2). Elam and Media were not the great military powers at the time of Isaiah that they would yet be in the future day when, as part of the Persian Empire, they would become the destroyers of Babylon.

At this juncture in the book of Isaiah, some scholars are quick to point out that Isaiah could not have written this accurate assessment of the future fall of Babylon because it would not happen for two hundred more years. We who believe in continuing revelation through prophets readily associate the word *prophet* with *prophesy*, which means "to predict (a future event)," and *seer*, which is defined as "a person with the supposed power to foretell the future."[39]

Watch in the Watchtower

Prophets prophesy! In so doing, they are not bound in any way by the constraints that people sometimes attempt to impose upon them to restrict their words only to spiritual matters. Prophets are often pained by what they must speak.

Of the "burden" he was obliged to speak to Babylon, Isaiah said, "Therefore are my loins filled with pain: pangs have taken hold upon me, as the pangs of a woman that travaileth: I was bowed down at the hearing of it; I was dismayed at the seeing of it. My heart panted, fearfulness affrighted me: the night of my pleasure hath he turned into fear unto me" (Isa. 21:3–4). And yet, he went boldly forward in his mission and took up his appointed station as the Lord's watchman: "Prepare the table, watch in the watchtower, eat, drink: arise, ye princes, and anoint the shield. For thus hath the Lord said unto me, Go, set a watchman, let him declare what he seeth" (Isa. 21:5–6).

As the Lord's watchman, Isaiah went wherever the Lord wanted him to go, spoke to whomever He wanted him to speak, and declared whatever message He wanted him to deliver, including "the burden of Dumah" and "the burden upon Arabia" (Isa. 21:11, 13).

Watchman, What of the Night?

Prophets of all ages go where the Lord wants them to go and do what He wants them to do. They and other appointed leaders are the watchmen on the tower.

The darkness of the night was an especially important time for communities to have dependable and true watchmen perched high up on the watchtowers to sound the warning cry against danger. The evil influences of ancient Babylon are a type for the growing influences of sinful Babylon in our day. We are in serious danger from spiritual Babylon wherein so many of the people of the world "seek not the Lord to establish his righteousness, but every man walketh in his own way, and after the image of his own god, whose image is in the likeness of the world, and whose substance is that of an idol, which waxeth old and shall perish in Babylon, even Babylon the great, which shall fall" (D&C 1:16).

The destruction of ancient Babylon is a type for the destruction that must and will come to spiritual Babylon in our day. In spiritual Babylon the whims and fashions of the ungodly may glimmer in the sun for a moment as an enticing sea of opulence, but they will quickly evaporate, leaving residents stranded in the dark of the night in the midst of a wasteland of death and evil. To live in Babylon is to live in darkness. To ignore the watchmen on the tower is spiritual death.

From a loving God who desires to warn, rescue, and save His children comes the solemn question, repeated for emphasis: "Watchman, what of the night? Watchman, what of the night?" (Isa. 21:11). Gratefully, our watchmen know the danger of the darkness and counter with the true light of the restored gospel.

As the voice of Babylon cries, "Take what is yours; get all you can!" our watchmen from the towers plead, "Serve one another; share your bounty." Babylon proclaims, "This is the latest in fashion; be popular," our watchmen counsel, "Be modest, be wise, seek to please the Lord." As the voice of the barren mores of the lustful world entices us—"Follow your lusts"—the Lord speaks eternal, saving truth: "Be chaste." As the agitators of world power and politics scream, "Fight with all your might," the Prince of Peace invites us to "be peacemakers."

"What of the night?" Will we seek society in the mirage of the dark desert of Babylon? Or will we strive to see "things as they really are" (Jacob 4:13) by living to make and keep protective covenants with our Heavenly Father?

CHAPTER TWENTY-TWO
ELIAKIM—GOD SHALL CAUSE TO ARISE

A FEW WEEKS PRIOR TO the time of this writing, our stake held a special conference. The announcement of this meeting caused some wonderment, particularly when we were told that a member of the Quorum of the Twelve Apostles was to be with us. Personally, I knew that whatever else might happen, he would share his testimony of the divinity of the mission and Atonement of Jesus Christ, which is, as Peter taught, central to the calling: "Must one be ordained to be a witness with us of his resurrection" (Acts 1:22).

In the meeting, our welcome visitor told us that our special conference was part of an effort on the part of the Brethren to be among the Saints more often than regular conference visits. We were grateful for the extra effort of this busy, inspired leader to go above and beyond his normal travels of the world and come testify to us of Christ, which he did in a powerful way.

Wholly Gone Up to the Housetops

Prophets teach and testify of Christ with cause for rejoicing when their message is well received and cause for mourning when it is rejected. Isaiah, who had been addressing the various nations in teaching and testifying of Christ, had cause to mourn as he now spoke to Jerusalem with "a message of doom" to them for their rebelliousness: "The burden of the valley of vision. What aileth thee now, that thou art wholly gone up to the housetops? Thou that are full of stirs, a tumultuous city, a joyous city: thy slain men are not slain with the sword, nor dead in battle" (Isa. 22:1–2).

The flat-top roof architecture of the Jerusalem homes often provided a place for both celebrating and mourning. Unrighteous partying leads to sorrow. Isaiah's reaction to their going "wholly to the housetops" tells us that their partying was not of clean, wholesome sociality but of rebellion and neglect of the more weighty matters of life. And Isaiah mourned for them: "Therefore said I, Look away from me; I will weep bitterly, labour not to comfort me, because of the spoiling of the daughter of my people" (Isa. 22:4). They were not currently being slain by external swords of battle but by the internal shafts of neglect, rebellion, and apostasy. Mourning would soon follow with their Babylonian captivity.

Ye Have Not Looked unto the Maker

The visiting authority at our conference counseled us in the usual temporal preparations for the times in which we live, but mostly he counseled us in spiritual matters. He urged us to be grateful, to have hope, and to live the gospel.

Judah, in the frightful shadow of the threat of the pending Assyrian invasion, had made some wise temporal preparations (see Isa. 22:8–11). They had miraculously constructed an underground "ditch," or tunnel, to bring the life-giving waters of the Gihon spring inside the protective walls of Jerusalem: "Ye made also a ditch between the two walls for the water of the old pool." However, they had been derelict in spiritual matters. "But ye have not looked unto the maker thereof, neither had respect unto him that fashioned it long ago" (Isa. 22:11). Nearly a century later, Jeremiah would reiterate this imagery in light of their continuing apostasy: "For my people have committed two evils; they have forsaken me the fountain of living waters, and hewed them out cisterns, broken cisterns, that can hold no water" (Jer. 2:13).

One of the false and damning philosophies, or "cisterns that can hold no water," that plagues all generations is the notion that repentance is not worth the effort. Satan whispers to the downtrodden, "It is too late, and it is too hard to repent! Just relax and party while you can." He and his servants tell us to "eat, drink, and be merry, for tomorrow we die; and it shall be well with us" (2 Ne. 28:7). And in Isaiah's words: "And behold joy and gladness, slaying oxen, and killing sheep, eating flesh, and drinking wine: let us eat and drink; for to morrow we shall die" (Isa. 22:13).

The truth of the matter is that life will only be well with us if we choose to live a life harmonious with principles of spiritual wellness. To live such a life, we need to "draw water out of the wells of salvation" (Isa. 12:3) and look unto our Maker. Rather than assume that "tomorrow we die," we are better served to recognize that tomorrow we live, and that how we live depends upon the degree of our acceptance of the living water, or of the doctrine, mission, and the Atonement of Jesus Christ. Judah's only hope was to turn their hearts to Christ as illustrated by "Eliakim," a type of

Christ. Such conversion of the heart is the hope of all truth-seeking people in all times.

Eliakim: God Shall Cause to Arise

The haughty and wicked Shebna held an important position of royal treasurer of Judah. Unfortunately, he fell prey to Satan's age-old trap of aspiring "to the honors of men" (D&C 121:35) and in so doing misused his position and resources in vainly constructing himself a grand tomb. The Lord rebuked him: "What hast thou here? and whom hast thou here, that thou hast hewed thee out a sepulchre here, as he that heweth him out a sepulchre on high, and that graveth an habitation for himself in a rock?" (Isa. 22:16). The result of such an attitude of arrogance among Judah and its leaders would result in them being tossed about "like a ball" and taken captive by Assyria, where the supposed might of their horses and chariots would "be the shame of thy lord's house" (Isa. 22:18).

The Lord would take the governing power from Shebna and lay it upon the worthy priest, Eliakim: "And it shall come to pass in that day, that I will call my servant Eliakim the son of Hilkiah" (Isa. 22:20). The life of Eliakim, the worthy servant, serves as a parallel or type for Christ, whom "God shall cause to arise" (footnote 20a). This understanding of Eliakim as a representative and reminder of Christ now brings us to one of the great Messianic prophecies of Isaiah. Let's examine some of this wonderful parallel imagery.

"And I will clothe him with thy robe, and strengthen him with thy girdle" (Isa. 22:21). Christ is both the king and the high priest. At his coronation a king is clothed so as to symbolize his power and authority. In the temple, vested, or covered, in sacred clothing, we receive the promise that through faithful living we may become kings and queens—as presiding parents of an eternal posterity.

As discussed, one meaning of *atonement* is "to cover." Religious scholar Dennis L. Largey points out that "a Hebrew correlate of *redemptio* and *lytrosis* is KPhRM ('atonement'), a plural noun referring to protective 'coverings' (its literal meaning) for human lives. The major symbols of protection are regal robes and royal embraces."[40] What sweet symbolism— to be clothed in regal robes and royal embraces! How often have we gone to the temple seeking comfort and direction and felt the encircling arms of our Savior's love?

The scriptures are filled with this comforting image of being encircled about. Alma told us that Christ "sendeth an invitation unto all men, for the arms of mercy are extended towards them, and he saith: Repent, and I will receive you" (Alma 5:33). Mormon lamented, "O ye fair ones, how could ye have rejected that Jesus, who stood with open arms to receive you!" (Morm. 6:17). Amulek taught, "And thus mercy can satisfy the demands of justice, and encircles them in the arms of safety" (Alma 34:16). In Nephi's great soul-searching psalm, he pleads, "O Lord, wilt thou encircle me around in the robe of thy righteousness!" (2 Ne. 4:33). He made this plea with confidence that the blessing would be granted, for prior to this, he had proclaimed, "But behold, the Lord hath redeemed my soul from hell; I have beheld his glory, and I am encircled about eternally in the arms of his love" (2 Ne. 1:15).

"And I will commit thy government into his hand" (Isa. 22:21). To sweeten the prospect of Christ being our king—the leader of our government—we may simply consider the contrast of the un-Christian aspects of the governments of our current world. With Christ as our king, rather than fiscal irresponsibility, our resources will be protected and managed under true principles of consecration and stewardship. Rather than immorality among our leaders, we will have chastity. Our governance will be conducted in honesty rather than dishonesty, love and compassion rather than hatred, peace rather than war, simplicity rather than complicated and inefficient bureaucracy, and honor and integrity rather than scandal and vice. Humility and a sincere desire to serve and lift one another will replace the hubris of seeking high position for motives of self-promotion and unholy striving for power and gain.

When the governing of the nations is committed into the hand of Christ, the rightful and righteous king, all people of the earth will enjoy the freedom dreamed of for millennia.

"And he shall be a father to the inhabitants of Jerusalem, and to the house of Judah" (Isa. 22:21). Christ is a Son and a Father. He is the Firstborn spirit of and the Only Begotten Son in the flesh of Heavenly Father. He is a father in the sense that He is the father of our salvation. Abinadi posed an important question about Christ when he asked, "And now what say ye? And who shall be his seed?" He then answered, "For these are they whose sins he has borne; these are they for whom he has died, to redeem them from their transgressions, And now, are they not his seed? (Mosiah 15:10, 12). We are His seed. He is our "spiritual" father, or the father of our salvation.

"And the key of the house of David will I lay upon his shoulder; so he shall open, and none shall shut; and he shall shut, and none shall open" (Isa. 22:22). David, as king of Israel, held the key, or authority, to rule his subjects. His word was law, and he sometimes misused his power. Christ, having descended from the house of David, was the legal and lawful heir to King David's political throne, but His mission was to a higher calling. From His Heavenly Father, He inherited the "keys of hell and of death" (Rev. 1:18). He never abused His power, being true to His commission: "He that is holy, he that is true, he that hath the key of David, he that openeth, and no man shutteth; and shutteth, and no man openeth" (Rev. 3:7).

As we are humble and obedient, Christ locks temptation and evil away from us. He protects us from Satan's influence and destructive powers. Our sincere plea is the same as Nephi's: "May the gates of hell be shut continually before me, because that my heart is broken and my spirit is contrite! O Lord, wilt thou not shut the gates of thy righteousness before me, that I may walk in the path of the low valley, that I may be strict in the plain road!" (2 Ne. 4:32).

Because of His Atonement, and through temple worship and covenants, our Savior unlocks the gift of eternal life. He unlocks the grave and locks away spiritual and physical death. He delegates His keys to His servants, who have the power to bind and seal families together eternally. Through Him, these same blessings are made possible for those in the spirit world. He opens the doors of His protective power to be upon those who make and keep sacred covenants with him.

"And I will fasten him as a nail in a sure place; and he shall be for a glorious throne to his father's house" (Isa. 22:23). *"I will fasten him as a nail in a sure place.* This image pertains to Christ's crucifixion. 'The nail fastened in a sure place,' remains a mystery to the world, and will, but the wise understand."[41] A "nail in a sure place" has reference to the method of the crucifixion of Christ. The cruel killers who employed crucifixion had many methods. Some victims were tied to the crosses. Some were nailed. We know Christ was nailed and has shown as a sign—and will do so again—the nail prints of His sacrifice. Scientific studies of victims of crucifixion have shown that some not only had nails driven through hands and feet but also through their wrists to ensure that their body weight would not tear them from the cross.

"And they shall hang upon him all the glory of his father's house, the offspring and the issue, all vessels of small quantity, from the vessels of cups, even to all the vessels of flagons" (Isa. 22:24). "His father's house" is a comprehensive, inclusive phrase for all of God's children, small and great.

Christ has invited "all to come unto him and partake of his goodness" (2 Ne. 26:33). His Atonement was "an infinite and eternal sacrifice" (Alma 34:10). He descended below all things and rose above all things.

Our conference visitor taught us that Christ did not *just* suffer for our sins but for all the unfairness and injustice of all people of all the world of all time. As the result of His foreordained mission of being hung on the cross, all glory is hung upon Him. In Him, we have the potential for eternal life.

"In that day, saith the Lord of hosts, shall the nail that is fastened in the sure place be removed, and be cut down, and fall; and the burden that was upon it shall be cut off: for the Lord hath spoken it" (Isa. 22:25). Shortly before the betrayal and arrest of Christ, He prayed to His Father, "I have glorified thee on the earth: I have finished the work which thou gavest me to do" (John 17:4). As the moment of His death arrived, he said, "It is finished" (John 19:30), and he "cried with a loud voice . . . Father, into thy hands I commend my spirit" (Luke 23:46). With His agony now complete, the nails were removed, and His body was prepared for burial. As His body lay in the tomb, He went in spirit body to the world of spirits to organize the work of preaching the gospel to those who had died. Within a few days, He would exercise His keys of power over death and come forth from the grave. He then taught and prepared His chosen leaders to take the glorious gospel message forward to the ends of the earth until such time as "the Lord hath performed his whole work upon mount Zion and on Jerusalem" (Isa. 10:12). He will continue, on occasion, to show the nail prints in His hands and feet as symbols of His atoning sacrifice until all of God's children of all ages have heard His saving message and acknowledged Him as their Lord, King, and Savior.

CHAPTER TWENTY-THREE
MERCHANDISE SHALL BE HOLINESS

As Isaiah speaks of Tyre, a "mart of the nations" (Isaiah 23:3), we may learn of the hazards of wealth not obtained in the Lord's way nor with His purpose.

An oft-repeated story of capturing monkeys is illustrative of the attitude of greed that permeates so much of society. As the story goes, a hole just large enough for the extended hand of a monkey is drilled in the end of a coconut shell. The other end of the shell is secured to a tree or a stake in the ground. A particular variety of nuts that are a favorite food of the monkey is placed inside the shell. As the monkey reaches his hand into the shell and procures a nut, his clenched fist now becomes too large to be removed from the hole. Even as the trapper advances to capture the monkey, the desire to retain the prize outweighs the desire to flee and be free. The monkey holds fast to his prize and thus loses his freedom.

At the time of this writing, much of the world is recovering from a deep recession. Some would say that the recession is even lingering and worsening. Although many noble, honest, and successful people are working hard to reverse the trend, it is apparent that there are also many corrupt people who are profiteering from the plight of others. Like the monkey, they hold fast to their exorbitant treasures without regard for their own spiritual welfare or the physical and spiritual welfare of humanity. The merchandise of the world presents a powerful lure to seduce them into a lifestyle of opulence, greed, selfishness, and corruption. This is in stark contrast to the Lord's plan that wealth is granted "for the intent to do good—to clothe the naked, and to feed the hungry, and to liberate the captive, and administer relief to the sick and the afflicted" (Jacob 2:19).

The Burden of Tyre

Isaiah now presents his "burden of Tyre": "The burden of Tyre. Howl, ye ships of Tarshish; for it is laid waste, so that there is no house, no entering in: from the land of Chittim it is revealed to them" (Isa. 23:1). The burden of Tyre is the same message Isaiah has delivered to the other corrupt nations: repent or be destroyed.

As Assyria and Babylon were the prevailing powers on land, Tyre and Sidon were the dominant powers at sea. Tyre was a powerful Phoenician port city on the Mediterranean and was famous for its wealth, shipping prowess, and successful merchandising. Buyers and sellers of every imaginable commodity were attracted to this internationally successful marketplace, and as is generally the case of worldly marts, every sin and evil imaginable ran rampant there. To its patrons, Tyre was perceived as a "joyous city, whose antiquity is of ancient days," but her misguided motive would ultimately "carry her afar off to sojourn" (Isa. 23:7). Tyre, as a woman lamenting her reproach, would be humiliated and become barren as though she had never been a greatly populated city of commerce. "Be thou ashamed, O Zidon: for the sea hath spoken, even the strength of the sea, saying, I travail not, nor bring forth children, neither do I nourish up young men, nor bring up virgins" (Isa. 23:4).

As is often the case when people lose sight of the principles of true character, honesty, and compassion, those principal merchants were lauded with phony accolades: "Who hath taken this counsel against Tyre, the crowning city, whose merchants are princes, whose traffickers are the honourable of the earth?" (Isa. 23:8). It seems to be a favorite pastime of the dishonorable to shower one another with undeserved praise.

There is No More Strength

Those who seek their own honor but fail to seek to honor the Lord and His purposes experience His chastening hand. Upon the residents of Tyre, who perceived themselves as honorable, "the Lord of hosts hath purposed it, to stain the pride of all glory, and to bring into contempt all the honourable of the earth" (Isa. 23:9). The sad awakening of Tyre's citizenry, who perceived themselves to be so strong, was the Lord's pronouncement, "There is no more strength. . . . Howl, ye ships of Tarshish: for your strength is laid waste" (Isa. 23:10, 14).

The puzzlement of truth-loving people of our age, and of every age, is why civilizations do not grasp the connection between their rebellion and the Lord's chastisement. Tyre was conquered but then had seventy years of respite to ponder and consider their errors. But then, "like the dog to his vomit, or like the sow to her wallowing in the mire" (3 Ne. 7:8), they returned to their pride and unrighteous merchandising and were again conquered: "And it shall come to pass in that day, that Tyre shall be forgotten seventy years, according to the days of one king: after the end of seventy years shall Tyre sing as an harlot. Take an harp, go about the city, thou harlot that hast been forgotten; make sweet melody, sing many songs, that thou mayest be remembered. And it shall come to pass after the end of seventy years, that the Lord will visit Tyre, and she shall turn to her hire, and shall commit fornication with all the kingdoms of the world upon the face of the earth" (Isa. 23:15–18).

Once again, the chastening hand of the Lord was upon Tyre, as it comes upon all who seek not His purposes. Although we mortals may grow impatient with waiting for justice to be served, it will be served. The day came to Tyre and the day will come to our society when the riches and resources of the earth will be reallocated from the wicked and put fully to the Lord's holy purposes.

Holiness to the Lord

The Lord delights in blessing His people. He would have us live lives of abundance and plenty if we could only so qualify by our humility and our love and service one to another. Of the "fulness of the earth. . . . the herb, and the good things which come of the earth, whether for food or for raiment, or for houses, or for barns, or for orchards, or for gardens, or for vineyards" we are told that "it pleaseth God that he hath given all these things unto man" (D&C 59:16–17, 20). We are further told, "And it is my purpose to provide for my saints, for all things are mine. But it must needs be done in mine own way. . . . For the earth is full, and there is enough and to spare" (D&C 104:15–17).

I was once asked a sincere question by a lady who was not a member of the Church: "Why does your church spend so much on the building of expensive temples rather than helping the poor of the world?" In my answer, I tried to give her a perspective of our great welfare and humanitarian programs and how we join hands with many others around the world in providing resources and services to those in need. I then explained the purpose of the temple and how we have a specific charge and mission to provide the opportunities for eternal life to as many people of the world as will accept the invitation. Many organizations, including our Church, can and do offer temporal provision. But only the true and living Church can provide the ordinances of eternal life.

It is true that our temples are magnificent and beautiful. The Church generously allocates sufficient resources in providing houses dedicated to the righteous purpose of "holiness to the Lord." Remember that in the Lord's economy, there is "enough and to spare." There is ample provision for the temporal and spiritual well-being of all. In his burden of Tyre, Isaiah gave its citizens a portent of the coming day and of the full implementation of the Lord's economy when the treasures of the earth would be dedicated fully to the Lord's purposes: "And her merchandise and her hire shall be holiness to the Lord: it shall not be treasured nor laid up; for her merchandise shall be for them that dwell before the Lord, to eat sufficiently, and for durable clothing" (Isa. 23:18).

When all people accept and honor our Savior as our King and our Lawgiver, all will eat "sufficiently" of the abundance of the delicious, wholesome food provided us. We will also enjoy living water in abundance. All will enjoy the blessing of a beautiful wardrobe of pleasant, comfortable, modest, and durable clothing. We will joy in our eternal wearing of the fine linen of righteousness. The Lord is truly pleased to give us His abundance if we will just please Him by our lives and actions, for "in nothing doth man offend God, or against none is his wrath kindled, save those who confess not his hand in all things, and obey not his commandments" (D&C 59:21).

It is sad that the people of Tyre and the greedy and proud of all generations struggle to learn of the true nature of the economy of God and of His purposes for His resources in the lives of His children. In the temple, we make covenants to properly use the Lord's resources—to care for the poor and to share the gospel message with all people. The desire of our Heavenly Father is for all to seek the gospel path and the blessings thereof and proclaim, "Holiness to the Lord" by our words and actions.

CHAPTER TWENTY-FOUR
THE LORD OF HOSTS SHALL REIGN IN MOUNT ZION

I ONCE HEARD A STORY of a father who was trying to read his newspaper but was being interrupted by his young son. To occupy his son, the father ripped a map of the world out of the paper, tore it in pieces to make a puzzle, and then put his son to the task of solving the puzzle. To the father's amazement, the son quickly returned with the puzzle solved. When the father inquired as to how he had figured it out so quickly, the son replied, "Oh, it was easy. On the back of the map of the world was a picture of a family. I just put the family together, and the world took care of itself."

The world is, in a sense, disjointed and upside down. Families are being torn apart. Our Heavenly Father and our Savior, who created the world, know how to fix it. They will turn it right side up once again, with all in perfect order, in preparation for the glorious millennial day. Individuals and families who keep their covenants will survive the apocalyptic day and endure to enjoy eternal peace and joy.

They Have . . . Broken the Everlasting Covenant

Isaiah proclaimed, "The earth also is defiled under the inhabitants thereof; because they have transgressed the laws, changed the ordinance, broken the everlasting covenant" (Isa. 24:5). The everlasting covenant has fulfillment in the ordinances of the holy temple.

The Lord beckons His children to the temple that they may be blessed by the provisions of the everlasting covenant. Satan's motive is to destroy eternal life, and so he lures those who follow him away from the temple and the covenants made therein. He has been so successful in veiling truth with error that vast multitudes of people have become so entangled in evil that they cannot escape on their own: "Therefore hath the curse devoured the earth, and they that dwell therein are desolate: therefore the inhabitants of the earth are burned, and few men left" (Isa. 24:6). Satan is a treacherous tyrant who delights in the misery of others: "The treacherous dealers have dealt treacherously; yea, the treacherous dealers have dealt very treacherously" (Isa. 24:16).

He Turneth the Earth Upside Down

Isaiah scholars often refer to chapters 24 through 27 as "Apocalyptic Isaiah." The word *apocalypse* connotes the cleansing destructions to come upon the wicked preceding the Second Coming of Christ. It also means "to unveil," "to reveal," and "to uncover." In these chapters, the Lord unveils, or reveals, how He will deal with treacherous Israel and how He will reward those who repent. The nature of apocalyptic writing is to speak of divine intervention. The wicked have made such a mess of the world and tied it in so many complex knots that they cannot, of their own doing, untangle the web that has been created. We of the Church, of course, continue our missionary efforts and work at our goal of establishing Zion and striving to teach the principles of salvation to as many people as possible, but the world will not get better by itself. Christ will come to make things right: "Behold, the Lord maketh the earth empty, and maketh it waste, and turneth it upside down, and scattereth abroad the inhabitants thereof" (Isa. 24:1).

His judgment will be just and fair, "as with the people, so with the priest; as with the servant, so with his master; as with the maid, so with her mistress; as with the buyer, so with the seller; as with the lender, so with the borrower" (Isa. 24:2). The Lord's cleansing of the earth will be thorough: "The land shall be utterly emptied, and utterly spoiled: for the Lord hath spoken this word" (Isa. 24:3).

When we speak of the end of the earth, it is helpful to consider that the earth itself will be changed from its current fallen state to a paradisiacal state and then to a celestial state. When we speak of the end of the world, it helps to remember that the world equates with Babylon, or wickedness. Under the Lord's plan of corrective justice, both the earth and the world will be put right: "The earth mourneth and fadeth away, the world languisheth and fadeth away, the haughty people of the earth do languish" (Isa. 24:4).

The bawdy and profane noise of the ungodly will come to an end: "The mirth of tabrets ceaseth, the noise of them that rejoice endeth, the joy of the harp ceaseth" (Isa. 24:8). The drunken of the earth will be sobered: "They shall not drink wine with a song; strong drink shall be bitter to them that drink it" (Isa. 24:9). The false and hollow happiness of those who refuse to accept or who break the everlasting covenant will flee:

"There is a crying for wine in the streets; all joy is darkened, the mirth of the land is gone" (Isa. 24:11).

In this day of trembling and destruction, the Lord majestically exerts His power in the cleansing of the earth: "The earth is utterly broken down, the earth is clean dissolved, the earth is moved exceedingly. The earth shall reel to and fro like a drunkard, and shall be removed like a cottage; and the transgression thereof shall be heavy upon it; and it shall fall, and not rise again. And it shall come to pass in that day, that the Lord shall punish the host of the high ones that are on high, and the kings of the earth upon the earth" (Isa. 24:19–21).

The Lord of Hosts Shall Reign in Mount Zion

As the wicked and unprepared lament the loss of their treasure, those who are prepared understand the earth being "removed like a cottage." The wicked and their cottages are being burned and purged from the earth to make way for the terrestrial and, ultimately, the celestial abode of the righteous. Malachi taught that the wicked who are to be burned will be left with "neither root nor branch" (Malachi 4:1), meaning that they will lose their ancestry (root) and their posterity (branch).

At the time of the Restoration of the gospel, the Lord instructed Joseph Smith through the Angel Moroni that He would send Elijah to the earth to restore the power to seal families—roots and branches—together. "If it were not so, the whole earth would be utterly wasted at his coming" (D&C 2:3). If there were to be no sealing of families, the purpose of the earth would not be accomplished.

In Heavenly Father's plan, the purpose of the earth will not be wasted. He will seek out the righteous as "the shaking of an olive tree, and as the gleaning grapes when the vintage is done" (Isa. 24:13). He will gather them to Zion where they may worship Him and prepare to receive the gift of eternal life He has for them. "The Lord of hosts shall reign in mount Zion, and in Jerusalem, and before his ancients gloriously" (Isa. 24:23).

CHAPTER TWENTY-FIVE
A FEAST OF WINES ON THE LEES

ISAIAH EXPOUNDS THE SWEET DOCTRINE associated with the imagery of "wines on the lees well refined" (Isa. 25:6). Our Savior offered the perfect illustration of this imagery during His ministry on the earth. At a marriage in Cana, Jesus performed His first recorded public miracle. His mother, who was in an important hostess role, came to Him to lament that they were out of wine. He responded by instructing the servants to fill six stone pots with water, then present them to the governor of the feast. When the governor tasted "the water that was made wine," he marveled at the quality thereof by exclaiming, "Every man at the beginning doth set forth good wine; and when men have well drunk, then that which is worse: but thou hast kept the good wine until now" (John 2:9–10).

Not only did Jesus turn water to wine, but He did so with perfection. Perfection is His nature. Of Himself, He said, "Therefore I would that ye should be perfect even as I, or your Father who is in heaven is perfect" (3 Ne. 12:48). To His disciples, He exhorts, "Be ye therefore perfect, even as your Father which is in heaven is perfect" (Matt. 5:48). He would not give an impossible commandment. The nature of His "perfect atonement" (D&C 76:69) is to ultimately make perfect all of our imperfections.

Faithful and True

As we continue our discussion of the apocalyptic Isaiah scriptures in this chapter we learn how our Savior seeks the perfection of His people. It may be confusing to some that a psalm of praise such as chapter 25 be considered "apocalyptic." Many people's perception of the apocalypse is doom, gloom, fright, terror, and destruction. However, we remember that *apocalypse* also means "to unveil." In the book of Revelation, also known as the Apocalypse, and in these chapters of Isaiah, the Lord not only unveils the destruction of the wicked but also the glorious salvation of those who choose to be obedient and righteous.

Here Isaiah exclaims, "O Lord, thou art my God: I will exalt thee, I will praise thy name; for thou hast done wonderful things; thy counsels of old are faithfulness and truth" (Isa. 25:1). Not only is our Savior faithful and true, but these two words are titles for Him in the New Testament. John the Revelator, in describing Jesus, said, "And I saw heaven opened, and behold a white horse; and he that sat upon him was called Faithful and True, and in righteousness he doth judge and make war" (Rev. 19:11).

In a world that seems powered by mistrust, we may have perfect trust in our Savior. Granted, in our limited view of things it appears that the wicked often prosper while the righteous suffer. However, our Savior works with an eternal perspective, and in His own due time and according to His justice and mercy, all things will be made perfectly right and true. Those who seek their own false gods will come to naught; their cities and defenses will do nothing for them: "For thou hast made of a city an heap; of a defenced city a ruin: a palace of strangers to be no city; it shall never be built. . . .Thou shalt bring down the noise of strangers, as the heat in a dry place; even the heat with the shadow of a cloud: the branch of the terrible ones shall be brought low" (Isa. 25:2, 5).

And, of course, the righteous that attune themselves to true principles and strive to live lives congruent with what they know to be true will recognize and feel the ever-present grace of our Savior: "For thou hast been a strength to the poor, a strength to the needy in his distress, a refuge from the storm, a shadow from the heat, when the blast of the terrible ones is as a storm against the wall" (Isa. 25:4).

In This Mountain

As we now continue this psalm of praise, let us consider the phrase "In this mountain" (Isa. 25:6), which we may relate to the holy temple, as in "the mountain of the Lord's house" (Isa. 2:2) previously discussed. Mount Zion refers to old Jerusalem and also to the New Jerusalem spoken of in modern revelation: "And it shall be called the New Jerusalem, a land of peace, a city of refuge, a place of safety for the saints of the Most High God; And the glory of the Lord shall be there, and the terror of the Lord also shall be there, insomuch that the wicked will not come unto it, and it shall be called Zion" (D&C 45:66–67). Temples are to be found in both Jerusalems.

In the chapter heading, we read, "In mount Zion the Lord shall prepare a gospel feast of rich food (Isa. 25). "Mount Zion" may cue us to the temple. In my preface to this book, I defined *temple inspiration* as "insights I personally see in the scripture when I read with the perspective of seeking truths related to the temple." In this chapter, I would like to share a few examples of gospel principles and temple inspirations as we ponder the work of our Savior and His perfect Atonement.

"And in this mountain shall the Lord of hosts make unto all people a feast of fat things . . . full of marrow, of wines on the lees well refined" (Isa. 25:6). In our day of prosperity and overindulgence, we may equate "fat" with something unhealthy and undesirable. In Isaiah's day of scarcity and depravation, "fat" carried a more pleasant connotation of prosperity and blessings. In the spiritual sense, "fat" is the desirable condition of having an abundance of truth and light readily within our grasp.

To the Missouri Saints who had suffered much and were about to suffer much more, the Lord gave a blessing of hope and reassurance: "For verily I say unto you, blessed is he that keepeth my commandments, whether in life or in death; and he that is faithful in tribulation, the reward of the same is greater in the kingdom of heaven. Ye cannot behold with your natural eyes, for the present time, the design of your God concerning those things which shall come hereafter, and the glory which shall follow after much tribulation. For after much tribulation come the blessings. Wherefore the day cometh that ye shall be crowned with much glory; the hour is not yet, but is nigh at hand" (D&C 58:2–4).

The enduring desire of the Saints was to build a temple wherein they could be crowned with the "much glory" spoken of. The Lord further promised them, "And also that a feast of fat things might be prepared for the poor; yea, a feast of fat things, of wine on the lees well refined, that the earth may know that the mouths of the prophets shall not fail; Yea, a supper of the house of the Lord, well prepared, unto which all nations shall be invited" (D&C 58:8–9).

The "supper of the house of the Lord" has reference to the time of the uniting of the righteous with Christ at His Second Coming. Only those who have made and kept covenants by wearing the fine linen of righteousness will be part of this gathering: "And to her was granted that she should be arrayed in fine linen, clean and white: for the fine linen is the righteousness of the saints. And he saith unto me, Write, Blessed are they which are called unto the marriage supper of the Lamb" (Rev. 19:8–9).

"Wine on the lees well refined" references the knowledge and skill of a master winemaker. "Lees" are the settlings, or the sediment, that collect in the bottom of the vat during the fermentation or aging process. The wine nearest the settlings absorbs more flavor from them. Sometimes the settlings are stirred throughout the whole to more widely disperse the flavor. If the wine is left too long on the lees, it may become bitter. The master winemaker knows when to stir, when to let it be, and when to extract the wine from the vat. The lees are eventually removed and discarded as dross.

Through the restored gospel and the ordinances and covenants thereof, the Lord gives us a feast of all that is needed to gain eternal life. Through daily life and trial, He refines us and perfects us in preparation for the blessings of eternal life. The Savior's miracle at the marriage feast in Cana was a portent of His power to change all things. He works with His children to bring about change. He loves, chastens, and watches over us with utmost care and concern. He knows when to stir, when to let us be, and when to remove the lees. If we come unto Him with all of our heart, He keeps us from bitterness, hatred, and evil, and enables us to become perfect and to enjoy perfect, eternal life.

"And he will destroy in this mountain the face of the covering cast over all people, and the veil that is spread over all nations" (Isa. 25:7). My wife did not hear of the restored gospel until late in her young adult years. At the tragic death of her young nephew, her life questions became more deep and pressing. Religious leaders from whom she sought counsel essentially taught that such things were "mysteries" and not intended to be known by us. The truth of the matter is that God delights in revealing His mysteries and drawing back the veil that covers the earth in darkness. As my wife was presented with the true gospel, joined the Church, worshipped with the Saints, studied the scriptures, prayed for inspiration, and went to the temple, her questions were answered. The mysteries were made known to her.

"For thus saith the Lord—I, the Lord, am merciful and gracious unto those who fear me, and delight to honor those who serve me in righteousness and in truth unto the end. Great shall be their reward and eternal shall be their glory. And to them will I reveal all mysteries, yea, all the hidden mysteries of my kingdom . . . even the wonders of eternity shall they know" (D&C 76:5–8). By making and keeping our covenants, we serve God "in righteousness and in truth." In the temple, His holy mountain, He imparts His knowledge and makes plain to us the eternal truths that remain as mysteries to the unprepared.

"For in this mountain shall the hand of the Lord rest, and Moab shall be trodden down under him, even as straw is trodden down for the

dunghill" (Isa. 25:10). I once lived in a community that was often covered in a blanket of smog. I was not aware of this until one day, while on a hike high up in the surrounding mountains, I was able to look down at my community and see the ugly fog resting like a blanket over the valley.

From the spiritual heights of the temple, the sins and evils of the world—of "Moab"—are made more visible. For example, as we learn principles of consecration and stewardship, we see selfishness and unjust governance in a sharp contrast. As we come to understand the eternal nature of the law of chastity, the lustful pursuits and practices of the immoral are discerned in their true damning darkness. Though we live daily in the shadow of the great and spacious building of pride, we may climb to the spiritual heights of the temple and therein learn humility in its purest form and practice.

From the glorious heights of the temple, the Lord will cleanse the earth of wickedness: "And I heard a great voice out of the temple saying to the seven angels, Go your ways, and pour out the vials of the wrath of God upon the earth" (Rev. 16:1). If the governor of the marriage feast was impressed at the changing of a few pots of water into wine, what might he think to see the changing of our fallen, telestial world into a glorious terrestrial, then celestial abode for the righteous Saints?

And to consider an even greater miracle, how about the changing of a human soul—of making it possible for those with "a broken heart and a contrite spirit" to become "unspotted from the world" and go on a forward course to "receive his reward, even peace in this world, and eternal life in the world to come" (D&C 59:8–9, 23). All of this is accomplished as we transcend the smog of the fallen world and receive the pure light and knowledge of the restored gospel.

CHAPTER TWENTY-SIX
SALVATION FOR WALLS AND BULWARKS

Several decades ago, as happens fairly regularly, a false prophet predicted the end of the world to occur on a particular date. I knew a young man who spent the specified weekend with his family barricaded in an old army bunker in the desert. Upon his return, I was surprised to learn of their adventure and also that he spoke so openly about it. I tried to convey to him the doctrine of the Second Coming, the role of living and true prophets, and the need for *spiritual* preparation as our priority.

Salvation for Walls and Bulwarks

The Lord, in His time frame and according to His plan, destroys wickedness from the earth. Those who follow Him will be protected by Him. "In that day shall this song be sung in the land of Judah; We have a strong city; salvation will God appoint for walls and bulwarks" (Isa. 26:1). Although this is a specific song of praise from the land of Judah, the principles of receiving the Lord's protection have universal application.

I once watched a thoughtful and well-produced film documentary series about the history of the civil rights movement in the United States entitled *Eyes on the Prize*. The obvious implication of the title is that keeping a focus on the ultimate goal of freedom and equality lends strength and courage to endure the trials along the way. Our desired prize as God's children is the salvation—the "immortality and eternal life" (Moses 1:39)—that He promises us.

Our protection—our "walls and bulwarks"—as we seek our prize of salvation, is our faith in the plan of our Heavenly Father for us. In seeking these protective walls and bulwarks, we have the legacy of countless faithful Saints who have gone before us and kept their eyes on the prize of salvation: "All these had departed the mortal life, firm in the hope of a glorious resurrection, through the grace of God the Father and his Only Begotten Son, Jesus Christ" (D&C 138:14).

We may safely and confidently give our complete trust to our Savior. As we do so, we receive strength, not just for a moment or a day, but always and forever: "Thou wilt keep him in perfect peace, whose mind is stayed on thee: because he trusteth in thee. Trust ye in the Lord for ever: for in the Lord Jehovah is everlasting strength" (Isa. 26:3–4). *Trust* is the Old Testament equivalent of "faith." Faith in Jesus Christ is the first principle of the restored gospel. Faith in Him thus becomes the first priority of our lives.

For He Bringeth Down the Lofty City

An oft-repeated theme of Isaiah continues in this chapter as he describes the humiliation and destruction of the wicked: "For he bringeth down them that dwell on high; the lofty city, he layeth it low; he layeth it low, even to the ground; he bringeth it even to the dust. The foot shall tread it down, even the feet of the poor, and the steps of the needy" (Isa. 26:5–6). The rulers of Babylon, who seem so mighty and powerful, will be as the dust from whence they came.

Those who lust for Babylon will eventually come to acknowledge their sin: "Lord, when thy hand is lifted up, they will not see: but they shall see, and be ashamed for their envy at the people; yea, the fire of thine enemies shall devour them" (Isa. 26:11).

We, of the modern world, marvel at and are blessed by the advent of laser surgery wherein light is controlled and focused by a skilled surgeon to destroy diseased tissue while preserving healthy tissue. Our Savior, the Light of the World, who inspired the genius for the development of laser surgery, will have no problem in seeking out and removing the wicked from among the righteous. Neither darkness of night nor bunkers of concrete and steel will offer protection to those who do evil. Salvation is only found in righteousness. The course of righteousness is a journey to the temple.

Come My People, Enter Thou into Thy Chambers

I now continue my discussion from the previous chapter by sharing some of my temple inspirations along with the other gospel principles taught in this chapter.

"Salvation will God appoint for walls and bulwarks" (Isa. 26:1). Our gospel covenants protect us, prepare us for, and guide us toward salvation. In the temple, we receive specific promises of protection. As we leave the temple and go into the world, we carry with us constant reminders of our covenants. As we heed these reminders and keep our covenants, we stand protected, as if by a bulwark, against evil.

"Open ye the gates, that the righteous nation which keepeth the truth may enter in" (Isa. 26:2). I recently toured a large cathedral. A few days later, I was in conversation with a lady who was a member of the church of the cathedral I had toured. I thought she would be interested, so I told her all about it. She then gave me an unexpected response: "Isn't it interesting that we let you in our churches but you do not let us in yours." (Obviously, she was referring to our temples.) I responded, "Everyone is invited to come to our temple, but there are some qualifiers that need to be fulfilled." All who prepare themselves through righteousness are invited to "enter in" the temple.

"Thou wilt keep him in perfect peace, whose mind is stayed on thee" (Isa. 26:3). Everything about the temple bespeaks peace to our souls. As we keep our minds and hearts in tune with the Lord's will and truth, we continue in the spirit of peace, even through troubled times.

I remember well a time of dark trial in my own life. During that period of much study, prayer, and soul searching, I had the time and opportunity to attend the temple regularly. I now reflect upon those times with gratitude and wonder at how I felt such welcome peace in such a turbulent time. The more we focus our lives on the Savior, the more peace we feel.

"Jehovah is everlasting strength" (Isa. 26:4). Trusting Jehovah strengthens us. Through temple worship, we learn more of the true nature of the Godhead. We are given the promise and blessing of their enabling grace to see us through our mortal trials. In Them, we have everlasting strength.

"The way of the just is uprightness: thou, most upright, dost weigh the path of the just" (Isa. 26:7). Only through uprightness may we qualify for the blessings of the temple. Sometimes we unduly condemn ourselves. In temple worship, we do not proclaim our own worthiness, but rather we seek judgment from the official judge in Israel, the bishop. He speaks and acts for the Lord in weighing our worthiness and in authorizing us to enter the temple.

"O Lord, have we waited for thee; the desire of our soul is to thy name" (Isa. 26:8). Through temple worship, we feel the true yearnings of our innermost soul. Such desire is to return to live with and be like our Heavenly Father. In the temple, He places His name upon us, thereby sealing us to Him, to live with Him eternally. The deep desire of our soul is to have His name upon us and to have a life as He has.

"Lord, thou wilt ordain peace for us: for thou also hast wrought all our works in us" (Isa. 26:12). Someday in the eternities, we will look back with perfect eternal perspective and understand how Christ "wrought all our works in us." Through our acceptance of and conversion to gospel truth, continued faith, prayer, study, and following the promptings of the

Holy Ghost, we chart a course, through the temple, and on to eternal life. In the temple, the culminating purpose of the Lord for our lives is taught. Our preparation for salvation is there outlined for us.

"Thy dead men shall live . . . and the earth shall cast out the dead" (Isa. 26:19). The sweet salvation of the dead centers in the perfect Atonement of our Savior. Through the vicarious ordinances of the temples, the full blessing of our Savior's victory over death and hell is extended to those who have died without a knowledge of the gospel.

"Come, my people, enter thou into thy chambers, and shut thy doors about thee: hide thyself as it were for a little moment, until the indignation be overpast" (Isa. 26:20).

In our homes, our chapels, and our temples, we may shut the doors of the world and bask in the peace and joy of pure gospel light as revealed to our own soul. As ancient Israel closed their doors while the destroying angel passed over them, we may gain the same retreat and protection through our making and keeping of gospel covenants. As we emerge from our silent chambers, the Lord will guide us forward on our mortal journey and will be to us as a protective wall and a sure bulwark against those who would destroy all that is good and eternal. The strength we gain in our quiet and safe places prepares us for the ongoing personal battles we all face. President David O. McKay taught, "The greatest battle of life is fought within the silent chambers of your own soul."[42]

CHAPTER TWENTY-SEVEN
TAKE ROOT, BLOSSOM, AND BUD

HERE ISAIAH CONTINUES HIS APOCALYPTIC decree of the final fate of Satan and his followers: "In that day the Lord with his sore and great and strong sword shall punish leviathan the piercing serpent, even leviathan that crooked serpent; and he shall slay the dragon that is in the sea" (Isa. 27:1).

For centuries, a legend has been perpetrated of a monster living in a lake in the Scottish Highlands. This mythical creature has been described as a dragon, a monster fish, a sea serpent, and a water beast. In our modern day, it is most commonly known as the Loch Ness Monster. Some affectionately call it Nessie. This legendary lake monster has been the focus of much speculation, many pranks, and numerous scary stories around the campfire.

The very real being known as Satan or Lucifer has existed since the premortal life. Many in our world have assigned him the same status as the Loch Ness Monster—a mythical being. Some have used talk of Satan as an attempt to frighten people into being good. Others view him as nothing more than a fable that provides a clever masquerade persona. Satan exploits the advantage given him by this bewilderment: "And behold, others he flattereth away, and telleth them there is no hell; and he saith unto them: I am no devil, for there is none—and thus he whispereth in their ears, until he grasps them with his awful chains, from whence there is no deliverance" (2 Ne. 28:22).

At the core of our theology is Heavenly Father's great plan of happiness juxtaposed with Lucifer's destructive desire to thwart that plan. If Lucifer can convince someone he does not exist, he succeeds in moving the very real battle of good and evil into a pretend realm equal to that of a video game or Halloween dress-up. If we think him a myth and treat him as such, he wins.

Left Like a Wilderness

In mythology, "leviathan" and "dragon" are sea monsters and are used as symbols of chaos and evil. Anciently, water was also a symbol of chaos and evil. This imagery is consistent with that of John the Revelator, who said, "And I stood upon the sand of the sea, and saw a beast rise up out of the sea, having seven heads and ten horns, and upon his horns ten crowns, and upon his heads the name of blasphemy" (Rev. 13:1). We sometimes, consistent with this symbolic imagery, speak of the "sea of evil" in our world.

In His cleansing of Satan and his evil designs from the earth, God takes action in perfect justice and mercy and not in unbridled anger: "Fury is not in me." Those who neglect the counsel of the Lord and try to protect their own treasures by their own designs will be destroyed along with their defenses: "Who would set the briers and thorns against me in battle? I would go through them, I would burn them together. . . . Yet the defenced city shall be desolate, and the habitation forsaken, and left like a wilderness" (Isa. 27:4, 10). The destruction of the defenses of the wicked is so complete that there are, figuratively, barely enough sticks left for women to have a small cooking fire: "When the boughs thereof are withered, they shall be broken off: the women come, and set them on fire" (Isa. 27:11).

In ancient mythology, leviathan is made impotent and in a jealous rage fights against the gods who create life. In real life, Satan is impotent—he cannot create life. He has lost his opportunity for eternal life. He will never be married, never have a family, and never gain eternal life. In his jealous rage, he tries to destroy the potential of God's children for eternal life. In his effort to destroy eternal life, Satan enlists great armies of evil-minded people who support his destructive work of leading people away from their divine potential.

"He that made them will not have mercy on them, and he that formed them will show them no favor" (Isa. 27:11). The phrase "will not have mercy" signifies how, in our limited mortal view, we might perceive the destroying of the wicked. Isaiah is declaring that the Lord means business. And He does. But we must remember that God always acts with a perfect blend of justice and mercy. He loves even His rebellious children and will prune them from His vineyard to enhance their repentance and development and to protect and preserve the righteous. The righteous will, in the due time of the Lord, be able to enjoy their righteous associations without distraction from the wicked.

Take Root, Blossom, and Bud

Those who turn their hearts to follow the Lord will receive His tender nurturing: "In that day sing ye unto her, A vineyard of red wine. I the Lord do keep it; I will water it every moment: lest any hurt it, I will keep it night and day" (Isa. 27:2–3). He waters us "every moment" with His living water that is as "a well of water springing up into everlasting life" (John 4:14). He watches over us night and day. He nurtures a gospel-loving people that they might grow and prepare to take the gospel to all the earth: "He shall cause them that come of Jacob to take root: Israel shall blossom and bud, and fill the face of the world with fruit" (Isa. 27:6).

"Fruit" represents "the blessings of salvation" (Isa. 27:6, footnote b). We of Israel are often referenced as "chosen Israel." God does not love His chosen people more than He loves others. He loves all equally and desires all to have equal claim upon the blessings of salvation, or eternal life. Through the efforts of the chosen, however, the gospel is taught to the world. As a leader of mine used to say, "We are chosen to wash feet forever," referencing the role-modeling of our Savior when He washed the feet of the Twelve and taught them, "If I then, your Lord and Master, have washed your feet; ye also ought to wash one another's feet" (John 13:14). We are chosen to bless others. In so doing, we help secure their salvation as well as our own.

We "take root" by becoming firmly rooted in the doctrines and principles of the gospel. As our roots deepen to this level, we lose the characteristics of the natural man and develop the Christlike life and attitude that allows us to have righteous influence with others. As we become rooted in gospel truth, we recognize idolatry and see it for what it really is. When we are deeply rooted in the gospel, we trust that the Lord will destroy the false gods of the world: "He maketh all the stones of the altar as chalkstones that are beaten in sunder, the groves and images shall not stand up" (Isa. 27:9). With deep roots, we are able to draw out the strength and endurance we need to help lift others out of addictive and enslaving idolatry.

With deep roots, we come to see others as our Heavenly Father sees them. We recognize the worth of individual souls. We more fully understand and connect to our own roots and branches, or our ancestry and posterity. We then understand why the gathering of Israel is an individual, one-by-one work that occurs on both sides of the veil: "And it shall come to pass in that day, that the Lord shall beat off from the channel of the river unto the stream of Egypt, and ye shall be gathered one by one, O ye children of Israel" (Isa. 27:12).

Worship the Lord in the Holy Mount

Granted, all of this talk of destroying idolatry, and gathering, and salvation may seem as strange mythology to many in the world. Our doctrine and practice of building temples and performing temple ordinances undoubtedly seems mysterious to many people. But once we know our Heavenly Father's plan and purpose, it makes perfect sense, and its fulfillment becomes as vital as the air we breathe or the water we drink. Simply stated, we seek the gathering of Israel with the motive of helping them gain salvation through Jesus Christ. Saving ordinances for the living and the dead are performed in the temple—thus, in all our gathering, we strive to bring people to Mount Zion, the holy temple.

In a prophetic discourse on the purpose of the gathering of Israel, Joseph Smith taught, "The main object was to build unto the Lord a house whereby He could reveal unto His people the ordinances of His house and the glories of His kingdom, and teach the people the way of salvation; for there are certain ordinances and principles that, when they are taught and practiced, must be done in a place or house built for that purpose."[43]

Isaiah proclaimed, "And it shall come to pass in that day, that the great trumpet shall be blown, and they shall come which were ready to perish in the land of Assyria, and the outcasts in the land of Egypt, and shall worship the Lord in the holy mount at Jerusalem" (Isa. 27:13).

The yearning desire of our Savior to save all who will accept of His invitation is not a myth. It is a view of things "as they really are, and of things as they really will be" (Jacob 4:13).

CHAPTER TWENTY-EIGHT
A TRIED STONE, A SURE FOUNDATION

Isaiah continues his ministry of inviting Israel to make Christ their "sure foundation" (Isa. 28:16).

For eleven years, my grandfather was the construction foreman of the Mammoth Dam water-storage facility in the mountains east of my hometown in central Utah, supervising his crew, who labored tirelessly stone by stone and bar by bar to construct this great dam. This project provided a good living for grandpa and his family. Then, in June of 1917, disaster struck. Grandpa was at home when news came that the not-yet-completed dam was failing. The newspaper reported that he "almost ruined a fast horse" in his effort to get to the site. The washout killed one woman and destroyed the access roads to several downstream coal mines. The engineers blamed wartime sabotage. Portions of the dam and of the water tower still stand as reminders of the long-ago tragedy.

My father began taking me to visit the ruins when I was very young. I have taken my children there. When I served as bishop, we took our youth there so they could also learn a massive object lesson. From a new perspective formed by the passage of years and the erosion of the streambed, it's apparent that the dam failed not from sabotage but because the foundation was not solidly anchored on bedrock. The lesson is simple. I call it the "Metaphor of the Mammoth." It is well expressed in this scripture: "Remember, remember that it is upon the rock of our Redeemer, who is Christ, the Son of God, that you must build your foundation . . . which is a sure foundation, a foundation whereon if men build they cannot fall" (Hel. 5:12).

Woe to the Crown of Pride

Prophets of all ages have taught us to seek Christ as the foundation of our lives. Lehi, in his dream of the tree of life, saw "a great and spacious building; and it stood as it were in the air, high above the earth" (1 Ne. 8:26). The interpretation of the great and spacious building was given to Nephi when he desired to see what his father had seen: "And the large and spacious building, which thy father saw, is vain imaginations and the pride of the children of men" (1 Ne. 12:18).

What a fitting description of pride: vain imaginations. If pride is our life's guide, we may well come to imagine that we can find happiness in wickedness. Sin is an illusion—a mystical, seductive palace floating in the air without cornerstone or foundation. Christ is our only sure foundation.

The Lord has warned of the evils and consequences of pride through prophets of all ages. Isaiah said, "Woe to the crown of pride, to the drunkards of Ephraim, whose glorious beauty is a fading flower, which are on the head of the fat valleys of them that are overcome with wine! . . . The crown of pride, the drunkards of Ephraim, shall be trodden under feet: And the glorious beauty, which is on the head of the fat valley, shall be a fading flower" (Isa. 28:1, 3–4). John the Revelator saw the wicked with their prideful "crowns like gold" (Rev. 9:7). In contrast, he saw the exalted Saints "cast their crowns [of eternal life] before the throne" of God (Rev. 4:10).

Those who seek and wear crowns of pride, adorning themselves in the immodest attire of the world and seeking the immoral pleasures thereof, will ultimately come to destruction. Their evil trysts and fancy feasts will lose all allure, for "they err in vision, they stumble in judgment. For all tables are full of vomit and filthiness, so that there is no place clean" (Isa. 28:7–8). The phony crowns of the world may seem to glimmer as gold but in reality are fading, withering crowns of pride. The path of wickedness may seem to have a bright beginning but soon leads to sorrow and darkness.

Line upon Line

True crowns of glory shine eternally in true gospel light. Through our Savior, we may gain crowns of glory, even eternal life. "In that day shall the Lord of hosts be for a crown of glory, and for a diadem of beauty, unto the residue of his people" (Isa. 28:5). This work of granting eternal life to those who prepare themselves is accomplished in dedicated homes, sacred places of worship, and holy temples that stand in stark contrast to the great and spacious buildings of the world, which have no true foundation. Pride leads to damnation. Humility and righteousness lead to eternal life.

Of the fact that we must begin our quest for eternal life in humility, Joseph Smith testified, "When you climb up a ladder, you must begin at the bottom, and ascend step by step, until you arrive at the top; and so it is with the principles of the Gospel—you must begin with the first, and go on until you learn all the principles of exaltation. It is not all to be comprehended in this world; it will be a great work to learn our salvation and exaltation even beyond the grave."[44]

Isaiah expounds on how we might learn most effectively: "Whom shall he teach knowledge? and whom shall he make to understand doctrine? them that are weaned from the milk, and drawn from the breasts. For precept must be upon precept, precept upon precept; line upon line, line upon line; here a little, and there a little" (Isa. 28:9–10). The covenants and knowledge required for exaltation are centered in Christ and His Atonement. As we mature in our understanding of the Atonement, we exercise faith and repentance by line and by precept in a steady, forward course. We are baptized and learn to follow the promptings of the Holy Ghost and are thereby properly guided as we endure to the end of our mortal test.

A Precious Corner Stone, a Sure Foundation

Those who seek company with the residents of the great and spacious building of pride do so at the peril of their own salvation. They trade truth for lies, reality for illusion, life for death, and heaven for hell: "Because ye have said, We have made a covenant with death, and with hell are we at agreement; when the overflowing scourge shall pass through, it shall not come unto us; for we have made lies our refuge, and under falsehood have we hid ourselves" (Isa. 28:15). They have no solid foundation and are left to the perils of every false wind of doctrine and gust of lustful vice that may blow their way.

Those who seek to follow the gospel path construct lives grounded on the bedrock of faith in Jesus Christ, who will guide, protect, and judge fairly: "Therefore thus saith the Lord God, Behold, I lay in Zion for a foundation a stone, a tried stone, a precious corner stone, a sure foundation: he that believeth shall not make haste. Judgment also will I lay to the line, and righteousness to the plummet: and the hail shall sweep away the refuge of lies, and the waters shall overflow the hiding place." In the Atonement of Christ, death and hell are conquered: "And your covenant with death shall be disannulled, and your agreement with hell shall not stand; when the overflowing scourge shall pass through, then ye shall be trodden down by it" (Isa. 28: 16–18).

There is an old saying of just reward: "You made your bed, now sleep in it." Those who reject the sure foundation of Christ and seek protection or covering from evil nations lose the peace and safety He offers. As they seek lodging in the great and spacious building, they find that their bed of iniquity is a misfit to the soul and offers no comfort or protection: "For the bed is shorter than that a man can stretch himself on it: and the covering narrower than that he can wrap himself in it" (Isa. 28:20). In contrast, as we come to understand and rely on the Atonement and seek out protection from our Savior, He covers us completely with His peace and guidance.

Our Savior is the perfect judge. He is "Faithful and True, and in righteousness he doth judge" (Rev. 19:11). His mission and purpose will be accomplished, however strange it may seem to the proud and worldly. "He may do his work, his strange work; and bring to pass his act, his strange act" (Isa. 28:21). He will render perfect judgment and will harvest and thresh the nations with His "threshing instrument" (Isa. 28:27).

Our Savior knows the end from the beginning and will accomplish His work. "Doth the plowman plow all day to sow? doth he open and break the clods of his ground?" (Isa. 28:24). Our Savior is the perfect plowman. He does not labor in idle purpose but prepares the seedbed of our soul for our growth and development. He sows, and He reaps. He will finish the work His Father sent Him to accomplish. We may trust Him in perfect faith. We may build our lives upon the sure foundation of His doctrine and Atonement. "This also cometh forth from the Lord of hosts, which is wonderful in counsel, and excellent in working" (Isa. 28:29).

CHAPTER TWENTY-NINE
A MARVELOUS WORK AND A WONDER

ONE OF ISAIAH'S MORE FAMILIAR prophecies is of the "marvellous work and a wonder" (Isa. 29:14) of the latter days. One of the more popular books in LDS literature by Elder LeGrand Richards takes its title from this passage.

After serving as a missionary, a bishop, and a mission president and before being called to the Quorum of the Twelve Apostles, Elder Richards was called on a six-month mission to New England. At a particular street meeting, a "noisy" and "extreme" sect came to heckle the missionaries. Elder Richards handled the matter with maturity and grace as he said to the disturbers, "Now, you folks would like to be gentlemen, wouldn't you? I'll tell you what we'll do. You give us twenty minutes to finish our meeting, and then we and the crowd will remain a half-hour to listen to you." All agreed. When their turn came, the disturbers used their time to attack the Church and the Book of Mormon: "Why, if you would let them, these Mormons would bind the Book of Mormon in the same cover with the Bible and ask us to take it and like it," they said.

At the end of the half hour, Elder Richards, who wisely used what the detractors had said to his advantage, announced to the crowd, "If you will come back next Tuesday at seven-thirty, I will tell you why we would bind the Book of Mormon in the same cover with the Bible and ask you to take it and like it. Bring your Bibles with you, for you will have no further use for them after that day, if you are not willing to accept the companion volume of scriptures which the Lord promised he would bring forth and put with your Bibles."[45] This bold approach enticed the crowd to return the following week, and the missionaries had much teaching success with many of them.

Also during this short-term mission, Elder Richards had an epiphany that greatly influenced his life and ministry. Once, as he discussed baptism by immersion with a lady, she replied, "What in thunder difference does it make?" He went away frustrated and discouraged, her question causing him to conduct some great soul searching. He concluded that he needed to be able to convince the people of the importance of the restored gospel or he was wasting his time. His biographer, Lucille Tate, writes, "The light of comprehension which came at that moment illuminated his whole being. Suddenly his years of gospel study, his lifelong committing of scriptures to memory, his preaching of the word, his faithful prayers, his seeking after spiritual excellence, his giving of self, and even his present cold disappointment and struggle—all these fused together in a burst of inspired comprehension and knowing."[46] As Elder Richards worked to clarify, write, and present the gospel message to those he taught, he set in place the foundation of his classic book, *A Marvelous Work and a Wonder*, which has so greatly blessed the missionary work of the Church for so many years.

Elder Richards and Isaiah got it right. The Book of Mormon: Another Testament of Jesus Christ stands with the Bible to teach and testify of the doctrines of the marvelous work and wonder of the Restoration of the gospel to the earth in latter days.

Behold, Ye Have Closed Your Eyes

The marvelous work and wonder of the restored gospel was to become absolutely essential to the reclaiming of apostate Judah and Israel. Isaiah here begins with a chastisement of Jerusalem—not just of the city but of God's chosen people, who have perverted the true gospel. The purpose of the temple in Jerusalem was to lead and guide the people to Christ. In their apostasy, they lost understanding of the purpose and blessings of the temple and followed a downward spiral of wrong choices that caused them to lose truth and temple blessings.

The results of their unwise choices would bring "heaviness and sorrow" and visitation "of the Lord of hosts with thunder, and with earthquake, and great noise, with storm and tempest, and the flame of devouring fire. And the multitude of all the nations that fight against Ariel." They would be left spiritually void, "as when an hungry man dreameth, and, behold, he eateth; but he awaketh, and his soul is empty: or as when a thirsty man dreameth, and, behold, he drinketh; but he awaketh, and, behold, he is faint" (Isa. 29:2, 6–8).

The Lord would "cover," or silence, the gifts of prophets and revelation: "For, behold, the Lord hath poured out upon you the spirit of deep sleep.

For, behold, ye have closed your eyes, and ye have rejected the prophets, and your rulers, and the seers hath he covered because of your iniquities" (2 Ne. 27:5).

Thy Speech Shall Whisper Out of the Dust

One such prophet who was silenced from speaking to Jerusalem was Lehi, who was led to the Americas and established a new colony of believers. The testimony of these believers, as contained in the Book of Mormon, would spring forth from plates preserved and buried in the ground to await the day of restoration: "And thy speech shall whisper out of the dust" (Isa. 29:4).

Isaiah foresaw the coming forth of the Book of Mormon and even foretold of a fascinating, specific event in the translation of the ancient plates wherein a learned man would declare that he could not read the book, "for it is sealed" (Isa. 29:11). Martin Harris obtained a copy of some of the characters from the translation of the plates from Joseph Smith and presented the writing to multiple language scholars, including Professor Charles Anthon of Columbia College. Professor Anthon studied the characters and, according to Martin, declared them to be authentic and even wrote him a certificate of authentication. After the fact, Professor Anthon inquired more about the origin of the writings, and when Martin told him the story, the scholar became agitated, retrieved the certificate, and tore it up. He told Martin to bring him the plates, and he would translate them himself. When Martin told him that a portion of the plates was sealed, Professor Anthon declared, "I cannot read a sealed book."[47]

Although readily available to the entire world, the Book of Mormon, unfortunately, remains "sealed" to many today, just as it was to Professor Anthon, by closed-minded prejudice. The Book of Mormon will not shout over the noisy crowd. It will "whisper out of the dust" so that all sincere and honest seekers who are willing to attune themselves to the message will be able to hear and discern the voice of truth proclaimed to a troubled world.

A Marvelous Work and a Wonder

The Savior's first charge to Joseph Smith in the First Vision was to join none of the churches established at that time. In His instruction, Jesus reiterated the message found in Isaiah chapter 29: "They draw near to me with their lips, but their hearts are far from me, they teach for doctrines the commandments of men, having a form of godliness, but they deny the power thereof" (JS—H 1:19).

The Savior then set in motion the events of the Restoration of the gospel, as foretold by Isaiah: "Therefore, behold, I will proceed to do a marvellous work among this people, even a marvellous work and a wonder: for the wisdom of their wise men shall perish, and the understanding of their prudent men shall be hid" (Isa. 29:14).

The keystone of the Restoration of the gospel is the Book of Mormon, coming forth as a refreshing voice from the dust to proclaim gospel truths. As Moroni visited Joseph, "he said there was a book deposited, written upon gold plates, giving an account of the former inhabitants of this continent, and the source from whence they sprang. He also said that the fulness of the everlasting Gospel was contained in it, as delivered by the Savior to the ancient inhabitants" (JS—H 1:34).

The "fulness of the everlasting Gospel" does not mean that the Book of Mormon serves as a complete history or geography of the ancient inhabitants of the land or as an organizational handbook for the Church. The fulness of the gospel refers to the doctrines we need to know about Jesus Christ and His gospel in order to understand that He is our Savior and Redeemer. The Book of Mormon brings sincere readers to Christ, and as a natural extension, to the holy temple, where we receive what is needed to chart our course for eternal life. The Book of Mormon guides us home to our Heavenly Father.

In the first verse of this chapter, Isaiah said in warning to Judah, who had abandoned the temple, "Woe to Ariel, to Ariel, the city where David dwelt!" (Isa. 29:1). The Hebrew translation of *Ariel* is "Hearth of God; i.e., the temple; translated as 'the altar' in Ezek. 43:15, second clause" (Isa. 29:1, footnote b). Through this message, we learn of the sacredness of the temple, or hearth, of God, and the importance of keeping it that way. Through the Book of Mormon and the doctrines of the marvelous work and wonder of the restored gospel, our Heavenly Father invites us to gather at His hearth, where we may warm our hearts with gospel truth and light. Such revealed truth and light corrects all of the strange notions and false doctrines perpetrated by those who work in darkness. And yet the restored gospel is so marvelous that even those who follow wrong paths may repent and come to the hearth of truth: "They also that erred in spirit shall come to understanding, and they that murmured shall learn doctrine" (Isa. 29:24).

In the holy house of our Heavenly Father, at His hearth, we receive the protection and guidance needed to see us safely through our mortal journey. The work of God, the "immortality and eternal life of man" (Moses 1:39), is accomplished through application of the first principles and ordinances of the gospel and through the ordinances of the temple. With gratitude, we praise Him with glory, sanctifying His name for his great and marvelous plan of happiness: "But when he seeth his children, the work of mine hands, in the midst of him, they shall sanctify my name, and sanctify the Holy One of Jacob, and shall fear the God of Israel" (Isa. 29:23).

CHAPTER THIRTY
THE LORD WILL WAIT, THAT HE MAY BE GRACIOUS

YEARS AGO, AS I SERVED as a branch president at the Missionary Training Center in Provo, Utah, we were blessed to hear from a general authority each Tuesday evening at a devotional. One particular evening, Elder Marion D. Hanks taught us a message that has remained a sweet insight for me these many years. He asked us a question: "Do you think God enjoys being God?" He then cited this scripture: "O then, my beloved brethren, come unto the Lord, the Holy One. Remember that his paths are righteous. Behold, the way for man is narrow, but it lieth in a straight course before him, and the keeper of the gate is the Holy One of Israel; and he employeth no servant there; and there is none other way save it be by the gate; for he cannot be deceived, for the Lord God is his name" (2 Ne. 9:41). Elder Hanks asked us if we knew why the Savior "employeth no servant there." At the time, I may have thought, *Well, so no one will sneak in.*

Elder Hanks then quoted this verse: "O ye fair ones, how could ye have departed from the ways of the Lord! O ye fair ones, how could ye have rejected that Jesus, who stood with open arms to receive you!" (Morm. 6:17) and taught us that this is why Christ "employeth no servant there," because it is He who waits "with open arms to receive" us.

He next taught us from Isaiah chapter 30 about how sometimes people want to hear only "smooth things" (Isa. 30:10), but the world needs more than smooth things—it needs the pure gospel, boldly proclaimed. He taught us that God enjoys His work by quoting this verse: "And therefore will the Lord wait, that he may be gracious unto you, and therefore will he be exalted, that he may have mercy upon you: for the Lord is a God of judgment: blessed are all they that wait for him" (Isa. 30:18). God enjoys His work because He likes being gracious and merciful to His children. He rejoices in helping us attain a life like His.

Speak unto Us Smooth Things

In lieu of seeking the protection, mercy, and grace of the Lord, rebellious Israel continued their futile pursuit of artificial peace and protection from warring and idolatrous neighbors. Having just come out of an unhealthy alliance with Syria, they now sought coalition with Egypt: "Woe to the rebellious children, saith the Lord, that take counsel but not of me; and that cover with a covering, but not of my spirit, that they may add sin to sin: That walk to go down into Egypt, and have not asked at my mouth; to strengthen themselves in the strength of Pharaoh, and to trust in the shadow of Egypt! Therefore shall the strength of Pharaoh be your shame, and the trust in the shadow of Egypt your confusion" (Isa. 30:1–3). Rather than seeking protective covering from the Lord, they sought covering from the shadow of the arm of flesh.

When I was a very young boy and still naïve to the commonplace pranks of my father, I was visiting a cemetery with him. He had me stand next to an above-ground vault and instructed me that if I would yell into the entrance, "What are you doing in there?" I would hear in reply, "Nothing, nothing, nothing at all!" I fell for his prank, following his instruction, and learned he was correct—I heard nothing at all. The Lord warned Israel, "For the Egyptians shall help in vain, and to no purpose: therefore have I cried concerning this, Their strength is to sit still" (Isa. 30:7). Those who seek counsel from dumb idol gods hear "nothing at all." Those who seek protection from unbelieving nations find that those nations "sit still" and do nothing for them.

Suppose the idol gods of wood and stone could speak? What would rebellious Israel want to hear? Certainly not the laws of God, for that would cramp their lifestyle. Sophisticated evil-doers want to hear only happy, "smooth" things. They want their sins justified: "This is a rebellious people, lying children, children that will not hear the law of the Lord: Which say to the seers, See not; and to the prophets, Prophesy not unto us right things, speak unto us smooth things, prophesy deceits: Get you out of the way, turn aside out of the path, cause the Holy One of Israel to cease from before us" (Isa. 30:9–11).

Isaiah further warned Israel of the decimation that would come to those who walked in their own way: "Wherefore thus saith the Holy One of Israel, Because you despise this word, and trust in oppression and perverseness, and stay thereon: Therefore this iniquity shall be to you as a breach ready to fall, swelling out in a high wall, whose breaking cometh suddenly at an instant. And he shall break it as the breaking of the potters' vessel that is broken in pieces; he shall not spare: so that there shall not be found in the bursting of it a sherd to take fire from the hearth, or to take water withal out of the pit" (Isa. 30:12–14).

For decades, many people nervously worried about the sufficiency and stability of the levee system holding the waters of Lake Pontchartrain away from much of the city of New Orleans. Then came hurricane Katrina and the realization of their greatest fears as the levee system failed. New Orleans experienced the worst natural disaster to date in the history of the United States. Ancient Israel's widespread idolatry was as a levee system ready to fail. The trust they had placed in their idol gods would not and did not protect them in the day of disaster. Spiritually trusting in anything except the saving power of the Lord, no matter how high and strong our earthly protections may seem, puts us at risk of spiritual harm. The only sure salvation is repentance and the building of protective barriers founded on the bedrock of the teachings and Atonement of our Savior.

The Lord Will Wait, That He May Be Gracious

Fortunately for us, one of the blessed character traits of our Savior is His patience. As we scurry around in our folly, praying for patience and wanting it now, He waits "that he may be gracious"—that He may apply His enabling grace to our quest for salvation. He allows us to experience the consequences of our choices and judges us fairly in the process, "for the Lord is a God of judgment." If we but learn to trust Him and accept His chastening when necessary, we come fully into the light of His love, for "blessed are all they that wait for him" (Isa. 30:18).

In His waiting for us, He never abandons us or lets us out of His sight. Even as we consume the "bread of adversity" and the "water of affliction" (Isa. 30:20), He remains constant with His hand "stretched out still" (Isa. 5:25), standing just behind us, ready to beckon us and lead us along the true path of peace and joy: "And thine ears shall hear a word behind thee, saying, This is the way, walk ye in it, when ye turn to the right hand, and when ye turn to the left" (Isa. 30:21).

As we walk in the way of the Lord, we gain the faith and courage to let go of our idolatry: "Ye shall defile also the covering of thy graven images of silver, and the ornament of thy molten images of gold: thou shalt cast them away as a menstruous cloth; thou shalt say unto it, Get thee hence" (Isa. 30:22). With this letting go of evil, we gain a replenishment of good: "Then shall he give the rain of thy seed, that thou shalt sow the ground withal; and bread of the increase of the earth, and it shall be fat and plenteous: in that day shall thy cattle feed in large pastures" (Isa. 30:23).

Truly, the Lord waits for us to turn to Him so He can bless us with His abundant grace and mercy!

Come into the Mountain of the Lord

My wife and I, like many other parents, have experienced the challenge of sometimes disobedient children. We have always loved them but sometimes did not like their actions. We have preached to them like Lehi of old: "And he did exhort them then with all the feeling of a tender parent, that they would hearken to his words, that perhaps the Lord would be merciful to them, and not cast them off." At other times, like Lehi, we have ceased "speaking unto them" (1 Ne. 8:37–38)—not stopped talking to them but rather just stopped preaching to them for a time. At times, we have gone out looking for them. Other times, we have waited at home for them to return.

Our Savior always waits for us to return. He beckons and invites but allows us time to repent—to turn around and seek Him and His path, which leads to His holy mountain and the protection and power of the temple and its saving ordinances and to eternal joy in this life and in the next: "Ye shall have a song, as in the night when a holy solemnity is kept; and gladness of heart, as when one goeth with a pipe to come into the mountain of the Lord, to the mighty One of Israel" (Isa. 30:29).

Sometimes we are flooded by the breaching of our manmade walls of pride and rebellion. But the Lord is patient, and when we finally remember who we are and come back to our true nature and destiny, as the prodigal son who "came to himself" (Luke 15:17), our Savior will be there for us. He welcomes us home to supreme light and truth—brighter than we could ever imagine in our wandering through mists of darkness: "Moreover the light of the moon shall be as the light of the sun, and the light of the sun shall be sevenfold, as the light of seven days, in the day that the Lord bindeth up the breach of his people, and healeth the stroke of their wound" (Isa. 30:26). In the "mountain of the Lord" or the holy temple, we learn of the purpose of the creation of the earth and the Restoration of the gospel, which is to bring us into the light of eternal life and to bind, or seal, us to our loved ones forever.

CHAPTER THIRTY-ONE
THE LORD OF HOSTS WILL DEFEND, DELIVER, AND PRESERVE

THERE SEEMS TO BE STRANGE irony ever present in the events of our fallen world. The terrorists who so brutally attacked the United States on September 11, 2001, sought to justify their actions as a holy crusade against a decadent nation. They, in their own ebb of brutality, torture, murder, and oppression, are certainly not qualified to pass judgment on any nation or people.

And yet there is much decline in all nations, and we do need to repent. Our call to repentance comes not from terrorists but from Heavenly Father through His prophets. In 1976, the United States was jubilantly celebrating two hundred years of independence and freedom. In June of that year, our Church President, Spencer W. Kimball, gave us a solemn message. He recounted the great blessings of the creation of our beautiful earth and spoke of our responsibility to live up to those blessings. He then spoke of the flood of evil enveloping our world and chastised us for our sins of idolatry, which he defined as follows: "Whatever thing a man sets his heart and his trust in most is his god; and if his god doesn't also happen to be the true and living God of Israel, that man is laboring in idolatry." He also taught, "We are a warlike people, easily distracted from our assignment of preparing for the coming of the Lord. When enemies rise up, we commit vast resources to the fabrication of gods of stone and steel—ships, planes, missiles, fortifications—and depend on them for protection and deliverance. When threatened, we become antienemy instead of pro-kingdom of God." President Kimball then gave us a great promise: "We forget that if we are righteous the Lord will either not suffer our enemies to come upon us . . . or he will fight our battles for us."[48]

The challenge of our fallen world is that many are not convinced of the need of turning to the Lord in righteousness—not everyone plays by the rules of the righteous. The nature of our world situation requires that we defend ourselves and others, but the principle is still true that the Lord will fight our battles for us as we turn wholly to Him. The day is coming when He will be our sole defense. In the meantime, we do the best we can to defend as needed.

Just weeks after the terrorist attacks of September 11, President Gordon B. Hinckley said,

> Those of us who are American citizens stand solidly with the president of our nation. The terrible forces of evil must be confronted and held accountable for their actions. . . .
>
> We are people of peace. We are followers of the Christ who was and is the Prince of Peace. But there are times when we must stand up for right and decency, for freedom and civilization, just as Moroni rallied his people in his day to the defense of their wives, their children, and the cause of liberty (see Alma 48:10). . . .
>
> Are these perilous times? They are. But there is no need to fear. We can have peace in our hearts and peace in our homes. We can be an influence for good in this world, every one of us.[49]

Woe to Them That Trust in Chariots

If we change "planes and missiles" to "horses and chariots," we have essentially the same message from Isaiah as from President Kimball: "Woe to them that go down to Egypt for help; and stay on horses, and trust in chariots, because they are many; and in horsemen, because they are very strong; but they look not unto the Holy One of Israel, neither seek the Lord!" (Isa. 31:1).

Nations often put their military prowess on parade for all to see. The rolling of tanks, the roar of fighter jets, the parading of big guns, and the precision march of well-equipped troops convey the message to others, "We are strong. We are powerful. We will conquer." The Lord's power, however, is manifest in such things as priesthood service, fasting, repentance, humility, and prayer: "Pray always, that you may come off conqueror; yea, that you may conquer Satan, and that you may escape the hands of the servants of Satan that do uphold his work" (D&C 10:5). The puny hand of man pales in comparison to the might of God. Isaiah warned, "Now the Egyptians are men, and not God; and their horses flesh, and not spirit. When the Lord shall stretch out his hand, both he that helpeth shall fall, and he that is holpen shall fall down, and they shall fail together" (Isa. 31:3).

As Birds Flying: Defend, Deliver, and Preserve

The Lord, in His ever-abounding love and in His own due time and manner, will defend and preserve the righteous. He will "arise against the house of the evildoers, and against the help of them that work iniquity" (Isa. 31:2).

A strong lion, intent on his prey, is not easily deterred by those who would oppose him. Our Savior, "The Lion of the tribe of Juda" (Rev. 5:5), is not *at all* deterred by those who would attempt to detract Him from carrying out the work and mission of His Father: "For thus hath the Lord spoken unto me, Like as the lion and the young lion roaring on his prey, when a multitude of shepherds is called forth against him, he will not be afraid of their voice, nor abase himself for the noise of them" (Isa. 31:4).

A mother hen flies swiftly to the protection of her chicks. As Jesus spoke of Himself in metaphor of a mother hen, He said, "How often would I have gathered thy children together, even as a hen gathereth her chickens under her wings, and ye would not!" (Matt. 23:37). In His love for us, He seeks to gather and protect His children under the canopy of protective wings: "As birds flying, so will the Lord of hosts defend Jerusalem; defending also he will deliver it; and passing over he will preserve it" (Isa. 31:5).

At the event now remembered as the Passover, our Savior defended ancient Israel from destruction by causing the plague of death to pass over those who covenanted with Him. He then delivered the Israelites from their bitter bondage. To the extent of their obedience, He preserved them in their new land and continues to preserve and gather them today.

Fire in Zion and Furnace in Jerusalem

As Jesus led the Israelites out of Egypt, He led them "to the mountain of the Lord's house" (Isa. 2:2)—first to Sinai, then with a Tabernacle in the wilderness, then on to a more permanent temple in Jerusalem, and today He leads us to temples throughout the world. He is intent on His mission of bringing souls to Mount Zion, or the temple: "So shall the Lord of hosts come down to fight for mount Zion, and for the hill thereof" (Isa. 31:4).

Modern detractors from the gospel cause, like the Assyrians of old, will ultimately come to fear the Lord and His power. They will scurry away in fright at the showing of the Lord's army marching under His banner: "Then shall the Assyrian fall with the sword, not of a mighty man; and the sword, not of a mean man, shall devour him: but he shall flee from the sword, and his young men shall be discomfited. And he shall pass over to his strong hold for fear, and his princes shall be afraid of the ensign, saith the Lord, whose fire is in Zion, and his furnace in Jerusalem" (Isa. 31:8–9). The Zion of New Jerusalem will have the same protection: "And the glory of the Lord shall be there, and the terror of the Lord also shall be there, insomuch that the wicked will not come unto it, and it shall be called Zion" (D&C 45:67).

We are engaged in a great battle for the souls of all people. We strive to invite and assist everyone to come out of the darkness of decadent society, repent of sin, and chart a forward and upward course toward the Lord and His holy mountain, where we may enjoy true and lasting peace and comfort. Those who will be fearful are those who walk in darkness and reject the Lord. We must take President Hinckley at his word that we have no need to fear. As we heed the beckoning call of the Lord and rally to His ensign to the nations, we gather to Zion. Through our gospel covenants, we gain strength, protection, and courage to face the evils of the world and to guide us toward a better world where the Lord will be our sole defense.

CHAPTER THIRTY-TWO
KING MESSIAH SHALL REIGN IN RIGHTEOUSNESS

ISAIAH CHAPTER 32 IS A sweet testament of how our Savior is the hope of those who seek Him and, as a great rock, a refuge to the weary.

On the Mormon pioneer trail, approximately halfway between Winter Quarters and Salt Lake City, Chimney Rock dominates the view of the vast plain. This magnificent 250-foot-tall rock "chimney" rises above the prairie floor and rests atop a 200-foot-high rounded base. This inspiring landmark could be seen for days by the weary Saints who would often stop there to mend, cook, and rest in the cool shadow of the rock. Many carved their names in the rock as a memorial to their passage.

One valiant sister did not quite make this milestone. Mary Murray Murdoch joined the Church in Scotland in 1851 at age sixty-seven after her husband was killed in a mining accident. She was a small woman of four feet seven inches and weighed about ninety pounds, thus earning her the nickname Wee Granny. John, one of her eight children, and his family left Scotland in 1852 and made the difficult journey to the Salt Lake Valley, where they saved enough money to bring Wee Granny to them. She sailed from Liverpool, England, to New York, rode a train to the Midwest, and joined the Martin Handcart Company at Iowa City. The difficult journey through the harsh prairie weakened Wee Granny to the point of exhaustion. On October 2, 1856, she died about ten miles east of Chimney Rock. Her tender, dying words are engraved on her memorial stone marker at the Chimney Rock visitors' center: "Tell John I died with my face toward Zion."[50]

It is reasonable that not only did Wee Granny die with her face toward Zion but with her heart yearning toward the blessings of the future temple, the center place of Zion, and the binding ordinances of families that occur therein. In 2001, four hundred fifty of her descendants gathered in

Scottsbluff, Nebraska, to commemorate her life and dedicate a headstone in her honor. On that occasion, Dallas Murdoch, one of her descendants, stated, "I am sure the Lord wants us to be bonded to our ancestors in order to withstand the temptations of an ever darkening world. That may be one reason it is so important we honor and revere their memory."[51]

Although Wee Granny did not quite make it to the great Chimney Rock or the Zion of the Salt Lake Valley, few would doubt that she safely arrived at the abode of her Savior, "the rock of [her] salvation" (Psalms 95:1). Though her body was covered by a crude grave in the prairie, her eternal soul was covered by the perfect Atonement. She undoubtedly had cause to exclaim, as did her biblical grandfather Abraham, "Therefore, eternity was our covering and our rock and our salvation" (Abr. 2:16).

As the Shadow of a Great Rock in a Weary Land

This chapter begins in Messianic praise: "Behold, a king shall reign in righteousness, and princes shall rule in judgment" (Isa. 32:1). The chapter heading indicates, "A king Messiah will reign in righteousness." Jehovah is then referred to as "a man" in verse 2, with explanation in the footnote that the "man" is "the king mentioned in [verse] 1." "And a man shall be as an hiding place from the wind, and a covert from the tempest; as rivers of water in a dry place, as the shadow of a great rock in a weary land" (Isa. 32:2; see also footnote 2a).

In these attributes of Christ, we have imagery of the protective power of the Atonement:

"As an hiding place from the wind." With due respect to destructive tornadoes and hurricanes, today's prevalent winds of adversity seem to be more spiritual than physical. Our protection from such comes from "King Messiah." We have the promise that if we will establish our lives upon the foundation principles of the gospel of Jesus Christ, the devil's winds will not destroy us: "Yea, his shafts in the whirlwind, yea, when all his hail and his mighty storm shall beat upon you, it shall have no power over you to drag you down to the gulf of misery and endless wo" (Hel. 5:12).

"A covert from the tempest." As we've learned, a consistent theme of the writings of Isaiah is his reference to the Atonement as a covering. We can live in a turbulent world and have inner, spiritual peace because of His "covert from the tempest." On the Sea of Galilee when the storm frightened and threatened His disciples, Christ serenely commanded, "Peace, be still. And the wind ceased, and there was a great calm" (Mark 4:39). Just as He calmed the sea, He can calm our spirits. We find our protective covering in Him. Our Savior lives in perfect peace and desires that we do likewise.

"As rivers of water in a dry place." One of the most refreshing doctrines of Christ is that He gives us the life-sustaining nourishment that comes from knowing the truth and from redemption of our sins. He offers us living water: "The water that I shall give him shall be in him a well of water springing up into everlasting life" (John 4:14).

"As the shadow of a great rock in a weary land." A sure spiritual foundation is the key to surviving the devil's scorching fires of destruction. The reason we are not burned by the flames of misery and wo is that Jesus Christ, the Rock of our Redeemer, protects us "because of the rock upon which ye are built, which is a sure foundation, a foundation whereon if men build they cannot fall" (Hel. 5:12). As we center our lives in Christ, He becomes our solid foundation. As we live His gospel, He becomes our protective shadow and shields us from the searing and damning rays of evil.

If we are willing to pay the price of studying and living the gospel, and if we seek out the protection of our Savior, He helps us see and hear gospel truth. "Wo," or sorrow, comes to those who "will not hear" and "will not see" (2 Ne. 9:31–32). Through proper exercise of our will, we may hear and see: "And the eyes of them that see shall not be dim, and the ears of them that hear shall hearken" (Isa. 32:3).

Rise Up, Ye Women That Are at Ease

Wo comes to all who refuse the voice of the Lord and earnestly seek selfish pleasure. Isaiah decreed, "Rise up, ye women that are at ease; hear my voice, ye careless daughters; give ear unto my speech" (Isa. 32:9). As discussed in chapter 3, Isaiah is not singling out women as the only ones with a problem, but he may be giving the message that "when your women are this bad, your whole society is in serious trouble." Also, the woman is the bride in the marriage metaphor, and the bride is the Church, or the Lord's covenant people.

Unlike Wee Granny, the covenant people of Isaiah's rebuking were not facing Zion. She is a worthy model for us in her undaunted faith in Christ— her keeping of her baptismal covenants, and her striving for Zion, where she could receive continued gospel blessings. One of our most significant life decisions lies in which way we will face.

To attain the Lord's blessings, Isaiah commended, "Tremble, ye women that are at ease; be troubled, ye careless ones; strip you, and make you bare, and gird sackcloth upon your loins" (Isa. 32:11). We are to be "stripped of pride" (Alma 5:28). We are to don the sackcloth of humility. We are to make ourselves bare from the "tinkling ornaments" of the world (Isa. 3:18).

Peaceful Habitations, Sure Dwellings, and Quiet Resting Places

Traveling to latter-day Zion is symbolic of traveling the road of salvation in any dispensation, which is a road of repentance. Undoubtedly, Wee Granny and her traveling companions started their journey of conversion with more worldly possessions than would ultimately fit into their small handcarts. They might have stayed and enjoyed the mortal fruits of their labors, but instead, they chose to let go of earth in order to grasp heaven.

The Greek root of the word *repentance* "denotes a change of mind, i.e., a fresh view about God, about oneself, and about the world. Since we are born into conditions of mortality, repentance comes to mean a turning of the heart and will to God and a renunciation of sin˙to which we are naturally inclined."[52] To face Zion is to regularly repent.

Wee Granny knew which direction she would face and kept facing it until the very end of her life. If we are to reach Zion, we need to be willing to sacrifice all things—to strip ourselves of pride and its adornments and leave such things to their natural fate. "Because the palaces shall be forsaken; the multitude of the city shall be left; the forts and towers shall be for dens for ever, a joy of wild asses, a pasture of flocks." If we are willing to let go and turn around and face Zion, "the spirit [will] be poured upon us from on high, and the wilderness be a fruitful field, and the fruitful field be counted for a forest" (Isa. 32:14–15).

The Lord delights in blessing His righteous children. He will give us the good things of the earth in such abundance as our faith and commitment will stand. But more than the things of this world, "the work of righteousness shall be peace; and the effect of righteousness quietness and assurance forever. And my people shall dwell in peaceable habitation, and in sure dwellings, and in quiet resting places" (Isa. 32:17–18). The sure promise of a Christ-centered life is that we may attain the best of all good things—the beauty and bounty of mortality and the glory and peace of eternity.

CHAPTER THIRTY-THREE
A TABERNACLE THAT SHALL NOT BE TAKEN DOWN

IN THIS CHAPTER, ISAIAH SPEAKS of the destructive fires upon the wicked and also of the divine fires upon the righteous who dwell with God in celestial glory.

Fire results when a combustible material is combined with a sufficient quantity of an oxidizer, such as oxygen gas, which combination is then ignited by a heat source sufficient to exceed the flash point of the oxidizer/fuel mix and sustain a chain reaction. Fire is extinguished when one or more of the elements of this formula is eliminated.

Man and nature use this fascinating and marvelous miracle for good or ill. Controlled fire in our automobile engines transports us from place to place. Small fires in our home furnaces provide warmth against the winter cold. On our stoves, finely controlled fire allows us to cook our food with precision. Arsonists use fire to destroy property. A wildfire can quickly ruin the lifetime construction efforts of man. But cleansing fire can facilitate renewal and regeneration of a forest and create an environment conducive to new growth and beauty.

As the Burnings of Lime

God, who created the elements and the miracle of fire, is the most quali-fied to control it for His purposes. He loves all of His children and desires eternal life for all. He teaches and exhorts with tenderness and mercy. "The Lord is exalted; for he dwelleth on high: he hath filled Zion with judgment and righteousness" (Isa. 33:5).

He uses and controls fire as needed to cleanse and purify the earth. Those who reject His commandments subject themselves to this cleansing fire: "For behold, saith the prophet, the time cometh speedily that Satan shall have no more power over the hearts of the children of men; for the day soon cometh that all the proud and they who do wickedly shall be as stubble; and the day cometh that they must be burned. For the time soon cometh that the fulness of the wrath of God shall be poured out upon all the children of men; for he will not suffer that the wicked shall destroy the righteous" (1 Ne. 22:15–16). The rebellious who will not hear the voice of the Lord shall be left as useless, lifeless chaff: "Ye shall conceive chaff, ye shall bring forth stubble: your breath, as fire, shall devour you" (Isa. 33:11).

What may seem to man as total destruction is merely a step forward in the process of God, who works for the salvation of all of His children. Limestone can be burned by fire to produce lime plaster and mortar, common staples in construction materials through the ages. As we consider that the rebellious "shall be as the burnings of lime: as thorns cut up shall they be burned in the fire" (Isa. 33:12), we need to keep an eternal perspective. We realize that those destroyed in mortality will yet live on as spirits to receive further refining and tutoring by a loving and caring Heavenly Father who never falters in His desire to bring His children to live with Him in everlasting burnings, or life eternal. A rebellious life destroyed in a mortal fire can be transformed, through the power of the Atonement, into a better life in the realm hereafter.

Who Shall Dwell in Everlasting Burnings

The Lord uses His fire to bring reward and protection to the righteous: "Wherefore, he will preserve the righteous by his power, even if it so be that the fulness of his wrath must come, and the righteous be preserved, even unto the destruction of their enemies by fire. Wherefore the righteous need not fear; for thus saith the prophet, they shall be saved, even if it so be as by fire" (1 Ne. 22:17).

The righteous that seek the Lord will be saved: "O Lord, be gracious unto us; we have waited for thee: be thou their arm every morning, our salvation also in the time of trouble" (Isa. 33:2). Such people who "wait for" or center their faith and hope in Christ, gain the blessing of a different kind of fire—even the "everlasting burnings" of eternal, Godlike life: "Who among us shall dwell with the devouring fire? who among us shall dwell with everlasting burnings?" (Isa. 33:14).

In modern revelation, we learn more of the nature of those who dwell in everlasting burning or fire: "They reside in the presence of God, on a globe like a sea of glass and fire, where all things for their glory are manifest, past, present, and future, and are continually before the Lord" (D&C 130:7) To live in a sea of fire is to live a Godlike life in an eternal realm where the joy and light of our premortal, mortal, and postmortal lives combine to provide us a life of perfect peace and gladness, light, and knowledge.

Who is to live in the everlasting burnings of eternal life? How do we prepare for such a life? In answer, we are charged to come unto Christ and learn to understand and rely on His perfect Atonement. As we do so, we prepare ourselves for the blessings of our endowment in the holy temple.

What is the worthiness standard for entrance into the holy temple and ultimately into eternal life in the celestial kingdom? Our temple recommend interview may serve as a guide wherein authorized priesthood leaders, directed by the Holy Ghost, assesses our worthiness through a series of questions about our testimony, our faith, our morality, our family responsibilities, and our honesty. In the language of Isaiah, this worthiness assessment may thus be stated, "He that walketh righteously, and speaketh uprightly; he that despiseth the gain of oppressions, that shaketh his hands from holding of bribes, that stoppeth his ears from hearing of blood, and shutteth his eyes from seeing evil" (Isa. 33:15).

What are the blessings of living a worthy life? "He shall dwell on high: his place of defence shall be the munitions of rocks: bread shall be given him; his waters shall be sure. Thine eyes shall see the king in his beauty: they shall behold the land that is very far off" (Isa. 33:16–17).

A Tabernacle That Shall Not Be Taken Down

Forty-six years elapsed from the day President Brigham Young thrust his cane into the ground and declared, "Here we will build the Temple of our God,"[53] until the completed Salt Lake temple was dedicated by President Wilford Woodruff on April 6, 1893. During these decades of growth and struggle, the Saints faced serious opposition, not the least of which was the coming of the army of the United States to put down the so-called "Mormon rebellion."

When the army arrived, the temple construction was at the below-ground level of the foundation. Under directive of President Young, the Saints completely buried the temple site and gave it the appearance of a plowed field. With the outbreak of the Civil War, the army departed. The dirt was then removed from the temple foundation and, to their dismay, the workmen discovered that several of the large foundation stones were cracked. After considering all aspects of this disappointing delay, President Young directed that the faulty stones be removed and replaced.

Some years later, President Young recounted his decision to replace the foundation stones and said, "When the temple is built I want it to stand through the millennium, in connection with many others that will yet be built, that the Elders may go in and labor for the dead who have died without the gospel, back to the days of Adam."[54]

What a comforting thought that despite "earthquakes, that shall cause groaning," "the waves of the sea heaving themselves beyond their bounds" (D&C 88:89–90), the failing of "men's hearts," and the condition wherein "the love of men shall wax cold, and iniquity shall abound" (D&C 45:26–27), righteous Saints who have held firm to their faith will perform the Lord's saving work in the holy temples throughout the earth. After the cleansing of the earth by fire, this sacred temple work will carry on into the glorious millennial day.

In 587 B.C., the conquering Babylonians destroyed King Solomon's temple in Jerusalem. Later, Jesus prophesied to His disciples of the destruction once again of the rebuilt temple: "See ye not all these things? verily I say unto you, There shall not be left here one stone upon another, that shall not be thrown down" (Matt. 24:2). A few decades later, the Romans fulfilled this prophesy by completely destroying the Jerusalem temple.

Although the physical structure of the Kirtland Temple still stands, its spiritual purpose and use were "thrown down" by apostasy and persecution as the Saints moved on. The Saints were driven from the Nauvoo Temple by evildoers, and the temple itself was completely thrown down by storms of nature and by manmade violence. In our modern day, the unenlightened often attempt to throw down the purpose of our temples through protest and legal wrangling.

But the Lord is true to His word. Those who worthily prepare for temple worship will have the sure privilege of "a tabernacle that shall not be taken down" (Isa. 33:20). "This [part of the verse] refers to the tabernacle of Moses, a portable temple that was a large tent with stakes and cords. . . . The entire verse speaks about latter-day Zion and informs us that the temples of the Lord will be surrounded and upheld by the stakes of Zion, which are gathering places of the Lord's people."[55]

We now have and will always have temples in our midst where we may feel peace, seek healing of our sorrows and forgiveness for our sins, and perform the sacred ordinances of salvation. "Look upon Zion, the city of our solemnities: thine eyes shall see Jerusalem a quiet habitation, a tabernacle that shall not be taken down; not one of the stakes thereof shall ever be removed, neither shall any of the cords thereof be broken. But there the glorious Lord will be unto us a place of broad rivers and streams; wherein shall go no galley with oars, neither shall gallant ship pass thereby. For the Lord is our judge, the Lord is our lawgiver, the Lord is our king; he will save us" (Isa. 33:20–22).

What sweet assurance we have to know that no matter how bad the world may become before the day of cleansing fire, we may always rely on the Atonement of Christ and worship in His holy temple. This privilege will continue from now until the day when our very earthly realm becomes always and forever as the temple—until the day when we shall dwell in "everlasting burnings."

CHAPTER THIRTY-FOUR
SEEK YE OUT THE BOOK OF THE LORD

A FEW WEEKS PRIOR TO this writing came news of a terrible school shooting wherein many small children were murdered in their classrooms. This and each new act or wave of violence seems to cause me to more fervently join in thought with John the Revelator, who concluded his vision with his sentiment about the Second Coming of Christ—"Even so, come, Lord Jesus" (Rev. 22:20).

Rolled Together As a Scroll

Chapters 34 and 35 are the concluding chapters of Apocalyptic Isaiah. The nature of apocalyptic literature is to portray a day of divine intervention in the cleansing of a corrupt world. We can have hope and encouragement as we come to understand that Christ holds the keys and governs the affairs of the world: "I am alive for evermore, Amen; and have the keys of hell and of death" (Rev. 1:18). Christ will come and revoke Satan's power in preparation for the glorious millennial day.

In these chapters, Isaiah is foretelling the Day of Judgment at the Second Coming of the Lord. The wicked who have committed unauthorized and apostate sacrifices will now be punished and destroyed for their evils: "The sword of the Lord is filled with blood, it is made fat with fatness, and with the blood of lambs and goats, with the fat of the kidneys of rams: for the Lord hath a sacrifice in Bozrah, and a great slaughter in the land of Idumea" (Isa. 34:6). As we learn in latter-day scripture, Idumea often represents the world: "The Lord . . . shall come down in judgment upon Idumea, or the world" (D&C 1:36). Isaiah warns how thorough the cleansing of the world in preparation for His coming will be: "Let the earth hear, and all that is therein; the world, and all things that come forth of it. For the indignation of the Lord is upon all nations, and his fury upon all their armies: he hath utterly destroyed them, he hath delivered them to the slaughter" (Isa. 34:1–2).

At the time of the destruction of God upon the wicked, the heavens will be "rolled together." Ancient scrolls were rolled on two sticks. The reader would roll the sticks back and forth to examine the scroll and to search the text. He would then open the sticks wide at the desired place of reading. Upon completion of the reading, the scroll would be closed as the sticks were rolled together. Along with the physical changes of heaven and earth, the time of the wicked will soon be past, and the books of their evil deeds will be closed: "And all the host of heaven shall be dissolved, and the heavens shall be rolled together as a scroll: and all their host shall fall down, as the leaf falleth off from the vine, and as a falling fig from the fig tree" (Isa. 34:4).

The Cormorant and the Bittern Shall Possess It

Isaiah continues to expound on how the earth is to be cleansed of wickedness: "And the streams thereof shall be turned into pitch, and the dust thereof into brimstone, and the land thereof shall become burning pitch. It shall not be quenched night nor day; the smoke thereof shall go up forever: from generation to generation it shall lie waste; none shall pass through it for ever and ever (Isa. 34:9–10). The once-thriving societies of the wicked will be left desolate: "But the cormorant and the bittern shall possess it; the owl also and the raven shall dwell in it. . . . and it shall be an habitation of dragons, and a court for owls. . . . The wild beasts of the desert . . . the screech owl also shall rest there. . . . there shall the vultures also be gathered" (Isa. 34:11–15). These birds of prey, along with dragons (jackals) and wild beasts are lonely scavengers and symbolize the desolate condition of the telestial world once the telestial people have been removed. The earth will be left barren and purged of evil preparatory to the great transformation to a paradisiacal and then on to a celestial realm.

The spirits of the wicked continue to live in the spirit world after death. The wicked who died in the flood in the day of Noah, for example, were not annihilated into a state of nonexistence. They had their place of residence changed from mortal earth to spirit prison, where they could eventually be taught the gospel and receive further opportunity to exercise agency and hopefully choose the right. The wicked suffer God's "endless" punishment until such time as their wickedness is burned away.

From modern revelation, we learn the true doctrine related to the false sectarian notion that the wicked suffer and burn in hell forever. Endless punishment is not so named because it never ends—it is named for God, whose name is "Endless." "For, behold, the mystery of godliness, how great is it! For, behold, I am endless, and the punishment which is given from my hand is endless punishment, for Endless is my name. Wherefore—Eternal punishment is God's punishment. Endless punishment is God's punishment" (D&C 19:10–12).

This "earth will be renewed and receive its paradisiacal glory" (A of F 1:10) and then go on to receive celestial glory. The wickedness now prevalent on earth will never return—not ever.

Seek Ye Out the Book of the Lord

How do we gain residence on a renewed and glorified earth where we will no longer need to seek out safe haven from the evils of our present fallen world? We plant our feet firmly on the gospel path and chart our course to the holy temple. We seek to have our names written in the Lord's book of life: "Seek ye out of the book of the Lord, and read" (Isa. 34:16). The glorious blessing of eternal life is made possible for those who have their names written in this book through the perfect Atonement of Jesus Christ: "These are they whose names are written in heaven, where God and Christ are the judge of all. These are they who are just men made perfect through Jesus the mediator of the new covenant, who wrought out this perfect atonement through the shedding of his own blood" (D&C 76:68–69).

What is the promise of seeking out the temple and the saving ordinances thereof? "No one of these shall fail; none shall want her mate; for my mouth it hath commanded, and my spirit it hath gathered them" (Isa. 34:16). To "want" a mate is to lack a mate. To *not* want a mate may represent having our mate sealed to us forever, along with our children and loved ones. This blessed state of existence—this forever dwelling with our families away from death and evil—will not end but will be ours forever and ever. What an awesome thought!—especially in context of our fallen world, where all around us is in decay and prone to death. Once we have successfully endured the trials of mortality, our eternal life endures forever: "They shall possess it for ever, from generation to generation shall they dwell therein" (Isa. 34:17).

CHAPTER THIRTY-FIVE
THE WAY OF HOLINESS

SOME TIME AGO, MY WIFE and I had an experience that caused me to consider Isaiah's prophecy that "the desert shall rejoice, and blossom as the rose" (Isa. 35:1). We traveled to the Kennedy Space Center in Florida to witness one of the final few launches of the space shuttle. We were disappointed that the shuttle was delayed several times and did not launch while we were there. However, we were delighted to experience a fascinating and informative tour of the space center and to personally meet and visit with a veteran astronaut.

The disappointing delay of the launch provided us an unanticipated opportunity to visit the Orlando temple. We are always impressed at the beautiful landscaping of the Lord's temples but felt that this particular setting was exceptional. My wife articulated our feelings well when she said that this was her first experience "up close and personal" with a temple in a more southern climate. The grounds were lush with palm trees, gorgeous flowers, flowering bushes, and other vegetation of many varieties. As is always true of temple grounds, everything was clean and well groomed.

The beautiful grounds could symbolize God's kingdom and the destiny of the earth to blossom as a rose in the coming millennial day. Everything about the temple and worship therein is designed to teach us of the true nature of God and the life He lives and desires to share with us.

The Desert Shall Rejoice

The Lord prospers the hand of Saints who strive to live righteously. Just as the faithful who gathered to Zion turned a mosquito-infested swamp on the Mississippi river into Nauvoo, the City Beautiful, they subsequently transformed the dusty sagebrush valley of the Great Salt Lake into a pleasant, habitable, and productive community.

The environment of "vultures, cormorants, and brambles" portrayed in Isaiah chapter 34 will, through the effects of the restored gospel, become a pleasant realm of health and beauty. In the millennial day, "the wilderness and the solitary place shall be glad for them; and the desert shall rejoice, and blossom as the rose. It shall blossom abundantly, and rejoice even with joy and singing: the glory of Lebanon shall be given unto it, the excellency of Carmel and Sharon, they shall see the glory of the Lord, and the excellency of our God" (Isa. 35:1–2).

This millennial transformation of the earth is a transitional step in the process of the earth ultimately becoming celestial. Of that day, John the Revelator saw in vision "a pure river of water of life, clear as crystal. . . . and on either side of the river, was there the tree of life, which bare twelve manner of fruits . . . and the leaves of the tree were for the healing of the nations. And there shall be no more curse" (Rev. 22:1–3). What joy to look in every direction and see the tree of life—and not face the mocking pride of the great and spacious building that has so plagued the fallen world.

Although our present mortal view of the earth presents us a rather pessimistic view of increasing pollutions and depleting resources, we renew our faith with the knowledge that God is in charge and has created "enough and to spare." Our planet is not on a crash course to annihilation but rather on a transformative path to celestialization. Of course, we need to care for our world and manage it in the Lord's "own way" (D&C 104:16–17), but our greater task is to properly nurture our souls in preparation for the blessings of residing in a celestial realm.

Strengthen the Weak Hands

In the true nurturing of our own souls, we prepare to fulfill God's purpose to nurture the souls of others. In response to Peter's positive affirmation of his love for his Savior, he was repeatedly instructed to turn his love outward to others: "Feed my sheep" (John 21:15–17). We are blessed with talents that we may use them to bless others.

Isaiah charged, "Strengthen ye the weak hands, and confirm the feeble knees. Say to them that are of a fearful heart, Be strong, fear not; behold your God will come with vengeance, even God with a recompence; he will come and save you" (Isa. 35:3–4).

We often comfort those who are ill or sorrowful by reminding them of the beauty of the earth. We take them flowers or walk with them in nature or watch a sunset with them to assure them of God's power and love. He created such things to buoy us up: "Yea, all things which come of the earth, in the season thereof, are made for the benefit and the use of man, both to please the eye and to gladden the heart. . . . to strengthen the body and to enliven the soul" (D&C 59:18–19).

At a deeper level, we "strengthen the weak hands and confirm the feeble knees" by teaching, testifying, and leading others to the foundational source of all beauty and life—even to Jesus Christ, the creator of all things.

We, as God's children, have an innate understanding of and longing for gospel truth and for a knowledge of our place in Heavenly Father's plan. At the space center reception, where we visited with the astronaut who had spent a total of 373 days in space, I asked him how his experiences in space had influenced his belief in God. His reply, in his own words and style, was a basic affirmation of the truths that "man is nothing" (Moses 1:10) and that "all things denote there is a God . . . all the planets which move in their regular form do witness that there is a Supreme Creator" (Alma 30:44).

Our Savior, the source of living water, gives life to all things. All things testify of Him. He creates the rose and causes it to bloom through life-giving water. He provides living water to the souls created by His Father. Through Him "the eyes of the blind shall be opened, and the ears of the deaf shall be unstopped. Then shall the lame man leap as an hart, and the tongue of the dumb sing: for in the wilderness shall waters break out, and streams in the desert. And the parched ground shall become a pool, and the thirsty land springs of water" (Isa. 35:5–7).

The Way of Holiness

Christ is not only the living water to our parched souls but the way to eternal life, the *only* way. In the Doctrine and Covenants, we learn of fantastic happenings associated with the gathering of Israel, including the return of the ten lost tribes: "The great deep . . . shall be driven back into the north countries . . . the earth shall be like as it was in the days before it was divided. . . . they shall smite the rocks, and ice shall flow down at their presence. And an highway shall be cast up in the midst of the great deep. . . . And the boundaries of the everlasting hills shall tremble at their presence" (D&C 133:23–27, 31).

In the scriptures, we are not always sure what is literal and what is figurative, but the figurative often teaches us much truth. Rather than speculating about a massive freeway with all lanes full of returning Israelites, let us consider the highway of truth and conversion that all people must travel to gain eternal life. Elder Bruce R. McConkie taught, "In the literal sense of the word, the Ten Tribes will not return with armies and trumpets and banners; with the ice flowing down at their presence; on a highway spanning oceans and continents over which their legions shall march in regal majesty. Their return will be marvelous, with miracles attending. They will tread the highway of righteousness, and it will be as though a nation had been born in a day, because the wicked will have been destroyed and the Lord himself will be reigning on earth. The return of the Ten Tribes is, of course, a Millennial event."[56]

As impressive as is a walk through the grounds of the Orlando temple and of all temples, the real beauty is the spiritual journey that happens inside the temple. Therein, dedicated Saints walk the path of salvation—the highway of righteousness. This path begins with faith in Jesus Christ and leads to repentance and the gate of baptism. As we keep our baptismal covenants and follow the guidance of the Holy Ghost, our forward path—the way of holiness—leads us through the temple on our way to eternal life: "And an highway shall be there, and a way, and it shall be called The way of holiness; the unclean shall not pass over it; but it shall be for those: the wayfaring men, though fools, shall not err therein" (Isa. 35:8)

If we keep our feet firmly planted on this way of holiness and cling firmly to the iron rod of guidance and truth, we need not fear the times of darkness or trial that will surely come our way. Just as our physical earth will blossom as the rose and become wholly and completely beautiful in the millennial day, as we diligently walk in the way of holiness, our souls will become wholly and completely pure. Our sorrows and heartaches will be left behind as burdens are discarded to lighten the load of weary travelers: "No lion shall be there, nor any ravenous beast shall go up thereon, it shall not be found there; but the redeemed shall walk there. And the ransomed of the Lord shall return, and come to Zion with songs of everlasting joy upon their heads: they shall obtain joy and gladness, and sorrow and sighing shall flee away" (Isa. 35:9–10).

CHAPTER THIRTY-SIX
WE TRUST IN THE LORD OUR GOD

As Isaiah recounts the history of the siege of Jerusalem, he may prompt us to consider the strength of our own trust in the Lord in the face of our personal desires and the dangers and trials we encounter. We may find illustration of this in the training of the Arabian horse.

The Arabian horse has a long and rich history and is often spoken of as the champion of all breeds. Its strength and value come from selective breeding and from the development of strict discipline and exact obedience to the commands of its master. A young colt is treated, in many ways, like a member of the family. It is nurtured with excellent food, much love, compassion, and respect. Through the process of growth and maturation, the developing colt is constantly trained to come to the master at the ringing of its bell.

Once a horse is strong and mature, it is put to the final test. The master secures the horse away from, but in sight of, its water source. The horse is left in this secured spot until it becomes thirsty. It is then set free, and as it charges toward the refreshing water, the master rings the bell. The horse passes this ultimate test if it turns away from the water and comes to the master. In so doing, it then receives the sustaining drink, plus the extended honor and favor of the master. It is then selected for nobler causes.[57]

As mortals we face a similar test. Will we charge full ahead in undaunted pursuit of what we want at present, or will we respond with discipline to the call of our Master and trust in His wisdom? Will we trade what we want most—our eternal rewards—for what we want at the moment? If we are willing to come unto Christ, we receive the food and drink of His creations and the living water of His Atonement and gift of salvation.

Sennacherib, King of Assyria

We now come to a significant historical bridge in the book of Isaiah. Chapters 36 through 39 mark a pivotal transition in the history wherein the

Assyrian threat disappears as the Babylonian threat increases on the horizon. Sadly, Judah and Israel have continued in seeking out false gods and thus reap the rewards of their disobedience. However, some of the people of Judah now finally turn to their Master and receive the protection He has promised them all along.

The historical setting of this chapter is 701 B.C., with Assyria coming up against Jerusalem. By 721 B.C., the ten northern tribes have been conquered by Assyria and subsequently carried into bondage. The majority of the southern tribe of Judah has also been conquered and carried captive: "Now it came to pass in the fourteenth year of king Hezekiah, that Sennacherib king of Assyria came up against all the defenced cities of Judah, and took them" (Isa. 36:1).

Hezekiah is a righteous king who breaks the tradition of his predecessors by humbling himself, going to the temple, turning to his Master, and appealing to the prophet for guidance. He seeks to shake off the bondage of Assyria and in so doing riles their anger and draws them to Jerusalem, where they intend to complete their conquest of Judah.

Sennacherib, the wicked king of the Assyrians, worships in the false temples of the idol gods, pursues his lustful desires and his tendencies toward vanity, and is confused about the true nature of the one true God and even mistakes himself as a near-god. Of this time of his coming up against Jerusalem and surrounding cities, Sennacherib, in his own words, proclaims in self-aggrandizement:

> The awesome splendor of my lordship overwhelmed Lul-li, king of Sidon. . . . The terrifying nature of the weapon of . . . Ashur my lord overwhelmed his strong cities. . . .
>
> The kings . . . brought me sumptuous presents as their abundant audience-gift, fourfold, and kissed my feet.
>
> As for Sidqa, king of Ashkelon . . . his family gods, he himself, his wife, his sons, his daughters, his brothers, and all the rest of his descendants, I deported and brought him to Assyria. . . .
>
> As for Hezekiah, the Judean, I besieged forty-six of his fortified walled cities and surrounding smaller towns, which were without number. Using packed-down ramps and applying battering rams, infantry attacks by mines, breeches, and siege machines, I conquered them. . . . He himself I locked up within Jerusalem, his royal city, like

a bird in a cage. I surrounded him with earthworks, and made it unthinkable for him to exit by the city gate. . . .

He, Hezekiah, was overwhelmed by the awesome splendor of my lordship.[58]

Sennacherib, of course, fails to mention that Hezekiah, the "caged bird," totally escaped him.

What Confidence Is This Wherein Thou Trustest?

The Assyrians, like all evil empires, are masters of intimidation and coercion. In modern parlance, we could label some of their tactics as "psychological warfare." King Sennacherib sends his commanding general and ambassador, Rabshakeh, to meet with the emissaries of King Hezekiah: "And the king of Assyria sent Rabshakeh from Lachish to Jerusalem unto king Hezekiah with a great army. And he stood by the conduit of the upper pool in the highway of the fuller's field" (Isa. 36:2).

Rabshakeh attempts to devastate their confidence by proclaiming the greatness of the Assyrian king and his army and belittling the strength of Judah and their past efforts at joining with Egypt: "And Rabshakeh said unto them, Say ye now to Hezekiah, Thus saith the great king, the king of Assyria, What confidence is this wherein thou trusteth? I say, sayest thou, (but they are but vain words) I have counsel and strength for war: now on whom dost thou trust, that thou rebellest against me? Lo, thou trustest in the staff of this broken reed, on Egypt; whereon if a man lean, it will go into his hand, and pierce it: so is Pharoah king of Egypt to all that trust in him" (Isa. 36:4–6).

Rabshakeh continues his attempt to shake the faith of Judah and lessen their trust in Hezekiah and in Jehovah by accusing Hezekiah of destroying some of Judah's places of worship: "But if thou say to me, We trust in the Lord our God: is it not he, whose high places and whose altars Hezekiah hath taken away, and said to Judah and to Jerusalem, Ye shall worship before this altar?" (Isa. 36:7). Yes, Hezekiah has centralized worship at the temple in Jerusalem and in so doing has indeed destroyed some of the high places dedicated to Jehovah—but he has done so because they have been contaminated by false idol worship. Hezekiah is trying to turn the people's hearts to Jehovah through pure worship. Rabshakeh's blasphemous words portray his complete ignorance and indifference toward the one true God. It is as if he is saying, "Are you sure you want Hezekiah to lead you? Are you sure your God will protect you? Isn't the Lord the very same God that Hezekiah has offended by destroying high places and altars that honored him?"

Rabshakeh further taunts, "Now therefore give pledges, I pray thee, to my master the king of Assyria, and I will give thee two thousand horses, if thou be able on thy part to set riders upon them." He then tells a blatant and blasphemous lie: "The Lord said unto me, Go up against this land, and destroy it" and then threatens a famine so terrible that the only thing Judah would have to eat would be "their own dung" (Isa. 36:8, 10, 12).

Rabshakeh continues his lying intimidation by promising the people a better life under Assyrian rule: "Hearken not to Hezekiah: for thus saith the king of Assyria, Make an agreement with me by a present, and come out to me: and eat ye every one of his vine, and every one of his fig tree, and drink ye every one the waters of his own cistern. Until I come and take you away to a land like your own, a land of corn and wine, a land of bread and vineyards" (Isa. 36:16–17).

We Trust in the Lord Our God

King Hezekiah is not swayed by the lying flatteries of the Assyrians but rather stands firm in his faith in God and trusts Him to arise in their defense. It is interesting to note the identity of the ambassador King Hezekiah sends to meet with Rabshaketh: "Then came forth unto him Eliakim, Hilkiah's son" (Isa. 36:3). We recall from chapter 22 that Eliakim symbolically represents the Savior. In fact, his name means "God shall cause to arise" (Isa. 22:20, footnote a). Just as our Savior standing before wicked King Herod "answered him nothing" (Luke 23:9), Eliakim offers no response to evil Rebshakeh: "But they held their peace, and answered him not a word: for the king's commandment was, saying, Answer him not" (Isa. 36:21). Hezekiah is not interested in negotiating with these evil terrorists. His righteous motive is to convince his people to pass their test and turn away from the fading mirage of false hope and toward their one true God, even Jesus Christ.

King Sennacherib and his ambassadors, in all of their bluster, miss the point of the great protective power of the true Savior, who stands ready to fight Judah's battles as soon as they will turn unto Him. King Hezekiah, by his actions, heeds the call of his true master and proclaims to the Assyrians, "We trust in the Lord our God" (Isa. 36:7). As we will see in the next chapter, the Assyrians will soon witness the majesty and power of this one true God.

CHAPTER THIRTY-SEVEN
INTO THE HOUSE OF THE LORD

CHURCH LEADERS AND MEMBERS OFTEN seek the solace and inspiration of the temple for strength and direction in facing the trials and opportunities of life.

Into the House of the Lord

As mentioned in the previous chapter, King Hezekiah, unlike his father, reverenced the temple and had a sense of its powerful potential. His father, wicked king Ahaz, had decimated the temple in pursuit of his idolatry: "And Ahaz gathered together the vessels of the house of God, and cut in pieces the vessels of the house of God, and shut up the doors of the house of the Lord, and he made him altars in every corner of Jerusalem" (2 Chronicles 28:24).

King Hezekiah corrected the evil deeds of his father. He repaired the temple and restored the Levites as its proper stewards: "And he did that which was right in the sight of the Lord. . . . He in the first year of his reign, in the first month, opened the doors of the house of the Lord, and repaired them. And he brought in the priests and the Levites, and gathered them together into the east street, And said unto them, Hear me, ye Levites, sanctify now yourselves, and sanctify the house of the Lord God of your fathers, and carry forth the filthiness out of the holy place" (2 Chronicles 29:2–5).

Today, we are sanctified by the Lord as we keep our gospel covenants and live up to the standards of worthiness for temple worship. As we enter the temple for guidance and protection in our lives, we shed the unnecessary baggage of the fallen world and seek out increased spirituality in the sacred precincts of the Lord's house.

Now with the Assyrian threat at his doorstep and his people in such awful danger, as reported by Eliakim (see Isaiah 36:22), Hezekiah humbly seeks refuge and inspiration in the temple and guidance from the prophet

Isaiah: "And it came to pass, when king Hezekiah heard it, that he rent his clothes, and covered himself with sackcloth, and went into the house of the Lord. And he sent Eliakim, who was over the household, and Shebna the scribe, and the elders of the priests covered with sackcloth, unto Isaiah the prophet the son of Amoz" (Isa. 37:1–2).

Hezekiah pleads with the Lord to acknowledge the blasphemy of Sennacherib: "Incline thine ear, O Lord, and hear; open thine eyes, O Lord, and see: and hear all the words of Sennacherib, which hath sent to reproach the living God" (Isa. 37:17). He then petitions the Lord for protection: "Now therefore, O Lord our God, save us from his hand, that all the kingdoms of the earth may know that thou art the Lord, even thou only" (Isa. 37:20).

Be Not Afraid

We are blessed with answers to our prayers through many means: scripture study, dreams, feelings, the ministrations of others, guidance from priesthood leaders, and the words of our prophets. Hezekiah received his answer from the Lord through Isaiah. It was a most welcome and sweet message in fulfillment of the Lord's promise that He would preserve and protect His people if they would trust in Him: "And Isaiah said unto them, Thus shall ye say unto your master, Thus saith the Lord, Be not afraid of the words that thou has heard, wherewith the servants of the king of Assyria have blasphemed me" (Isa. 37:6).

The seemingly invincible rulers of the earth are easily subjected to the Lord's strength. As a young man, I was impressed as I witnessed a large, powerful ox being controlled and directed by a relatively small and weak man through means of a few tugs on a simple steel ring installed in its nose. Isaiah proclaimed how the Lord would punish and direct Sennacherib and his Assyrian hosts: "But I know thy abode, and thy going out, and thy coming in, and thy rage against me. Because thy rage against me, and thy tumult, is come up into mine ears, therefore will I put my hook in thy nose, and my bridle in thy lips, and I will turn thee back by the way by which thou camest" (Isa. 37:28–29).

The Lord then promises the faithful and repentant of Judah that their farms and vineyards, having been abandoned during the time of the Assyrian siege, will soon be productive once again: "And this shall be a sign unto thee, Ye shall eat this year such as groweth of itself; and the second year that which springeth of the same: and in the third year sow ye, and reap, and plant vineyards, and eat the fruit thereof" (Isa. 37:30). In further promise, the Lord proclaims that the faithful who have fled Jerusalem in the wake of the Assyrian threat will return to their city and to their temple: "For out of Jerusalem shall go forth a remnant: and they that escape out of Jerusalem shall come up upon mount Zion; the zeal of the Lord of hosts shall do this" (JST, Isa. 37:32).

He continues: "And the remnant that is escaped of the house of Judah shall again take root downward, and bear fruit upward" (Isa. 37:31). We may find a dual meaning here, with the imagery of roots and fruit. As Judah repents and seeks the blessings of eternity, their "roots," or ancestry, are secured to them. Their "fruit," or posterity, will reap the blessings of their obedience.

The Lord now reaffirms His constant protective promise to all who will abandon their idolatry and trust in Him. Specifically of the Assyrian king, the Lord said, "He shall not come into this city, nor shoot an arrow there, nor come before it with shields, nor cast a bank against it. By the way that he came, by the same shall he return, and shall not come into this city, saith the Lord. For I will defend this city to save it for mine own sake, and for my servant David's sake" (Isa. 37:33–35).

One of my pleasant memories of President Gordon B. Hinckley was his aura of eternal optimism. He would often face challenges with the attitude of "Go forward with faith, and it will all work out." For years, I worried about my parents—their aging, their deteriorating health, and their dwindling finances. But my family kept our faith and tried to do our best for them. And sure enough, things worked out. They lived good lives and, although they faced serious challenges, when the time came for their deliverance from mortality, they passed on to the next world in relative peace.

We now come to a great pivotal verse in the writings of Isaiah where things all work out for the remnant of Judah. Throughout the entire prophecy so far, we have studied the repeated theme that if Judah and Israel will trust in the Lord, He will protect them. Now, He fulfills His promise in a single, significant night: "Then the angel of the Lord went forth, and smote in the camp of the Assyrians a hundred and fourscore and five thousand; and when they arose early in the morning, behold, they were all dead corpses" (Isa. 37:36).[59]—Imagine that!—185,000 troops of the most terrible army on the planet simply gone! Although we are not told how it was done, we know that it was done by a faithful and true God who keeps His promises.

The House of Nisroch

As prophesied, King Sennacherib was not to be killed just yet, but he was to return "by the way that he came" (Isa. 37:34). He went home, without his great army, to the shelter of his idol temple, to the protection of his idol gods, and to the company of his idolatrous sons. Let's see how it worked out for him: "So Sennacherib king of Assyria departed, and went and returned, and dwelt at Nineveh. And it came to pass, as he was worshipping in the house of Nisroch his god, that Adrammelech and Sharezer his sons smote him with the sword; and they escaped into the land of Armenia: and Esar-haddon his son reigned in his stead" (Isa. 37:37–38). So it was that this great and powerful king—especially in his own estimation—was dumber than an ox, after all. For even "the ox knoweth his owner and the ass his master's crib" (Isa. 1:3).

In contrast, how blessed we are when we choose to worship a true God, in His true and holy house, and to therein be sealed for time and all eternity to sons and daughters who seek to honor and protect us by their righteous lives.

CHAPTER THIRTY-EIGHT
SING IN THE HOUSE OF THE LORD

WHAT A WELCOME BLESSING IT would be to know from the Lord that we would live to accomplish our life's work. King Hezekiah received a promise from the Lord that his life would be extended: "Behold, I will add unto thy days fifteen years" (Isa. 38:5).

In Charles Dickens' classic story *A Christmas Carol,* Ebenezer Scrooge is given a great opportunity—he is permitted to look into the future. After an adult lifetime of being sour and stingy in his personal and business affairs, Ebenezer receives a visit from his former partner, Jacob Marley, who appears from the dead and presents him with the ghosts of Christmas past, present, and future. This reality-check prompts Ebenezer to change his course. He diligently goes to work to correct his former mistakes and use his genius to bless lives rather than to curse them as in times past.

The Prophet Joseph Smith was uncertain about his future but, unlike Ebenezer Scrooge, had spent his life seeking truth and serving others. He gained sweet reassurance from the blessing of his dying father.

"Joseph, my son, you are called to a high and holy calling. You are even called to do the work of the Lord. Hold out faithful and you shall be blest and your children after you. You shall even live to finish your work." At this, Joseph cried out, weeping, "Oh! My father, shall I?" "Yes," said his father, "you shall live to lay out the plan of all the work which God has given you to do. This is my dying blessing upon your head in the name of Jesus. I also confirm your former blessings upon your head; for it shall be fulfilled. Even so, Amen."[60]

Sweet is the assurance of a future with opportunity to learn, grow, and serve.

I Have Walked before Thee in Truth

King Hezekiah had the courage to change the wicked traditions of his predecessors. He had worked diligently to persuade Judah to heed the prophet and to prepare against the Assyrian threat, and he desired enough time to see his efforts to completion. Then he became ill, "sick unto death." Isaiah confirmed his fate to him: "Thus saith the Lord, Set thine house in order: for thou shalt die, and not live" (Isa. 38:1).

Perhaps Hezekiah felt that he had invested too much in helping his people to just die and leave them. So he petitioned the Lord in humble prayer to let him live: "Then Hezekiah turned his face toward the wall, and prayed unto the Lord, And said, Remember now, O Lord, I beseech thee, how I have walked before thee in truth and with a perfect heart, and have done that which is good in thy sight. And Hezekiah wept sore" (Isa. 38:2–3). He was in a unique position of being one of only a very few kings of Judah of this era who could present a positive case to the Lord as to why he should have his life prolonged.

I Have Heard Thy Prayer

The Lord has the power to intervene in matters of natural events and in the lives of men. Someday we will better understand why He changes the course of some events and not of others. In the instance of Hezekiah's petition to live, the Lord grants him an extension—time to accomplish his righteous desires[61]: "Then came the word of the Lord to Isaiah, saying, Go, and say to Hezekiah, Thus saith the Lord, the God of David thy father, I have heard thy prayer, I have seen thy tears: behold, I will add unto thy days fifteen years. And I will deliver thee and this city out of the hand of the king of Assyria: and I will defend this city" (Isa. 38:4–6).

The Lord then gave Hezekiah a great sign that He would keep His promises: "And this shall be a sign unto thee from the Lord, that the Lord will do this thing that he hath spoken; Behold, I will bring again the shadow of the degrees, which is gone down in the sun dial of Ahaz, ten degrees backward. So the sun returned ten degrees, by which degrees it was gone down" (Isa. 38:7–8).

The Lord, who created the heavens, uses them on a grand scale to teach us of His plans and purposes. The Assyrians, at the time, were the greatest mortal empire on earth. They lived in the pride and arrogance of their wickedness and focused their idolatry on, among other things, the sun. And yet they neglected to acknowledge the real power source of the sun, the power of the one true God. Jesus Christ, the *Son*, spoke His word and, either figuratively or literally, moved the *sun*. Before long, He would speak His powerful word and annihilate the sun-worshippers, the Assyrians. The Son is indeed a "mighty God" (Isa. 9:6).

I Will Praise Thee

Through the Lord's gracious blessing, Hezekiah recovered from his illness. He then expressed a psalm of gratitude to His Savior for His bounteous mercy. The balance of the chapter is essentially Hezekiah's psalm: "The writing of Hezekiah king of Judah, when he had been sick, and was recovered of his sickness" (Isa. 38:9).

Hezekiah begins his psalm with a review of his lament at the prospect of an early death: "I am deprived of the residue of my years." Just as a shepherd moves his tent from one location to another, Hezekiah felt that the tent of his life would be moved to the next world: "Mine age is departed, and is removed from me as a shepherd's tent." As a weaver completes a tapestry and then cuts it from the loom, he felt he would be cut off or separated from his mortality: "I have cut off like a weaver my life: he will cut me off with pining sickness: from day even to night wilt thou make an end of me." Being the great king that he was, he may have expected to die in heroic battle with his enemies pursuing him "as a lion," but his illness caused him to "chatter" as "a crane or a swallow" and "mourn as a dove" (Isa. 38:10–14).

Hezekiah now shifts his tone from mourning to praise and thanksgiving. We turn to the Joseph Smith Translation for clarity on these next verses. Hezekiah's bitterness is changed to joy at the blessing of the healing he receives: "What shall I say? He hath both spoken unto me, and himself hath healed me. I shall go softly all my years, that I may not walk in the bitterness of my soul" (JST, Isa. 38:15).

He praises His Redeemer and the life-giving Atonement that overcomes death and hell: "Oh, Lord, thou who art the life of my spirit, in whom I live; so wilt thou recover me, and make me to live; and in all these things I will praise thee. Behold, I had great bitterness instead of peace, but thou hast in love to my soul, saved me from the pit of corruption, for thou hast cast all my sins behind thy back" (JST, Isa. 38:16–17).

The Lord is willing to forgive us—to cast our sins behind His back. The Prophet Joseph Smith expounded this doctrine of love and forgiveness for us as he explained how we feel toward all of God's children when we've experienced such unconditional love ourselves: "The nearer we get to our heavenly Father, the more we are disposed to look with compassion on perishing souls; we feel that we want to take them upon our shoulders, and cast their sins behind our backs. My talk is intended for all this society; if you would have God have mercy on you, have mercy on one another."[62]

Sing in the House of the Lord

As Hezekiah recovered from his illness and sought direction for his future in his continuing role of leading Judah to safety, he naturally longed for communion in the holy temple: "The Lord was ready to save me; therefore we will sing my songs to the stringed instruments all the days of our life in the house of the Lord" (Isa. 38:20).

In his quest to be healed of his illness, which evidently included a boil, he did what he could for himself first. Isaiah had instructed him to "take a lump of figs, and lay it for a plaster upon the boil" (Isa. 38:21). He then needed to do what he could not do for himself and, under the law of Moses, go before a priest to be pronounced clean. In preparing to enter the temple, Hezekiah wondered, "What is the sign that I shall go up to the house of the Lord?" (Isa. 38:22).

As we ask the question of what we must do to enter the house of the Lord, our answer is the same as was Hezekiah's. We do what we must do to repent and look to the Lord for cleansing and to His servants to declare us worthy to enter the temple: "Who shall ascend into the hill of the Lord? or who shall stand in his holy place? He that hath clean hands, and a pure heart; who hath not lifted up his soul unto vanity, nor sworn deceitfully. He shall receive the blessing from the Lord, and righteousness from the God of his salvation" (Psalms 24:3–5).

CHAPTER THIRTY-NINE
PEACE AND TRUTH IN MY DAYS

LIFE IS OFTEN BITTERSWEET. DARK clouds regularly traverse our quest for peace and joy: "For it must needs be, that there is an opposition in all things" (2 Ne. 2:11). The people of Judah, under King Hezekiah, stood on the threshold of a time of enjoyment of Judah's freedom from their longtime Assyrian oppression. However, the threat of Babylon still loomed in their distant future.

A Present to Hezekiah

Following King Hezekiah's illness and near death, the son of the king of Babylon came to him bearing gifts and letters: "At that time Merodach-baladan, the son of Baladan, king of Babylon, sent letters and a present to Hezekiah: for he had heard that he had been sick, and was recovered" (Isa. 39:1). This Babylonian prince was perhaps attempting to secure a union with Hezekiah against the Assyrians (remember that the events of chapter 39 likely occur before the conquest of Assyria discussed in chapter 37).

Hezekiah, in his hospitality, gave the prince a grand tour of his kingdom: "And Hezekiah was glad of them, and shewed them the house of his precious things, the silver, and the gold, and the spices, and the precious ointment, and all the house of his armour, and all that was found in his treasures: there was nothing in his house, nor in all his dominion, that Hezekiah shewed them not" (Isa. 39:2).

Although we are uncertain as to the exact specifics of the report made by the prince to his father, the king of Babylon, and how the king handled the information received, we do know that the day would come in just over one hundred years when Babylon would return to completely plunder Jerusalem and carry the treasures and the people into captivity.

Nothing Shall Be Left

When Isaiah got word of the visit of Merodach-baladan, he sought out Hezekiah and inquired, "What said these men? and from whence came they unto thee? . . . What have they seen in thy house?" Hezekiah replied, "All that is in mine house have they seen: there is nothing among my treasures that I have not shewed them" (Isa. 39:3–4).

Isaiah then used this occasion to prophesy of the pending Babylonian captivity of Jerusalem: "Then said Isaiah to Hezekiah, Hear the word of the Lord of hosts: Behold, the days come, that all that is in thine house, and that which thy fathers have laid up in store until this day, shall be carried to Babylon: nothing shall be left, saith the Lord. And of thy sons that shall issue from thee, which thou shalt beget, shall they take away; and they shall be eunuchs in the palace of the king of Babylon" (Isa. 39:5–7).

Peace and Truth in My Days

How might Hezekiah have felt about such a dreary report of the future of his kingdom and his people? We can only guess at his complete perception, but we suppose that he had a positive outlook, just having been granted the gift of fifteen extra years of life. We also know that on the near horizon, he would witness the salvation of the righteous remnant of his people through the hand of the Lord in the smiting of the camp of the Assyrians. This near success may have tempered the darkness of the distant prophecy about the Babylonian captivity. In response to the prophecy of Isaiah, Hezekiah proclaimed, "Good is the word of the Lord which thou hast spoken. He said moreover, For there shall be peace and truth in my days" (Isa. 39:8).

In our area is a young man with Down syndrome. He regularly prays in our church meetings and endears the hearts of his listeners with the personal nature of his petitions and the love he has for his family. He often says, "Bless my mother and keep her okay *for now*." That is good perspective— gratitude for the bounty and protection we have *for now* and faith that the Lord will continue His protection and sustain those who serve Him.

Perhaps this portrays the feelings of King Hezekiah, as if he were to say, "We are grateful that we are okay *for now*, and trust that we and our families will continually be under thy watchful eye in the future."

CHAPTER FORTY
GET THEE UP INTO THE HIGH MOUNTAIN

ISAIAH CHAPTER 40 MARKS THE beginning point of Handel's *Messiah*, and it is significant that Handel's great oratorio begins with a focus on the central mission of Christ—to bring healing and comfort to all people through His Atonement.

Charles Jennens, an eighteenth-century English landowner and patron of the arts, had a powerful sense of the mission of the Messiah and worked diligently to compile a scriptural collection expressing his feelings. He then hoped that the great composer, George Frideric Handel, would put his collection to music. Of this inspired libretto, Charles wrote to his friend Edward Holdsworth, "Handel says he will do nothing next Winter, but I hope I shall perswade [sic] him to set another Scripture Collection I have made for him, & perform it for his own Benefit in Passion week. I hope he will lay out his whole Genius and Skill upon it, that the Composition may excel all his former Compositions, as the Subject excells every other Subject. The Subject is Messiah."[63]

Handel did just that. After pondering the marvelous collection of scriptural passages provided him, he went to work and applied his "whole genius and skill" to the project. It has been stated about Handel and his *Messiah* that after he had written the "Hallelujah Chorus," he called his servant and, with tearful eyes, said to him, "I did think I did see all Heaven before me and the great God Himself."[64]

Comfort Ye My People

Handel's *Messiah* begins, "Comfort ye, comfort ye my people, saith your God. Speak ye comfortably to Jerusalem, and cry unto her, that her warfare is accomplished, that her iniquity is pardoned: for she hath received of the Lord's hand double for all her sins" (Isa. 40:1–2). Chapter 40 serves as a preface for the balance of the book of Isaiah. The Assyrian threat has now vanished. Judah will yet face the Babylonian captivity, but for now there is respite due to their repentance in heed of Isaiah's charge to them—for now, their "warfare is accomplished."[65]

"Comfort ye" is written as an imperative. We are commanded to comfort one another. The plural pronoun *ye* is inclusive of all of us. We each share in the mission of bringing comfort to the entire world through the saving principles of the gospel of Jesus Christ. Thus, Handel's *Messiah* is profound in its message. The message is the same as that of the Church: Come unto Christ and receive comfort and then share that comfort with the world.

The phrase, "[They] received of the Lord's hand double for all her sins" is drawn from the imagery of the law of Moses: "If the theft be certainly found in his hand alive, whether it be ox, or ass, or sheep; he shall restore double. . . . If a man shall deliver unto his neighbor money or stuff to keep, and it be stolen out of the man's house; if the thief be found, let him pay double" (Exodus 22:4, 7). Judah had suffered for their sins and received "double," or a full measure, of justice. As a result, they repented and were brought under the saving wings of the Atonement of the Lord, who paid in full through His suffering. When we rebel, we receive full justice. When we repent, we receive full grace, mercy, and joy.

Prepare Ye the Way of the Lord

Isaiah now gives us a dual, Messianic prophecy. He speaks of the mortal ministry of Christ and also of His Second Coming and millennial reign: "The voice of him that crieth in the wilderness, Prepare ye the way of the Lord, make straight in the desert a highway for our God. Every valley shall be exalted, and every mountain and hill shall be made low: and the crooked shall be made straight, and the rough places plain: And the glory of the Lord shall be revealed, and all flesh shall see it together: for the mouth of the Lord hath spoken it" (Isa. 40:3–5).

As Christ began His mortal ministry, John the Baptist, as foretold by Isaiah, was sent to prepare the way: "In those days came John the Baptist, preaching in the wilderness of Judea, And saying, Repent ye: for the kingdom of heaven is at hand. For this is he that was spoken of by the prophet Esaias, saying, The voice of one crying in the wilderness, Prepare ye the way of the Lord, make his paths straight" (Matt. 3:1–3).

When a king traveled, it was customary to send a forerunner ahead of his entourage to herald his journey and to clear the highway of obstruction. In a spiritual sense, John the Baptist ministered to help people clear away their spiritual clutter through repentance and baptism in preparation of the coming of King Messiah, who would give them the higher law.

We of the modern Church are charged with the role of forerunners, under the direction of our prophets, to make straight the crooked ways of the world and remove the rough places from the path to eternal life in preparation for the Second Coming of Christ. In modern revelation, the Lord commanded, "Yea, open your mouths and they shall be filled, saying: Repent, repent, and prepare ye the way of the Lord, and make his paths straight; for the kingdom of heaven is at hand" (D&C 33:10). We are to help remove the "mountains" of prejudice and make the "rough places" of unbelief and sin smooth, or "plain." We are to edify people and assist them in rising above their "valleys" of discouragement and spiritual blindness. We are to teach, testify, and assist people in overcoming the common roadblocks to temple worship—things such as not paying tithes, abuses of the Word of Wisdom and the law of chastity, and doubts about the nature of God and of the role and divine calling of prophets.

Get Thee Up into the High Mountain

When I began my mission, like all missionaries, I went to the temple and received my endowment. A few weeks later, while we were in training at the old mission home in Salt Lake City, we went to the temple, where we were instructed in our duties by President Harold B. Lee. He taught us of our responsibility to boldly teach and testify of Christ and gather the honest in heart to the stakes of Zion.

Isaiah commends us to the temple, the "high mountain," and urges us to share boldly the message of our Redeemer: "O Zion, that bringest good tidings, get thee up into the high mountain; O Jerusalem, that bringest good tidings, lift up thy voice with strength; lift it up, be not afraid; say unto the cities of Judah, Behold your God!" (Isa. 40:9). In the holy temple, we are privileged to behold the power and salvation of God and Christ as we complete the ordinances of salvation, make eternal covenants, and receive the opportunity for the full blessing of the Atonement in our lives.

Elder Bruce C. Hafen taught, "A friend once said, 'If the temple is our holiest place of worship and learning, shouldn't it teach the Atonement, our most sacred and central doctrine? And to do that, shouldn't the endowment focus on the life of Christ rather than on the lives of Adam and Eve?' The temple endowment does teach the Atonement, but it focuses on Adam and Eve to teach the story of *receiving* the Atonement. The Savior's life is the story of *giving* the Atonement."[66] Through our temple worship and the keeping of our temple covenants, we more fully receive the Atonement in our daily lives and thoughts.

Christ will come as a true Shepherd with strength and power to nurture and guide His flock to His Father: "Behold, the Lord God will come with strong hand, and his arm shall rule for him: behold, his reward is with him, and his work before him. He shall feed his flock like a shepherd: he shall gather the lambs with his arm, and carry them in his bosom, and shall gently lead those that are with young" (Isa. 40:10–11).

To Whom Then Will Ye Liken God?

For nearly four decades, I have been an avid reader of a particular national news magazine. From my reading, I feel I have learned much about our world and have kept in touch with the important issues of our time. Interestingly, the magazine unwittingly publishes regular reminders of the puny strength and knowledge of man as compared to the grandeur of God. For example, a few years ago it ran a cover story about scientific exploration of space and concluded that we have come so far in our knowledge that we are fairly confident that there is evidence of water on some planets and that it is not unlikely that there is life out there somewhere. I could not repress a chuckle as I considered this scriptural passage: "And worlds without number have I created; and I also created them for mine own purpose; and by the Son I created them, which is mine Only Begotten" (Moses 1:33). How much further advanced science and scientists would be if they had the true nature of God and of His creations as the beginning point of their studies.

Isaiah asked some searching questions to guide us in consideration of the grandeur and power of God: "Who hath measured the waters in the hollow of his hand, and meted out heaven with the span, and comprehended the dust of the earth in a measure, and weighted the mountains in scales, and the hills in a balance? Who hath directed the Spirit of the Lord, or being his counsellor hath taught him? (Isa. 40:12–13). The glaringly obvious answer is that no mortal could even come close to comprehending God or to counseling Him in His work. Our task is "not to counsel the Lord, but to take counsel from his hand" (Jacob 4:10).

Isaiah continues his observations of God's might by striking at the root of the ongoing challenge of Judah and Israel—their persistent lure to idolatry: "To whom then will ye liken God? or what likeness will ye compare unto him? The workman melteth a graven image, and the goldsmith spreadeth it over with gold, and casteth silver chains" (Isa. 40:18–19). Isaiah then answers, "Hast thou not known? hast thou not heard, that the everlasting God, the Lord, the Creator of the ends of the earth, fainteth not, neither is weary? there is no searching of his understanding. He giveth power to the faint; and to them that have no might he increaseth strength" (Isa. 40:28–29). The true power and wisdom of God cannot be compared to anything known to any unenlightened mortal man.

With Wings as Eagles

Isaiah now offers a promise to those who, in acknowledging the Lord's power, seek His guidance in all things: "But they that wait upon the Lord shall renew their strength; they shall mount up with wings as eagles; they shall run, and not be weary; and they shall walk, and not faint" (Isa. 40:31).

We "wait upon the Lord" by centering our lives and our faith in Him. We hope for His coming, and we joyfully anticipate the establishment of His kingdom. He sustains us in our weaknesses. A "waiter" is one who serves another. As we wait upon the Lord, we serve Him by serving one another. As we diligently serve one another in the gospel cause, we have our strength renewed and, through the grace of Christ, we are able to accomplish the work He gives us to do.

In ancient Israel, the eagle was a symbol of deliverance from on high. Isaiah, in seeking for a symbol of deliverance, glory, and freedom, chooses the eagle. We, in our fallen condition, cannot begin to imagine the glorious blessings our Heavenly Father has in store for those who serve Him: "For since the beginning of the world have not men heard nor perceived by the ear, neither hath any eye seen, O God, besides thee, how great things thou hast prepared for him that waiteth for thee" (D&C 133:45).

CHAPTER FORTY-ONE
FEAR THOU NOT, FOR I AM WITH THEE

ISAIAH HAS A RICH LEGACY of courage and faith to draw from as he teaches and guides his people. The history of the house of Israel is a story of a people faced with severe trial and oppression but always blessed with the protective hand of the Lord when they choose to follow and serve Him.

After Moses had guided the children of Israel out of Egypt, he focused his efforts on obtaining the promised land and sent twelve men on a secret reconnaissance mission to assess the conditions there. Upon returning from their forty-day mission, the majority of these twelve spies gave Moses a grim and dismal report of strongly fortified cities and well-defended people, including some who looked like giants. Joshua and Caleb, however, trusted in the Lord's purpose for Israel and, in their faith, gave a positive report. Caleb said to Moses, "Let us go up at once, and possess it; for we are able to overcome it" (Num. 13:30).

The Israelites' general lack of faith and disobedience to the Lord's commandments caused a forty-year delay in their mission to possess their promised land. Through it all, however, Joshua and Caleb kept their faith. Caleb, at the age of eighty-five, continued to proclaim his trust in the Lord: "I wholly followed the Lord my God. . . . As yet I am as strong this day as I was in the day that Moses sent me. . . . Now therefore give me this mountain, whereof the Lord spake in that day" (Joshua 14:8, 11–12). As they prepared to wrest the promised land from the hands of its idolatrous inhabitants, the Lord told Joshua, "Only be thou strong and very courageous" (Joshua 1:7).

Later, as Israel was in possession of the promised land, they were besieged by a "great host" of the Syrian army. As the enemy troops, horses, and chariots encompassed their city, the servant of the prophet Elisha cried out to him in fear: "Alas, my master! how shall we do?" Elisha answered,

"Fear not: for they that be with us are more than they that be with them. And Elisha prayed, and said, Lord, I pray thee, open his eyes, that he may see. And the Lord opened the eyes of the young man; and he saw: and, behold, the mountain was full of horses and chariots of fire round about Elisha" (2 Kings 6:14–17).

Isaiah is undoubtedly inspired by this legacy of faith as he continues to guide and inspire ancient and modern Israel. Like Moses, Joshua, Caleb, and Elisha, Isaiah testifies of the true power vested in Christ and labors to bring Israel to Him in faith and commitment.

Keep Silence before Me

The Lord now speaks generally to the islands—the nations—of the earth. He admonishes them to trust Him and recognize Him as the one true God: "Keep silence before me, O islands; and let the people renew their strength: let them come near; then let them speak: let us come near together in judgment" (Isa. 41:1). He reminds all that He is "the Lord, the first, and with the last; I am he" (Isa. 41:4).

The Lord speaks a dual prophecy of two kings—Cyrus and Christ Himself—and their future influence with Israel: "Who raised up the righteous man from the east, called him to his foot, gave the nations before him, and made him rule over kings?" (Isa. 41:2). We will soon learn more of King Cyrus, a righteous king from the east who will rise up and free the Israelites from their Babylonian captivity. At His Second Coming, the Lord Himself will come from the east and will, as the King of Kings, rule over the kings of the earth.

Rather than heed the Lord's warning cry and trust in His promise of protection, the people of the world attempt to find comfort in one another: "They helped every one his neighbour; and every one said to his brother, Be of good courage." They persisted in the construction of false gods that would not save: "So the carpenter encouraged the goldsmith, and he that smootheth with the hammer him that smote the anvil, saying, It is ready for the sodering: and he fastened it with nails, that it should not be moved" (Isa. 41:6–7).

Fear Not, Be Not Dismayed

The Lord now turns His message from general admonishment of the nations of the earth to Israel, His covenant people: "But thou, Israel, art my servant, Jacob whom I have chosen, the seed of Abraham my friend. Thou whom I have taken from the ends of the earth, and called thee from the chief men thereof, and said unto thee, Thou art my servant; I have chosen thee, and not cast thee away" (Isa. 41:8–9).

Just a few days before this writing, we were discussing the twelfth chapter of Isaiah in my institute class, and I desired to have the class sing a hymn in illustration of the following passage: "Sing unto the Lord; for he hath done excellent things: this is known in all the earth" (Isa. 12:5). I asked for someone to consider a favorite hymn that would illustrate the excellent things the Lord has done, and one young lady appropriately chose "How Firm a Foundation" (*Hymns*, no. 85). We sang the hymn and were inspired by the strength and power of the music and the words of this beautiful song drawn from the Lord's promise to Israel if they would trust in Him: "Fear thou not; for I am with thee: be not dismayed; for I am thy God: I will strengthen thee; yea, I will help thee; yea, I will uphold thee with the right hand of my righteousness" (Isa. 41:10).

The right hand is the covenant hand. It is also a symbol of divine favor and power and of the Lord's sustaining of us in our trials. Through our covenants with our Savior, we are upheld on our mortal journey. The Lord continues His renewed promise of protection to His righteous followers and assures them that "they that were incensed against thee shall be ashamed and confounded: they shall be as nothing; and they that strive with thee shall perish." He then gives a sweet promise referencing again the covenant hand and His protective promises to us: "For I the Lord thy God will hold thy right hand, saying unto thee, Fear not; I will help thee" (Isa. 41:11, 13). As we consider the divine assistance we receive from our Heavenly Father's hand, our thoughts are directed to the temple and the protective covenants we make therein.

Thou Worm, Jacob

Isaiah teaches of how the Lord urges sincerity of heart and humility in those who desire to become implements for good in His hands. Levi Savage was a humble and faithful man. He joined the Church with his parents and, in process of gathering to Utah, joined the Mormon Battalion. After his military service, he returned to Utah, married, and he and his wife were blessed with a baby son. Within the year of the son's birth, his wife died, leaving Levi to raise the baby by himself. After another year, he was called on a four-year mission to Siam, accepted the call, and left his son in the care of his sister. At the conclusion of his mission, as he anxiously traveled homeward to be with his son, he joined the Willie handcart company and was appointed as a subcaptain. With the delayed departure of the company came the fear that they would not make it to the Salt Lake Valley before the severity of winter was upon them. As the company debated whether to promptly depart or stay at Winter

Quarters, Levi, speaking from experience in crossing the rugged plains and mountains, courageously spoke his opinion that they should stay and not attempt the crossing so late in the season. Upon being outvoted, Levi declared, "Seeing you are to go forward, I will go with you . . . will suffer with you, and if necessary, will die with you."[67]

En route, some traveling elders met with the handcart company, and when they learned that Levi had voiced opposition to the departure, one of them publicly rebuked him. Rather than bristle with pride and insist on discussing the true context of his opposition, Levi simply offered a humble apology for any discord he may have sown and committed to continue in his support of the company. Levi had gained courage and strength from the knowledge that God knew the true intent of his heart. His desire was to serve with faith and humility.

If we are humble, the Lord will bless us. He promised Israel, "Fear not, thou worm Jacob, and ye men of Israel; I will help thee, saith the Lord, and thy redeemer, the Holy One of Israel" (Isa. 41:14). The statement, "Thou worm Jacob," along with Moses's declaration "that man is nothing" (Moses 1:10) and Nephi's statement, "O how great is the nothingness of the children of men; yea, even they are less than the dust of the earth" (Hel. 12:7), are not declarations of man's worthlessness but are rather statements of humility. Humility is not worthlessness.

As we attain humility, we become instruments in the hand of the Lord in the gathering of Israel: "Behold, I will make thee a new sharp threshing instrument . . . thou shalt thresh the mountains. . . . Thou shalt fan them . . . thou shalt rejoice in the Lord, and shalt glory in the Holy One of Israel" (Isa. 41:15–16). A "fan" is a tool or device for winnowing grain. "To fan" is to harvest and separate out the seed from the chaff and symbolizes separating the righteous from the wicked and the humble from the proud. The poor and the needy who are humble, who come unto Christ and who "thirst" for His righteousness, will not be forsaken. Their thirst shall be quenched with water in abundance, granted by the Giver of living water: "I the God of Israel will not forsake them. I will open rivers in high places, and fountains in the midst of the valleys: I will make the wilderness a pool of water, and the dry land springs of water" (Isa. 41:17–18).

Their Molten Images Are Wind and Confusion

The prophet Elijah challenged the false gods of wicked king Ahab and even challenged the king himself to a contest of fire that they might discover the one true God. When Baal, Ahab's god, did nothing, Elijah chided, "Cry aloud: for he is a god; either he is talking, or he is pursuing, or he is in a journey, or peradventure he sleepeth, and must be awaked" (1 Kings 18:27).

The Lord now chides and challenges the false gods of Isaiah's day: "Produce your cause, saith the Lord; bring forth your strong reasons, saith the King of Jacob." The Lord challenges them to prophesy: "Shew us what shall happen." He asks them to speak history: "Shew the former things, what they be." He asks them to do something good—or even bad—to show they are alive: "Yea, do good, or do evil, that we may be dismayed, and behold it together" (Isa. 41:21–23). And of course, the idol gods did nothing because they "are all vanity; their works are nothing: their molten images are wind and confusion" (Isa. 41:29).

The true Messiah stands in stark and majestic contrast to the dumb and impotent idol gods. He comes as "one that bringeth good tidings" (Isa. 41:27).

CHAPTER FORTY-TWO
BEHOLD MY SERVANT

WITH THE BEGINNING VERSES OF chapter 42, we are now introduced to the first of four "servant songs" of Isaiah.[68] These beautiful poetic expressions teach us the true character of our Savior and of His nature to be of service to all of the Father's children. Although the servants are often identified with various people, the characteristics certainly match the character of Christ.

These words of Victor Ludlow are helpful in giving us a broader and more personal perspective for application of the servant songs: "Rather than categorically stating that Isaiah's servant songs apply only to one servant, we might be wise in recognizing that the characteristics of God's servant are best exemplified in Christ and are also demonstrated through the lives of all of God's righteous children. In short, the precise identity of the servant is not as important as studying his characteristics and seeking to develop them in our own lives."[69]

Wash One Another's Feet

A young woman was waiting in line in a busy airport. She was stranded by bad weather, was pregnant, and was threatening miscarriage. She was tending as best she could to a young toddler sitting on the floor. She later said, "Someone came towards us and with a kindly smile said, 'Is there something I could do to help you?' With a grateful sigh I accepted his offer." The stranger then proceeded to comfort the child and helped move the young mother to the head of the line so she could expedite her flight arrangements. He then helped her get settled on a bench and assured her that all was in order. The young mother later reported, "About a week later I saw a picture of Apostle Spencer W. Kimball and recognized him as the stranger in the airport."[70]

The years passed, and President Kimball received a letter:

> Dear President Kimball:
>
> . . . . I have just returned from my mission in Munich, West Germany. . . .
>
> I was sitting in priesthood meeting last week, when a story was told of a loving service which you performed some twenty-one years ago in the Chicago airport. The story told of how you met a young pregnant mother. . . . She was threatening miscarriage and therefore could not lift her child to comfort her. She had experienced four previous miscarriages, which gave added reason for the doctor's orders not to bend or lift.
>
> You comforted the crying child and explained the dilemma to the other passengers in line. This act of love took the strain and tension off my mother. I was born a few months later in Flint, Michigan.
>
> I just want to thank you for your love. Thank you for your example![71]

President Kimball was a living example of Christlike service. When Jesus's Apostles questioned "which of them should be accounted the greatest," He taught them, "He that is greatest among you, let him be as the younger; and he that is chief, as he that doth serve" (Luke 22:24, 26).

At the feast of the Passover, Jesus demonstrated this principle of service: "He riseth from supper, and laid aside his garments; and took a towel, and girded himself. After that he poureth water into a basin, and began to wash the disciples' feet, and to wipe them with the towel wherewith he was girded." He then taught, "If I then, your Lord and Master, have washed your feet; ye also ought to wash one another's feet" (John 13:4–5, 14). Jesus was a true servant!

Behold My Servant

In serving as His Father would have Him serve, Christ speaks and acts with great power yet in sublime reverence. In contrast to the noisy shouting and loud haggling of the world, He gently nurtures and imparts His truth to His children and softly beckons them to come unto Him and receive life eternal: "Behold my servant, whom I uphold; mine elect, in whom my soul delighteth; I have put my spirit upon him: he shall bring forth judgment to the Gentiles. He shall not cry, nor lift up, nor cause his voice to be heard in the street. A bruised reed shall he not break, and the smoking flax shall he not quench: he shall bring forth judgment unto truth. He shall not fail nor be discouraged, till he have set judgment in the earth: and the isles shall wait for his law" (Isa. 42:1–4).

In a world where many grow weary of trial and heartache and become discouraged and give up, Christ "does not fail nor be discouraged." To the downtrodden—the "bruised reed"—and to those gasping for spiritual breath—"the smoking flax"—He heals and resuscitates. Reeds are marsh plants that depend on abundant water. Flax was used as a wick for an oil lamp. A bruised reed would be limp, bent over, and ready to die. An oil lamp would have a smoking wick when the oil was nearly depleted. Christ provides refreshing and saving water and healing oil for those in need. He brings forth judgment unto truth. He suits "his mercies according to the conditions of the children of men" (D&C 46:15).

Christ came to earth to do the will of His Father. Even in His hour of greatest agony, He submitted His own will to that of the Father: "O my Father, if it be possible, let this cup pass from me: nevertheless not as I will, but as thou wilt" (Matt. 26:39).

And though He meekly submitted to the Father's will, when faced with the blasphemy of the world, He powerfully proclaimed His mission: "I have long time holden my peace; I have been still, and refrained myself: now I will cry like a travailing woman; I will destroy and devour at once." Those who cry out, "God is dead!" and live their lives in full disregard of His gospel will receive the powerful and reverberating echo of His might and justice: "I will make waste mountains and hills, and dry up all their herbs; and I will make the rivers islands, and I will dry up the pools" (Isa. 42:14–15).

Christ created the heavens and the earth. He did so to help His Father fulfill His purpose of providing opportunity for eternal life for His children. He constantly teaches us this purpose, that not only did He create the earth and "the heavens, and stretched them out" but He "giveth breath unto the people upon it, and spirit to them that walk therein" (Isa. 42:5).

Christ opens "the blind eyes, to bring out the prisoners from the prison, and them that sit in darkness out of the prison house" (Isa. 42:7). Just as the physically blind were healed by the Savior, those who are spiritually blind may be healed of their unbelief through faith in Christ: "For I will send my servant unto you who are blind; yea, a messenger to open the eyes of the blind, and unstop the ears of the deaf; And they shall be made perfect

notwithstanding their blindness, if they will hearken unto the messenger, the
Lord's servant" (JST, Isa. 42:19–20).

The Isles Shall Wait for His Law

As I've sought personal inspiration, I have enjoyed pondering this
chapter through the perspective of the teachings of the holy temple. I share
several examples of my ponderings, as follows:

**"He shall not cry, nor lift up, nor cause his voice to be heard in
the street"** (Isa. 42:2). Anyone can walk in the open streets of the world
and listen to the many conversations. However, if we have something really
important to say to someone, we generally seek privacy and quiet. The Lord
has much to say to us about His plan and beckons us to the temple to learn
of His ways. All people on the earth are invited to prepare themselves to
qualify for the blessings of the temple and enter therein to hear His voice of
instruction and blessing.

**"A bruised reed he shall not break and the smoking flax shall he not
quench"** (Isa. 42:3). In the temple, we may receive healing of our spiritual
bruises as we learn to understand and rely on the power of the Atonement.
If our testimonies are smoldering as smoking flax, they may be fanned
bright as we learn of our Heavenly Father and His plan for us and receive
replenishment through His life-giving "beauty for ashes" and "oil of joy" (Isa.
61:3).

"He shall not fail nor be discouraged" (Isa. 42:4). We may not
always trust every promise or relationship we make with mankind in the
fallen world. In the temple, however, we may fully trust every promise
given us by our Heavenly Father, who does not give up on us. His
covenants with us never fail. If we forfeit blessings, it is of our own
doing—He is "Faithful and True" (Rev. 19:11) in all of His doings.

"The isles shall wait for his law" (Isa. 42:4). In biblical context, "the
isles of the sea" generally refers to the far reaches of all the earth—not just
the islands. In our modern time, temples are now within reasonable reach
of most of the inhabitants of the world—the majority of Church members
now live within a few hours of a temple. The wait is now over for many
of the "isles" of the world that have anxiously looked for the Lord's law to
come to them through temple worship.

**"He that created the heavens, and stretched them out . . . giveth . . .
spirit to them that walk therein"** (Isa. 42:5). In the world, we pursue the
elusive answers as to how and when the heavens and the earth were created.
In the temple, we learn the sure truth, by Spirit and by word, of how, when,
and why the earth was created.

"I the Lord . . . will hold thine hand, and will keep thee, and give thee for a covenant" (Isa. 42:6). As we are willing, humble, and obedient, the Lord takes us by the hand and leads us to the temple, through the temple, and onward to eternal life, which life He promises us by His covenants.

"To bring out the prisoners from the prison" (Isa. 42:7). Through the mission and Atonement of Jesus Christ and by temple proxy ordinances for the dead, the faithful prisoners are set free: "The Son of God appeared, declaring liberty to the captives who had been faithful" (D&C 138:18).

"My glory will I not give to another, neither my praise to graven images" (Isa. 42:8). The temple is unencumbered by the iconic images of God found in so many other places. The appropriate and accurately portrayed symbolism of God and Christ in the temple focuses our worship on Them and Their true nature and mission rather than on images of Them.

"New things do I declare" (Isa. 42:9). One purpose of the temple, as taught us in the dedicatory prayer of the Kirtland temple, is for God to have a place to "manifest himself to his people" (D&C 109:5). When we go to the temple, we learn things "new" to us in our mortality—although we likely knew many of them in the premortal realm. In the temple, we learn of God's truth, which is "knowledge of things as they are, and as they were, and as they are to come" (D&C 93:24).

"Shout from the top of the mountains" (Isa. 42:11). At temple dedications, we participate in the sacred ceremonial act of shouting hosanna. This act of praise reminds us of the purpose of the temple and the connecting of this earth to our premortal life: "When the morning stars sang together, and all the sons of God shouted for joy" (Job 38:7). We also connect to our eternal life by shouting praise "with joy and rejoicing, and with hosannas to him that sitteth upon the throne forever and ever" (D&C 124:101).

"And I will bring the blind by a way that they knew not; I will lead them in paths that they have not known: I will make darkness light before them, and crooked things straight. These things will I do unto them, and not forsake them. . . . Hear, ye deaf; and look, ye blind, that ye may see (Isa. 42:16, 18). In the temple, we see with new spiritual eyes and hear the Spirit's voice as with new ears. In an ambiance of light and truth, we chart a path to celestial splendor and glory—a path that is new and distinct from the mortal paths of the telestial, fallen world we leave behind as we enter the temple.

"The Lord is well pleased for his righteousness' sake; he will magnify the law, and make it honourable" (Isa. 42:21). With a magnifying glass, we focus light and enhance and expand our vision. In the temple, as we learn the greater purpose of God's laws and make covenants to keep His commandments, we are made honorable and acceptable before Him and are able to see His purposes with greater clarity and light.

"Walk in his ways . . . obedient unto his law" (Isa. 42:24). The first principles and ordinances of the gospel chart our path to the temple. In the temple, we learn more of the Lord's ways and extend our spiritual path and sacred journey into eternity. As we obey God's laws and walk in His ways, we ultimately arrive where He is.

CHAPTER FORTY-THREE
BESIDES ME THERE IS NO SAVIOUR

THERE ARE MANY GREAT PHILOSOPHERS of the world, inspired by God, from whom we may learn much truth. Confucius said, "If a man takes no thought about what is distant, he will find sorrow near at hand." From Mohammed we are taught, "The best richness is the richness of the soul." William Shakespeare wrote, "This above all: to thine own self be true, and it must follow, as night the day, thou canst not then be false to any man." Buddha declared, "Even death is not to be feared by one who has lived wisely." Gandhi proclaimed, "A man is but the product of his thoughts—what he thinks, he becomes."

Although many purveyors of truth may inspire and guide us with wisdom, there is only one who can save us. King Benjamin said, "There shall be no other name given nor any other way nor means whereby salvation can come unto the children of men, only in and through the name of Christ, the Lord Omnipotent" (Mosiah 3:17).

Christ takes His stewardship of us seriously. Our salvation is His personal mission. He is our only Savior (see 2 Ne. 31:21; Mosiah 4:8; Acts 4:12).

O Jacob, O Israel

Despite Israel's[72] rebellion, Christ—their only Savior—continues to claim them as His own: "But now thus saith the Lord that created thee, O Jacob, and he that formed thee, O Israel, Fear not: for I have redeemed thee, I have called thee by thy name; thou art mine" (Isa. 43:1).

Because of the love of Christ for Israel, He preserves them for His own glory. He saved them from a pursuing pharaoh as they passed "through the waters" of the Red Sea. Shadrach, Meshach, and Abednego were blessed by the Lord's continuing promise that "when thou walkest through the fire, thou shalt not be burned; neither shall the flame kindle upon thee" (Isa. 43:2).

As those of scattered Israel learn of Christ and of His covenant and strive to receive and keep that covenant, then the promise of their gathering is fulfilled as declared through Isaiah: "Fear not: for I am with thee; I will bring thy seed from the east, and gather thee from the west. I will say to the north, Give up; and to the south, Keep not back; bring my sons from far, and my daughters from the ends of the earth" (Isa. 43:5–6).

Through years of apostasy, the children of Israel had spiritually closed their eyes and stopped their ears to the sweet whisperings of the gospel message. They still had their eyes and ears—they were just not *spiritually* using them. The Lord invites, "Bring forth the blind people that have eyes, and the deaf that have ears. . . . let them bring forth their witnesses, that they may be justified: or let them hear, and say, It is truth" (Isa. 43:8–9).

Beside Me, There Is No Saviour

A sad and all-too-common scenario of our present immoral world is to have someone we love and care about wander from the gospel path and wallow in the depths of hell for a time—even though they know better. It seems we can teach that wickedness is never happiness (see Alma 41:10), but it also seems that some must just learn for themselves rather than rely on the faith and testimony of prophets and other inspired loved ones. It is bitter to see someone wander. It is sweet to see them come home and reacquaint themselves with the truth they have always known.

Christ, our only Savior, is Alpha and Omega—the beginning and the end—"For I am the Lord thy God, the Holy One of Israel, thy Saviour" (Isa. 43:3).

Ye are my witnesses, saith the Lord, and my servant whom I have chosen: that you may know and believe me, and understand that I am he: before me there was no God formed, neither shall there be after me.

> I, even I, am the Lord; and beside me there is no saviour.
>
> I have declared, and have saved, and I have shewed, when there was no strange god among you: therefore, ye are my witnesses, saith the Lord, that I am God.
>
> Yea, before the day was I am he; and there is none that can deliver out of my hand: I will work, and who shall let it? (Isa. 43:10–13)

He is with us from cradle to grave. If we choose a course of idolatry, we will someday sadly come to know that He was with us before our wrong choices—"when there was no strange god among you"—meaning before the worshipping of false gods (Isa. 43:12). He will wait for us during our sufferings for our wrong choices, and He will be with us when we finally come to our senses.

Our modern bookshelves are crowded with publications offering solutions to all of our problems and cures for all of our ills. Our universities are well populated with professors who proclaim the proven ways of life. We revere great thinkers of the ages who have sincerely inspired generations to a better life. Politicians boldly proclaim the path to deliverance from our societal and economic woes. But any and all hope of salvation is vested in our Savior. All truth from any source centers in our one true God and in His Son, Jesus Christ, our only Savior.

Called By My Name

Christ is the father of our salvation. As we hear "the words of the prophets," hearken "unto their words," believe "that the Lord [will] redeem his people," and look forward to a "remission" of our sins, we become His seed: "I say unto you, that these are his seed, or they are the heirs of the kingdom of God" (Mosiah 15:11).

To become "heirs of the kingdom of God" is to come unto our Heavenly Father through Christ and receive the kind of life He has. Christ proclaimed, "Fear not: for I have redeemed thee, I have called thee by thy name; thou art mine." Our souls are of great worth to Him: "Since thou wast precious in my sight, thou hast been honourable, and I have loved thee." Because of His love for us, He calls us by His name and wants to give us His glory: "Even every one that is called by my name: for I have created him for my glory, I have formed him; yea, I have made him" (Isa. 43:1, 4, 7).

Isaiah continued his bold ministry in proclaiming the message of our Heavenly Father, through Christ, and the path He would have us walk to return to Him and gain eternal life: "Behold, I will do a new thing; now it shall spring forth; shall ye not know it? I will even make a way in the wilderness, and rivers in the desert." We are reminded that we are His and that He is perfectly possessive of us in His desire to save us: "This people have I formed for myself." Christ redeems us from sin and death: "I, even I, am he that blotteth out thy transgressions for mine own sake, and will not remember thy sins." The object of our daily walk through life is to remember His perfect Atonement and to seek His justification and sanctification with all our hearts: "Put me in remembrance: let us plead together: declare thou, that thou mayest be justified" (Isa. 43:19, 21, 25–26).

CHAPTER FORTY-FOUR
FOR I HAVE REDEEMED THEE

IN ISAIAH'S CONTINUED DISCUSSION OF the grandeur of God, he poses a profound question: "Is there a God beside me?" (Isa. 44:8). In the deep pondering of things spiritual, we are reminded that the greatest achievements of man pale in comparison to the creations and miracles of our one true God.

Some time ago, I read a fascinating book written by one of my favorite authors about the building of the great Brooklyn Bridge that spans the East River between Brooklyn and Manhattan, New York.[73] This engineering miracle has been called "the eighth wonder of the world" and is almost beyond imagination as we consider how the developers constructed forms for huge caissons upriver, floated them into place, and then sank and positioned them at the bridge site for the footings and foundations. The builders worked against seemingly impossible odds to engineer and develop the bridge and to construct the steel cables that would suspend the decking. Their rigorous specifications were six times stronger than necessary. Perhaps the most fascinating aspect of the project for me was the fact that its construction began in 1870—just a few years after the Civil War and well before the advent of so much of our modern technology. We marvel at the genius of human invention!

But by viewing things from a greater perspective we realize that it was God who created the river spanned by the bridge. It was He who gave the engineering genius to the developers to plan and execute the construction. And it was from the Lord's well-provisioned earth that the ore and stone were quarried and converted into steel and structure used to build the cables and towers.

God's miracles are more sublime than the greatest imaginations of man. Wendell Berry said, "Whoever really has considered the lilies of the field or the birds of the air and pondered the improbability of their existence *in this warm world within the cold and empty stellar distances* will hardly balk at the turning of water into wine—which was, after all, a very small miracle. We forget the greater and still continuing miracle by which water (with soil and sunlight) is turned into grapes."[74]

Is There a God Beside Me?

In all of Israel's struggles, if they would repent, they could look to their Creator with full assurance of absolute protection, guidance, and redemption: "Thus saith the Lord that made thee, and formed thee from the womb, which will help thee; Fear not, O Jacob, my servant; and thou, Jesurun, whom I have chosen." In their physical and spiritual drought, He, the giver of living water, offered the promise, "For I will pour water upon him that is thirsty, and floods upon the dry ground: I will pour my spirit upon thy seed, and my blessing upon thine offspring: And they shall spring up as among the grass, as willows by the water courses" (Isa. 44:2–4).

We receive or accept the living water as we seek the saving ordinances of the gospel and, in so doing, are led to the temple, where we make covenants and receive what we need to be "named" the children of God: "One shall say, I am the Lord's; and another shall call himself by the name of Jacob; and another shall subscribe with his hand unto the Lord, and surname himself by the name of Israel" (Isa. 44:5). We manifest that we are the Lord's through baptism and by renewing our baptismal covenants through the sacrament. We desire to be called by "the name of Jacob" and do so as we are "wrought upon and cleansed by the power of the Holy Ghost" (Moro. 6:4). We "subscribe with" our "hand unto the Lord" by seeking and receiving the higher ordinances and covenants of the temple. As we accept and live the terms of the new and everlasting covenant, we are given what we need to prepare us to ultimately receive the name of God, or to become heirs of His glory, which is eternal life.

Our Savior boldly proclaimed His absolute power—as vested in Him by His Father—in order to help us gain eternal life: "Thus saith the Lord the King of Israel, and his redeemer the Lord of hosts; I am the first, and I am the last; and beside me there is no God" (Isa. 44:6). Spoken from the lips of any mere mortal, such language would be blasphemy. Proclaimed from the mouth of our Savior, it is pure humility and spoken in total deference to the motive, will, and plan of the Father. This bold declaration is akin to the Lord's message to Abraham in reference to all other beings: "I am the Lord thy God, I am more intelligent than they all" (Abr. 3:19). He has superior intelligence to lead and guide us to a superior, eternal life. In His humility, he assures us that He has the capacity to take us there.

What glorious promises! Is there any god to compare to our one true God? Of course not! "Fear ye not, neither be afraid: have not I told thee from that time, and have declared it? ye are even my witnesses. Is there a God beside me? yea, there is no God; I know not any" (Isa. 44:8).

A Graven Image That Is Profitable for Nothing

Through the genius given from God to man, we are blessed to travel on highways, fly on airplanes, traverse rivers on bridges, live in temperature-controlled homes, and to enjoy much comfort and wholesome sociality with our loved ones.

Through the damning influence of Satan, mankind wastes precious resources in pursuit of idol gods that demean, seduce, and corrupt. Idolatry destroys our economy, our sociality, our peace, and our progress: "They that make a graven image are all of them vanity; and their delectable things shall not profit; and they are their own witnesses; they see not, nor know; that they may be ashamed. Who hath formed a god, or molten a graven image that is profitable for nothing?" (Isa. 44:9–10).

How foolish to consider that a man may take a tree and from it "burn . . . and warm himself . . . and baketh bread" and also from the same tree "maketh a god, and worshippeth it . . . and falleth down thereto. . . . and saith, Deliver me; for thou art my god." Consider the folly of one who would, in worship, "fall down to the stock of a tree" (Isa. 44:15, 17, 19). Granted, the pagan idolaters saw their wooden gods as *symbols* for gods, but the end result was the same. Their dumb symbols represented their dumb gods, "which neither see, nor hear, nor eat, nor smell" (Deuteronomy 4:28). Of course, if one's desire is to do unspeakable things, the last thing he would want is a god who speaks. In the day of trouble when the cry is "Deliver me," the idol god does what it was fashioned to do—remain still and silent.

For I Have Redeemed Thee

The Brooklyn Bridge is founded on two grand towers set deep into the bedrock of the river and rising high into the sky, as if to connect heaven and earth. These two towers are the pivotal structures of the bridge. From them, myriad cables span the river and support the decking.

Likewise, there are two grand pillars of doctrinal understanding that are essential to our progress toward eternal life. We must know who we are and what we must do, and we must know who God is and what He does for us.

We are His offspring—His creation: "Remember these, O Jacob and Israel; for thou art my servant: I have formed thee; thou art my servant: O Israel, thou shalt not be forgotten of me" (Isa. 44:21). We must learn of Him and accept of His plan for us.

God is our literal Father. Christ is our Savior. God formed us as individual souls. He organized covenant Israel. We are His people, and He will remember us. To know Jesus Christ, the Son, is to know God, the Father. Our Father has provided salvation for us through His Only Begotten Son: "I have blotted out, as a thick cloud, thy transgressions, and, as a cloud, thy sins: return unto me; for I have redeemed thee" (Isa. 44:22).

How damning and inane it would be to pay devotion to something we have created with our own hands. How divine and heavenly it is to worship our God, who created us. A correct knowledge of God and true devotion to Him gives us life: "And this is life eternal, that they might know thee the only true God, and Jesus Christ, whom thou hast sent" (John 17:3). Gaining a correct understanding of our Heavenly Father and His plan for us gives us much cause to rejoice: "Sing, O ye heavens; for the Lord hath done it: shout, ye lower parts of the earth: break forth into singing, ye mountains, O forest, and every tree therein: for the Lord hath redeemed Jacob, and glorified himself in Israel" (Isa. 44:23).

Cyrus, He Is My Shepherd

We have spoken some and will speak more of Isaiah's prophecy of the pending Babylonian captivity of Judah and the subsequent Persian conquest of Babylon under King Cyrus, who, after conquering Babylon, would allow the Jews to return to Jerusalem and rebuild their temple: "Thus saith Cyrus king of Persia, The Lord God of heaven hath given me all the kingdoms of the earth; and he hath charged me to build him an house at Jerusalem, which is in Judah" (Ezra 1:2).

Two centuries before this benevolence of King Cyrus, Isaiah related the words of the Lord concerning him: "That saith of Cyrus, He is my shepherd, and shall perform all my pleasure: even saying to Jerusalem, thou shalt be built; and to the temple, Thy foundation shall be laid" (Isa. 44:28). One of the most amazing occurrences in world history is the miraculous return of the Jews, as a people, to Jerusalem under the reign of King Cyrus. He truly did act as a shepherd of the Lord in this great cause of protecting and nurturing the Lord's people.

Also amazing is the notion that unbelieving critics will dither about the role of a prophet: "Oh my, Isaiah could not have written this portion of the book that bears his name, for he speaks of events well beyond the scope of his years." We do well to remember a few fundamentals: The work of God is greater than the puny work of mankind, and prophets prophesy beyond the scope of their years. They always have, and they always will, for "surely the Lord God will do nothing, but he revealeth his secret unto his servants the prophets" (Amos 3:7).

CHAPTER FORTY-FIVE
IN THE LORD HAVE I RIGHTEOUSNESS AND STRENGTH

Our doctrine of being "the only true and living church upon the face of the whole earth" (D&C 1:30) is not meant to be antagonistic toward anyone or any church but rather implies that we hold the priesthood authority of God to administer His ordinances of salvation to *all* people who will come and receive them. This doctrine does not mean that we claim a monopoly on truth or goodness—we accept any and all truth and goodness as part and portion of the whole truth and goodness of God.

Cyrus, Whose Right Hand I Have Holden

As mentioned in the previous chapter, King Cyrus—though not of covenant Israel—was a man of goodness and truth whom the Lord raised up to bless Israel:

> Thus saith the Lord to his anointed, to Cyrus, whose right hand I have holden, to subdue nations before him; and I will loose the loins of kings, to open before him the two leaved gates; and the gates shall not be shut;
>
> I will go before thee, and make the crooked places straight: I will break in pieces the gates of brass, and cut in sunder the bars of iron:
>
> And I will give thee the treasures of darkness, and hidden riches of secret places, that thou mayest know that I, the Lord, which call thee by thy name, am the God of Israel.
>
> For Jacob my servant's sake, and Israel mine elect, I have even called thee by thy name: I have surnamed thee, though thou hast not known me. (Isa. 45:1–4)

Although Cyrus did not worship Jehovah, He did respect Him. The Lord used Cyrus as an instrument in doing His work of restoring scattered

Judah to their homeland and to their temple. The Lord "anointed" him to this great work and held and led him by the hand in performing his noble mission. Cyrus was called the Lord's "shepherd" in that he brought the scattered sheep of Judah safely home. In all of this, Cyrus became a type and a shadow of the coming Messiah.

When King Cyrus finally conquered Babylon, he was privileged to examine the Savior's prophecy of him as this shepherd to restore the Jews and was thereby encouraged and guided in his divine mission. Josephus, the famed Jewish historian, helps us understand Cyrus's moment of discovery regarding this prophecy:

> Thus saith Cyrus the King:—"Since God Almighty hath appointed me to be king of the habitable earth, I believe that he is that God which the nation of the Israelites worship; for indeed he foretold my name by the prophets, and that I should build him a house at Jerusalem, in the country of Judea. . . .
>
> . . . This was known to Cyrus by his reading the book which Isaiah left behind him of his prophecies; for this prophet said that God had spoken thus to him in a secret vision:—"My will is, that Cyrus, whom I have appointed to be king over many and great nations, send back my people to their own land, and build my temple." This was foretold by Isaiah one hundred and forty years before the temple was demolished. Accordingly, when Cyrus read this, and admired the divine power, an earnest desire and ambition seized upon him to fulfill what was so written; so he called for the most eminent Jews that were in Babylon, and said to them, that he gave them leave to go back to their own country, and to rebuild their city Jerusalem, and the temple of God, for that he would be their assistant.[75]

Prophets prophesy. Heavenly Father orchestrates the building of His kingdom. Kings, who humble themselves, are put to the task of helping Heavenly Father in His work.

Woe unto Him That Striveth with His Maker

There is an old saying, "Don't bite the hand that feeds you." If a pet dog were to strike out at its master, who is only trying to feed and nurture it, we could assume that the dog misunderstands the intent of the master—or that the dog is mad. Anyone—and there are many in our world—who would strike out at the great plan of happiness and the saving truths offered us by our Savior through His Atonement must misunderstand true doctrine. Or perhaps they are "mad"—so stirred up to anger and prejudice by Satan that they refuse to embrace truth. Why would any reasonable person not grasp with gratitude the outstretched hand that is extended for rescue and salvation?

C. S. Lewis served as a great example of a Christian scholar from whom we learn much truth. He is revered and often quoted by our own LDS scholars and has done much to illustrate the sweet truths of the gospel. He taught:

> I have heard some people complain that if Jesus was God as well as man, then His sufferings and death lose all value in their eyes, "because it must have been so easy for him.". . . If I am drowning in a rapid river, a man who still has one foot on the bank may give me a hand which saves my life. Ought I to shout back (between my gasps) "No, it's not fair! You have an advantage! You're keeping one foot on the bank"? That advantage—call it "unfair" if you like—is the only reason why he can be of any use to me. To what will you look for help if you will not look to that which is stronger than yourself?
>
> Such is my own way of looking at what Christians call the Atonement.[76]

Of those who would scoff at the divine providence of the Savior, Isaiah proclaimed, "Woe unto him that striveth with his Maker! Let the potsherd strive with the potsherds of the earth. Shall the clay say to him that fashioneth it, What makest thou? Or thy work, He hath no hands? Woe unto him that saith unto his father, What begettest thou? or to the woman, What has thou brought forth?" (Isa. 45:9–10). One of our greatest life tasks is to learn, in humility, to be submissive to the will of our Heavenly Father.

Satan's quest is to pervert the doctrine of submissiveness. This crown-prince of counterfeit persuades people to challenge gospel truth. The question "What begettest thou?" is intended to cast doubt on the very nature of God and His spirit children.

As the creations of His hands, we can trust the Lord implicitly. We are blessed by total submission to His will. Our happiness is central to His plan. "Thus saith the Lord, the Holy One of Israel, and his Maker, Ask me of things to come concerning my sons and concerning the work of my hands command ye me. I have made the earth, and created man upon it: I, even my hands, have stretched out the heavens, and all their host have I commanded" (Isa. 45:11–12).

I Am the Lord, and There Is None Else

Here Isaiah continues his theme of inviting and encouraging all people to learn of and worship the one true God: "I am the Lord, and there is none else, there is no God beside me: I girded thee, though thou hast not known me: That they may know from the rising of the sun, and from the west, that there is none beside me. I am the Lord, and there is none else. I form the light, and create darkness: I make peace, and create evil: I the Lord do all these things" (Isa. 45:5–7; The Lord does not "create evil"; see endnote).[77]

Understanding that temple spires symbolically reach upward to connect earth with heaven, we can better understand the Lord's proclamation: "Drop down, ye heavens, from above, and let the skies pour down righteousness: let the earth open, and let them bring forth salvation, and let righteousness spring up together; I the Lord have created it." Again, the Lord reminds us of the heaven-earth connection: "For thus saith the Lord that created the heavens; God himself that formed the earth and made it; he hath established it, he created it not in vain, he formed it to be inhabited: I am the Lord; and there is none else" (Isa. 45:8, 18).

One of the most inspiring examples of the earth being connected to the purposes of heaven is found in the mission of Elijah. The Lord taught, "Behold, I will send you Elijah the prophet before the coming of the great and dreadful day of the Lord: And he shall turn the heart of the fathers to the children, and the heart of the children to their fathers, lest I come and smite the earth with a curse" (Malachi 4:5–6). When Moroni appeared to Joseph Smith during the Restoration of the gospel, he repeated this promise of Elijah and then declared the importance of the keys to be restored by Elijah: "If it were not so, the whole earth would be utterly wasted at his coming" (D&C 2:3). When Elijah actually came in his mission of restoring priesthood keys, Joseph and Oliver were again reminded of the importance of the promise of turning hearts from children to fathers: "Lest the whole earth be smitten with a curse" (D&C 110:15). This earth is intended to become the celestial, eternal abode of eternal families. Without the binding together of families for all of eternity, the eternal purpose of the earth would be for naught.

Many people in our fallen world are confused about the need to connect the things of heaven and earth—to seek after spiritual guidance and direction. Often people go on their way, basking in the idolatry of this earth, seeking whatever pleasures they may find. Some even align themselves with false "religious worship" in an attempt to justify wrong actions. Of all who seek evil, the Lord said, "They shall be ashamed, and also confounded, all of them: they shall go to confusion together that are makers of idols" (Isa. 45:16).

In stark contrast, all who seek the Lord and accept His Atonement and gospel of salvation will not be confused: "But Israel shall be saved in the Lord with an everlasting salvation: ye shall not be ashamed nor confounded world without end" (Isa. 45:17).

As I am at my computer writing this manuscript, I have many choices. For example, I may align my text to the left or right margins. I may also center all my text, leaving uneven margins. Or I may seek to justify my text by bringing it into balance and alignment at both margins. We have many choices in how we align our lives—we may seek the things of this world; we may seek uneven balance in fanaticism and untruth. Or we may seek the perfect harmony and balance offered us by the Lord through His true and living Church.

How do we do this? We seek the Lord through following His gospel plan. We flee the world with its fallen and damning idolatry: "Assemble yourselves and come; draw near together, ye that are escaped of the nations: they have no knowledge that set up the wood of their graven image, and pray unto a god that cannot save" (Isa. 45:20).

As we choose the course of truth and humbly align ourselves with the Lord's commandments, He will guide and justify us: "I have raised him up in righteousness, and I will direct all his ways. . . . Surely, shall one say, in the Lord have I righteousness and strength: even to him shall men come; and all that are increased against him shall be ashamed. In the Lord shall all seed of Israel be justified, and shall glory" (Isa. 45:13, 24–25). As we humbly acknowledge the saving power of the Atonement and reach out to grasp its glorious promise, the Lord will stretch out His hand and rescue us from the depths of darkness and will guide us safely on our way of return to our Heavenly Father and the life He prepares for us.

CHAPTER FORTY-SIX
I WILL CARRY AND WILL DELIVER YOU

IN A CLASSIC MOVIE, *SNOWBALL Express*, a man and his family inherit a remote, run-down mountain lodge. They decide to turn it into a ski resort and, with not much working capital, struggle with how to power the ski lift. They discover an old steam-powered donkey engine on the property, and then the man scurries around the community seeking a way to move the engine to the ski slope. His young son, after much effort, finally gains his attention and solves the problem with a simple statement of a rhetorical question: "If a donkey engine can pull a six-ton log out of the woods, why can't it pull *itself* up a hill?" The inanimate engine, with the miracle of steam power, had the capacity to move from one place to another. The inanimate wood and stone idol gods of Israel lacked the inherent power or capacity to do anything constructive or positive.

A Burden to the Weary Beast

Isaiah persisted in his mission to teach Israel of the evil and futility of their idolatry. He declares the obvious—that their idol gods, Bel and Nebo, were not even capable of moving themselves from one place to another but needed to be transported on wagons pulled by beasts of burden: "Bel boweth down, and Nebo stoopeth, their idols were upon the beasts, and upon the cattle: your carriages were heavy loaden; they are a burden to the weary beast. They stoop, they bow down together, they could not deliver the burden, but themselves are gone into captivity" (Isa. 46:1–2).

Isaiah continues with his message that worshiping false, manmade gods will not save us but will only bring us trouble and sorrow: "They lavish gold out of the bag, and weigh silver in the balance, and hire a goldsmith; and he maketh it a god: they fall down, yea, they worship. They bear him upon the shoulder, they carry him, and set him in his place, and he standeth; from his place shall he not remove: yea, one shall cry unto him, yet can he not answer, nor save him out of his trouble" (Isa. 46:6–7). Idolatry is a burdensome and helpless cargo.

Even to Hoar Hairs Will I Carry You

False gods that cannot reason, see, move, speak, nor hear fail in stark contrast to our one true God who knows all, sees all, hears all, and speaks His will. The Lord asked, "To whom will ye liken me, and make me equal, and compare me, that we may be like?" (Isa. 46:5). The answer is, of course, that no one and certainly no thing can compare with our Savior and the redemptive power of His atoning sacrifice. He proclaimed with inviting tenderness, "Hearken unto me, O house of Jacob, and all the remnant of the house of Israel, which are borne by me from the belly, which are carried from the womb: And even to your old age I am he; and even to hoar hairs will I carry you: I have made, and I will bear; even I will carry, and will deliver you" (Isa. 46:3–4). We need not spend our lives scurrying about seeking external power sources—we only need to look inward and upward to our Heavenly Father and our Savior and lean on their ample arms—they have sufficient strength and endurance to carry us for the entire journey to eternal life.

To fully access the Lord's sustaining power and to act in His strength, we need to repent of our sins and rise up and be men and women of faith: "Remember this, and shew yourselves men: bring it again to mind, O ye transgressors" (Isa. 46:8). Paradoxically, one way to "shew ourselves men" is to learn to be humble as the child. As we become humble and submit to the will of the Father, He opens our spiritual ears and eyes and gives us vision of our eternal potential.

The Lord declared to us, "The end from the beginning, and from ancient times the things that are not yet done, saying, My counsel shall stand, and I will do all my pleasure." His "pleasure," or His work, is to free us from our oppressors and grant us immortality and eternal life. In ancient times, when Judah wearied of their captivity and humbled themselves in seeking deliverance, the Lord called "a ravenous bird from the east, the man that executeth my counsel from a far country." This "ravenous bird" was Cyrus, who rapidly conquered Babylon, freed the Jews, and set them on a course back to Jerusalem and to the rebuilding of the temple (Isa. 46:10–11; footnote 11a).

I Bring Near My Righteousness

Isaiah, in his beautiful parallel poetic style, reaches out to all who wander and teaches them that, although they may now be far away, they may return and come near unto the Lord and, in Him, find the salvation that seemed beyond their reach: "Hearken unto me, ye stouthearted, that are far from righteousness: I bring near my righteousness; it shall not be far off, and my salvation shall not tarry: and I will place salvation in Zion for Israel my glory" (Isa. 46:12–13).

Undoubtedly, we all know people who, in their pursuit of the idolatry of the world, have found themselves far from their spiritual roots and far from the path leading to true happiness and eternal life. I will speak of one woman as composite example of many. This woman grew up active in gospel knowledge and service, married in the temple, and worked hard to care for her children and to teach them the ways of righteousness. Then her eyes were drawn to the glitter of the world. She traded the counsel of her one true God for the dumb and silly lure of idol gods. As her path veered away from the gospel, it took her away from her marriage and out of the Church. To those who knew her best, and likely even to herself, she might seem far from true and lasting happiness. And yet, in the eternal realm and view of God, she may be nearer than she can imagine. The journey back will be difficult but certainly possible.

All who are willing to become as humble as children and abandon the false gods of the fallen world may return joyfully to the path of happiness and salvation.

CHAPTER FORTY-SEVEN
THE LOSS OF CHILDREN AND WIDOWHOOD

I KNOW OF A GRAVE marker for a couple, both deceased, who did not accept, and perhaps did not have opportunity to receive, the restored gospel and the ordinances thereof. On the marker is the inscription "Together Forever." I also know of a young couple who are members of the Church but who chose not to follow the path leading to eternal marriage. They were married by civil authority. At their request, in the marriage ceremony the justice of the peace included the words "I unite you for time and all eternity."

Our hope, of course, for both of these couples is that they will yet fully accept the gospel and seek the blessings of celestial marriage. But just speaking the words or engraving them on a stone does not make it so. The Lord proclaimed, "And again, verily I say unto you, if a man marry a wife, and make a covenant with her for time and for all eternity, if that covenant is not by me or by my word, which is my law, and is not sealed by the Holy Spirit of promise, through him whom I have anointed and appointed unto this power, then it is not valid neither of force when they are out of the world, because they are not joined by me, saith the Lord" (D&C 132:18).

Our Heavenly Father is a God of order. He sets the terms of His covenants with us and offers these covenants to us by His invitation. The blessings of eternity may be granted only by Him and through proper authority, no matter how much some may try to rationalize to the contrary. Those who attempt to change His ordinances sentence themselves to spiritual loss and disappointment.

I Shall Not Sit As a Widow

In dualistic prophecy, Isaiah speaks of the overthrow of Babylon, ancient and modern, and of the ancient political power of Babylon and of modern materialism and worldliness: "Come down, and sit in the dust, O virgin daughter of Babylon, sit on the ground: there is no throne, O daughter of the Chaldeans: for thou shalt no more be called tender and delicate. Take the millstones, and grind meal: uncover thy locks, make bare the leg, uncover the thigh, pass over the rivers. Thy nakedness shall be uncovered, yea, thy shame shall be seen: I will take vengeance, and I will not meet thee as a man" (Isa. 47:1–3).

Sitting "uncovered" and "on the ground" grinding meal at the "millstones" is a description of the work of slaves and refers to the bondage and loss that would come upon Babylon at the time of its destruction. The people must have thought Isaiah mad to make such a bold pronouncement of destruction of an empire engaged in such a seemingly unconquerable rise to dominance and power. And yet, by the time of the rise of the Roman Empire, Babylon would be mostly reduced to the status of an insignificant outpost. They who conquered so many would in turn be conquered, left uncovered, and driven into bondage "over the rivers" because they would not accept the true God, their "redeemer, the Lord of hosts . . . the Holy One of Israel" (Isa. 47:4).

Babylon, or the worldliness of ancient times and of our modern world, is thrown quickly down at the day of the Lord's reckoning. Spiritual rebellion denies those of Babylon their potential for eternal life. The rebellious do not receive the blessings of being prepared as a bride to meet the Bridegroom, as described in the continuing marriage metaphor throughout the scriptures. The Lord will not meet them "as a man" (Isa. 47:3), or as the Bridegroom.

Greed, materialism, and evil are destructive in all their forms. In modern revelation, the Lord describes the sad fate of those who seek the things of Babylon: "They seek not the Lord to establish his righteousness, but every man walketh in his own way, and after the image of his own god, whose image is in the likeness of the world, whose substance is that of an idol, which waxeth old and shall perish in Babylon, even Babylon the great, which shall fall" (D&C 1:16). Through sin and evil, people forfeit the opportunity to be crowned kings and queens and are left to mourn in silence: "Sit thou silent, and get thee into darkness, O daughter of the Chaldeans: for thou shalt no more be called, The lady of kingdoms" (Isa. 47:5).

There is an old saying, "You can leave the Church, but you cannot leave it alone." We might also say that the saving principles of the gospel, once understood, will not leave us alone. People in rebellion are still reminded on occasion of eternal, saving truths. The fruit of the tree of life remains desirable above all other fruit. Even when someone is bent on sinning—"I shall be a lady [or a mistress] for ever"—he or she may still yearn for the promised blessings of eternity, insisting, "I shall not sit as a widow, neither shall I know the loss of children" (Isa. 47:7–8; footnote 7a).

The Loss of Children and Widowhood

However, the Lord's judgment is just, fair, and unbiased. He provides equal opportunity for all to join Him in eternal glory, but He lets those who sin know that they will suffer the loss of His favor as a result of the misuse of their agency: "Behold, the Lord esteemeth all flesh in one; he that is righteous is favored of God" (1 Ne. 17:35). To the lady who wistfully declares that she will be both a "mistress" and a mother in Zion, the Lord proclaimed: "But these two things shall come to thee in a moment in one day, the loss of children, and widowhood: they shall come upon thee in their perfection for the multitude of thy sorceries, and for the great abundance of thine enchantments" (Isa. 47:9). We cannot simply bequeath ourselves the gift of eternal life by wishing it so or by carving it in a memorial or by having it announced by civil authority.

The things of the temple and of eternity are unequivocally of God. Those who seek them outside of the Lord's prescribed course will realize glory lost. In pride and vanity, the haughty cry out, "I am, and none else beside me." To them, the Lord said, "For thou hast trusted in thy wickedness: thou hast said, None seeth me. Thy wisdom and thy knowledge, it hath perverted thee. . . . Therefore shall evil come upon thee; thou shalt not know from whence it riseth: and mischief shall fall upon thee; thou shalt not be able to put it off: and desolation shall come upon thee suddenly, which thou shalt not know" (Isa. 47:10–11).

Often, those who think they know, do not know. The Babylonians were "expert," in their own estimation, of speaking "truth" as revealed to them through the alignment of the stars or through the entrails of an animal. Their disciples, who tuned in to their fables and ignored the eternal truths of God, were to be left in the company of the useless wizards they so adored: "Stand now with thine enchantments, and with the multitude of thy sorceries, wherein thou hast labored from thy youth; if so be thou shalt be able to profit, if so be thou mayest prevail. . . . Let now the astrologers, the stargazers, the monthly prognosticators, stand up, and save thee from these things that shall come upon thee." Of course, the soothsayers and wizards were to be of no more help to them than the arm of flesh of the Moabites and the Egyptians. In the day of trouble, they would not even be able to save themselves, let alone someone else: "Behold, they shall be as stubble; the fire shall burn them; they shall not deliver themselves from the power of the flame: there shall not be a coal to warm at, nor fire to sit before it" (Isa. 47:12–14).

As people attempt to form their own plan of salvation, counterfeit their own vision of eternal glory, and walk their own imagined path to eternal life, they are left blinded, disappointed, lost, and remain unsaved: "Thus shall they be unto thee with whom thou hast labored, even thy merchants, from thy youth: they shall wander every one to his quarter; none shall save thee" (Isa. 47:15).

CHAPTER FORTY-EIGHT
THY PEACE AS A RIVER

WATER SUSTAINS LIFE. THE IMAGERY of water is a staple of gospel teaching. It is often a symbol of spiritual life. Jeremiah rebuked his people for having "hewed them out cisterns, broken cisterns, that can hold no water" (Jer. 2:13). We recall how, in chapter 8, Isaiah invited us to not refuse the "waters of Shiloah" (v. 6–7). Jesus proclaimed Himself as the source of living water.

Lehi and his family were called to leave Babylon—both physically, from the pending Babylonian destruction, and spiritually, from the world. Just a few years after leaving Jerusalem and arriving in the promised land, Lehi saw in vision that Jerusalem had indeed been destroyed by Babylon. But even in the wilderness and in the new world, while safely removed from physical Babylon, Lehi battled the influence of spiritual Babylon upon his family. As they came near a river running into the Red Sea, Lehi charged rebellious Laman, "O that thou mightest be like unto this river, continually running into the fountain of all righteousness!" (1 Ne. 2:9).

In Lehi's vision of the tree of life, he saw "a river of water; and it ran along, and it was near the tree of which I was partaking the fruit" (1 Ne. 8:13). Nephi later taught that the river was representative of "the depths of hell" (1 Ne. 12:16). As frightening as this was, they were given the assurance of a guiding and protective "rod of iron, and it extended along the bank of the river" (1 Ne. 8:19).

As Nephi grew into his stewardship as a teacher and prophet, his desire was to teach his family to leave spiritual Babylon and prepare for celestial glory by coming unto Christ, "the fountain of living waters" (Jer. 17:13). He explained his teaching plan: "But that I might more fully persuade them to believe in the Lord their Redeemer I did read unto them that which was written by the prophet Isaiah; for I did liken all scriptures unto us, that it might be for our profit and learning" (1 Ne. 19:23). He then launched into teaching them the writings of Isaiah, beginning with Isaiah chapter 48 (see 1 Nephi 20).

Out of the Waters of Judah

In chapter 48, Isaiah shifts his focus from the destruction of Babylon to the chastisement of covenant Israel: "Hear ye this, O house of Jacob, which are called by the name of Israel, and are come forth out of the waters of Judah, which swear by the name of the Lord, and make mention of the God of Israel, but not in truth, nor in righteousness" (Isa. 48:1). The Book of Mormon expounds the phrase "are come forth out of the waters of Judah" by adding "or out of the waters of baptism" (1 Ne. 20:1). Isaiah's teachings here apply to Church members who have covenanted, by baptism, to live the gospel. His message has application to covenant Israel of Isaiah's day, to the family of Lehi, and to us of modern Israel.

To "swear by the name of the Lord, and make mention of the God of Israel, but not in truth, nor in righteousness" is hypocrisy. The word *hypocrite* is of Greek origin. In Greek theater, men played all of the parts, including the wearing of masks in the women's roles. Thus, a hypocrite was one who was pretending to be someone he was not. Many in ancient and modern Israel desire the cultural and social association with the true Church but do not accept the obligation of obedience. They just want to appear to be of Israel but not accept the mantle of truth and righteousness. Hypocrites are unwilling to exit Babylon or leave behind the things of the world. They "call themselves of the holy city, and stay themselves upon the God of Israel" or, in other words, they "pretend to rely upon" the God of Israel (Isa. 48:2; footnote b). Of pretenders, the Lord said, "But the hypocrites shall be detected and shall be cut off, either in life or in death, even as I will; and wo unto them who are cut off from my church, for the same are overcome of the world" (D&C 50:8).

The Lord's message of chastisement continues: "I knew that thou art obstinate, and thy neck is an iron sinew, and thy brow brass" (Isa. 48:4). A neck like an "iron sinew" is a neck that does not bend or bow down in humble prayer. A brow of brass implies thickheadedness, or an unwillingness, to ponder and accept the counsel of God. Rather, the stubborn rationalize away inspired counsel and are prone to give credit to false gods of their own design and purpose, saying, "Mine idol hath done them, and my graven image, and my molten image, hath commanded them" (Isa. 48:5).

The Lord's constant desire for His children throughout the ages is to lead them from Babylon and into His gospel light so He can reveal to them higher laws for a higher life: "Thou hast heard, see all this; and will not ye declare it? I have shewed thee new things from this time, even hidden things, and thou didst not know them" (Isa. 48:6). "Hidden things" are things hidden from the pretenders who are unwilling to commit to gospel covenants. If we are humble and submissive to the Lord and get past our stiff necks and thickheadedness, He leads us into the light and into the temple where He pours eternal truth into our souls and where we receive the refreshing waters of sweet knowledge and instruction.

Behold, I Have Refined Thee

True to the teaching pattern of the Lord, He now follows His chastisement of Israel with a sweet, merciful invitation for them to return unto Him and rechart their course to eternal life: "For my name's sake will I defer mine anger, and for my praise will I refrain for thee, that I cut thee not off. Behold, I have refined thee, but not with silver; I have chosen thee in the furnace of affliction. For mine own sake, even for mine own sake, will I do it: for how should my name be polluted? and I will not give my glory unto another" (Isa. 48:9–11).

What is the "glory" that He guards so carefully? It is the exaltation of His children. We often reference this mission statement of our Heavenly Father: "For behold, this is my work and my glory—to bring to pass the immortality and eternal life of man" (Moses 1:39). Sealing us up unto eternal life is central to His primary mission. Our modern prophets have declared that Heavenly Father has placed families at the very center of His plan, which lays out the eternal destiny of all of His children.[78]

Through gospel study and ordinances, temple worship, and the guidance of the Holy Ghost, we learn that He holds in His hand the power to bring together heaven and earth: "Mine hand also hath laid the foundation of the earth, and my right hand hath spanned the heavens: when I call unto them, they stand up together." As we come near unto the Lord, we realize that His knowledge and power have been in place forever and are available to the righteous who will seek them: "Come ye near unto me, hear ye this; I have not spoken in secret from the beginning; from the time that it was, there am I: and now the Lord God, and his Spirit, hath sent me" (Isa. 48:13, 16).

As we worship the Lord and come to know the far-reaching impact of His blessings for us, we gain a great calming sense of who we really are and how all aspects of our lives blend into the potential of a perfect eternal life. In serving God and in keeping His commandments, we receive the constant and powerful blessings of peace, joy, and the assurance of His glory, to include the perpetuation of our families forever, as stated by the Lord in these verses: "O that thou hadst hearkened to my commandments! then had thy peace been as a river, and thy righteousness as the waves of the sea: Thy seed also had been as the sand, and the offspring of thy bowels like the gravel thereof; his name should not have been cut off nor destroyed from before me" (Isa. 48:18–19).

Go Ye Forth of Babylon

The wish of Father Lehi for Laman and for all of his children was that they would have peace as a river and the sweet assurance of eternal life. He led them away from the threat of conquering Babylon and also tried to lead them away from spiritual Babylon, or from the things of the world. Similarly, Isaiah taught, "Go ye forth of Babylon, flee ye from the Chaldeans." As we flee from worldliness and seek protection and direction in spirituality, we experience the reassuring joy of redemption: "With a voice of singing declare ye, tell this, utter it even to the end of the earth; say ye, The Lord hath redeemed his servant Jacob" (Isa. 48:20).

We may trust the Lord with perfect faith. He will protect, guide, and nourish us just as He has always done. Isaiah reminded Israel that "they thirsted not when he led them through the deserts: he caused the waters to flow out of the rock for them: he clave the rock also, and the waters gushed out." He also gave a stark reminder for those who fail to remember and recognize His hand in all things and who turn away from His protection and guidance: "There is no peace, saith the Lord, unto the wicked" (Isa. 48:21–22). Alma likewise taught his wayward son of the foolishness of thinking we can experience true joy outside the protective covering of the Atonement: "Behold, I say unto you, wickedness never was happiness" (Alma 41:10).

Just as wickedness never would and never will equate with happiness, righteousness always has and always will equate with eternal peace and joy. Even though there will be turns and obstacles along our course of mortality, if we keep our covenants, our progress toward eternal life, like a river, will be constant, our peace will be sure, and our joy will be full.

CHAPTER FORTY-NINE
YET WILL I NOT FORGET THEE

SEVERAL YEARS AGO, MY WIFE had our young daughter in a grocery cart as she shopped at a local store. She went through the check-out line, loaded her items into the car, and began the drive home. After driving for about a mile, she realized the embarrassing and terrifying fact that she had forgotten our daughter. She raced back to the store to gratefully find her eating an ice cream cone and safe in the arms of a helpful cashier who assured my wife that she had certainly not been the first mother to forget a child in their store.

Some may question, "How could this be possible; how could a mother forget her own child?" and yet, truth be known, we all have occasional distractions or memory lapses that could put us in a similar circumstance. We are mere mortals, after all. Our Savior queried, "Can a woman forget her sucking child, that she should not have compassion on the son of her womb?" While we may be thinking, "No, never!" He declared the reality of our mortal existence: "Yea, they may forget." He then offered a sweet, eternal, and sublime message of hope and assurance: "Yet will I not forget thee" (Isa. 49:15).

The perfect Atonement does not only redeem us from death and hell—it has the capacity to cover all of our mortal weakness, sorrows, indiscretions, offenses, our forgetfulness, deep heartaches, neglects, and anything that may cause us to fall short of God's glory. Joseph Smith, in his trial of sorrow in Liberty Jail, was reminded in relationship to all mortal heartache and circumstance: "The Son of Man hath descended below them all" (D&C 122:8).

A Polished Shaft

In praise of our Savior and His perfect Atonement, Isaiah now offers the second servant song. Isaiah's capacity for dual prophecy suggests that this passage may refer to other prophets, ancient and modern. Interestingly, Joseph Smith used a verse from this chapter of Isaiah—"And made me a polished shaft; in his quiver hath he hid me" (Isa. 49:2)—to describe himself:

> I am like a huge rough stone rolling down from a high mountain; and the only polishing I get is when some corner gets rubbed off by coming in contact with something else, striking with accelerated force against religious bigotry, priest-craft, lawyer-craft, doctor-craft, lying editors, suborned judges and jurors, and the authority of perjured executives, backed by mobs, blasphemers, licentious and corrupt men and women—all hell knocking off a corner here and a corner there. Thus I will become a smooth and polished shaft in the quiver of the Almighty.[79]

For my purpose, I would like to focus on the aspects of this servant song that relate to Christ Himself. The chapter heading tells us, "Messiah shall be a light to the Gentiles and shall free the prisoners." Christ was foreordained for His saving mission as foretold by prophets: "The Lord hath called me from the womb . . . formed me from the womb to be his servant." His message and mission was for the whole world: "Listen, O isles, unto me; hearken, ye people from far." He was made powerful in His speech and persuasion: "And he hath made my mouth like a sharp sword." He experienced refiner's fire through rejection and persecution: "In the shadow of his hand hath he hid me, and made me a polished shaft; in his quiver hath he hid me." His mission was to gather and redeem Israel: "The Lord . . . formed me from the womb to be his servant, to bring Jacob again to him." He was to provide salvation through the establishment of His everlasting covenant with Israel: "In an acceptable time have I heard thee, and in a day of salvation have I helped thee: and I will preserve thee, and give thee for a covenant of the people, to establish the earth, to cause to inherit the desolate heritages." His Atonement would set free those imprisoned by death and hell: "That thou mayest say to the prisoners, Go forth; to them that are in darkness, Shew yourselves. They shall feed in the ways, and their pastures shall be in all high places" (Isa. 49:1–9).

My Highways Shall Be Exalted

Our Savior, during His ministry to the Nephites, taught them of the mercy, love, and compassion with which He would gather scattered Israel. He then directly followed this teaching with His charge to us to study the teachings of Isaiah: "And now, behold, I say unto you, that ye ought to search these things. Yea, a commandment I give unto you that ye search these things diligently; for great are the words of Isaiah" (3 Ne. 23:1).

We are blessed to be living in the day of the Restoration of the gospel and the latter-day gathering of scattered Israel. Gratefully, we have the writings of Isaiah and other prophets to guide us. In fulfillment of Isaiah's words, we are seeing the nations of the earth opening their doors to the gospel cause. During the years since the gospel was restored, missionaries have appealed to rulers of governments who have, in many instances, and as Isaiah prophesied, proclaimed a greater degree of religious liberty and welcomed us to teach their people: "Kings shall see and arise, princes also shall worship, because of the Lord that is faithful, and the Holy One of Israel, and he shall choose thee" (Isa. 49:7).

The veil of mystery that so clouded the dark ages has been penetrated, and gospel light is shining forth, illuminating truth and the freedom associated with it. Those held captive by unbelief and false theology are coming to drink of the living water and eat of the bread of life. Multitudes are gathering to the protective covering wings of the knowledge, understanding, and healing power of the Atonement: "That thou mayest say to the prisoners, Go forth; to them that are in darkness, Shew yourselves. They shall feed in the ways, and their pastures shall be in all high places. They shall not hunger nor thirst; neither shall the heat nor sun smite them: for he that hath mercy on them shall lead them, even by the springs of water shall he guide them" (Isa. 49:9–10).

In modern revelation, we are told of this day of gathering Israel: "And the Lord, even the Savior, shall stand in the midst of his people, and shall reign over all flesh. And they who are in the north countries shall come in remembrance before the Lord. . . . And an highway shall be cast up in the midst of the great deep. . . . And in the barren deserts there shall come forth pools of living water; and the parched ground shall no longer be a thirsty land. And there shall they fall down and be crowned with glory, even in Zion, by the hands of the servants of the Lord, even the children of Ephraim. And they shall be filled with songs of everlasting joy" (D&C 133:25–33).

Of this path traveled by the tribes of Israel, Isaiah said, "And I will make all my mountains a way, and my highways shall be exalted" (Isa. 49:11). The exalted highway traversed by gathering Israel is the highway of righteousness. It leads to the mountains of Zion, or to the temples. In the temples, gathered Saints are given their endowment to prepare them for the crown of glory of eternal life in the celestial kingdom of God.

I Have Graven Thee upon the Palms of My Hands

When we recall the fact that a mortal mother might momentarily forget a child but that the Lord will not forget scattered Israel, we may ask, "Why will He not forget us?" He answers, "Behold, I have graven thee upon the palms of my hands; thy walls are continually before me" (Isa. 49:16).

The engraving on His palms has obvious reference to the Crucifixion and atoning sacrifice of the Savior—the pivotal point of the entire plan of salvation. Our Heavenly Father's mission is to bring about our immortality and eternal life. This is made possible through the perfect Atonement. Those who gain immortality and eternal life are "they who are just men made perfect through Jesus the mediator of the new covenant, who wrought out this perfect atonement through the shedding of his own blood" (D&C 76:69).

Having suffered for us in such a glorious cause, He will not forget us as He nurtures and guides us along our homeward path: "I will lift up mine hand to the Gentiles, and set up my standard to the people: and they shall bring thy sons in their arms, and thy daughters shall be carried upon their shoulders. And kings shall be thy nursing fathers, and their queens thy nursing mothers: they shall bow down to thee with their face toward the earth, and lick up the dust of thy feet; and thou shalt know that I am the Lord: for they shall not be ashamed that wait for me" (Isa. 49:22–23).

What sweet peace we have in our Savior's love and assurance that He will never forget us and that He will help us receive the eternal promises of our Heavenly Father.

CHAPTER FIFTY
HE IS NEAR THAT JUSTIFIETH ME

IMAGINE THIS SCENARIO: A MAN and woman fall in love, marry in the temple, serve faithfully in the Church, work hard, love and serve one another, have children, are happy together—and then tragedy strikes. Eyes wander, lust is inflamed, covenants are broken, the marriage ends in divorce, and loved ones mourn the betrayal of sacred family ties.

Now pause and consider this question: Who strayed from the marriage—the husband or the wife? My guess would be that most of us would instinctively think, the husband. Although this perception may be most generally accurate, we acknowledge that the reverse is also often true—there are many faithful husbands who are betrayed by unfaithful wives. Of this President Spencer W. Kimball taught:

> Once I had a "talents-and-pence," "mote-and-beam" situation when an injured husband finally persuaded his adulterous wife to come with him to my office. She admitted her guilt but justified herself in her losing interest in her own home in the fact that her husband was so righteous and fair and honorable that it gave her an inferiority complex. I asked her what he did to disturb her and justify her leaving her home and her children and him. She could find little fault with him. He provided well, was a good father, was kind and thoughtful, a good member of the Church, but because she had bad tendencies and impure thoughts, she felt inferior. Hers was the beam; hers was the 10,000-talent error; his was the mote and the 100-pence error.[80]

Ye Have Sold Yourselves

In the marriage metaphor, as taught by Isaiah, we find the straying wife with the beam—the ten thousand talent error. But unlike the husband in President Kimball's example, this husband does not have even a mote, for He is the perfect Bridegroom, the perfect Savior. He calls out to Israel, "Where is the bill of your mother's divorcement, whom I have put away? or which of my creditors is it to whom I have sold you? Behold, for your iniquities have ye sold yourselves, and for your transgressions is your mother put away" (Isa. 50:1).

Sadly, when a mother or a father strays, children often follow. So Christ speaks not only to the wayward bride but also to the children of Israel: "For your transgressions is your mother put away." He assures them that they, and their mother, left Him. He did not and would never leave them. As such, He sees the eternal potential of the wandering soul and, even in their rebellion, keeps His hand outstretched to them: "Is my hand shortened at all, that it cannot redeem?" (Isa. 50:2). We answer with a resounding "No!" He is always faithful, never abandoning, always inviting, ever hopeful.

This comforting and hopeful doctrine of Christ's ever-outstretched hand is reaffirmed for us in modern revelation. Although those who violate covenants and wander from their vows of faithfulness divorce themselves from promised blessing of eternal life and family, of root and branch— "For, behold, the day cometh that shall burn as an oven, and all the proud, yea, and all that do wickedly, shall be stubble; and the day that cometh shall burn them up, saith the Lord of hosts, that it shall leave them neither root nor branch,"— our Savior does not falter in His desire and efforts to save us: "Yet my arm was not shortened at all that I could not redeem, neither my power to deliver" (D&C 133:64, 67). He is the ever true servant, constantly seeking the will and work of His Father.

I Gave My Back to the Smiters

As we now come to the third servant song of Isaiah, we will continue to keep our focus on Christ as the servant.

Christ was blessed with eloquence, both in speaking to the proud and to the humble. He did not hesitate to condemn the hypocritical scribes and Pharisees, who He declared were "like unto whited sepulchres, which indeed appear beautiful outward, but are within full of dead men's bones, and of all uncleanness" (Matt. 23:27). But for the sincere and righteous who sometimes wearied of life's journey, He tenderly implored, "Come unto me, all ye that labour and are heavy laden, and I will give you rest"

(Matt. 11:28). He described His gift of eloquence thus: "The Lord God hath given me the tongue of the learned, that I should know how to speak a word in season to him that is weary: he wakeneth morning by morning, he wakeneth mine ear to hear as the learned" (Isa. 50:4).

Christ was given this gift because He was a willing sacrifice: "The Lord God hath opened mine ear, and I was not rebellious, neither turned away back" (Isa. 50:5). In all things, He was true to the will of His Father. Even when His burden seemed unbearable, He supplanted His own comfort with obedience to His divine, foreordained mission: "O my Father, if it be possible, let this cup pass from me: nevertheless not as I will, but as thou wilt" (Matt. 26:39).

In the horrible pain of His unjust trial and torture, His lonely suffering in Gethsemane, and in the agony of His Crucifixion, He endured His lot: "I gave my back to the smiters, and my cheeks to them that plucked off the hair: I hid not my face from shame and spitting" (Isa. 50:6). Why did He endure? Nephi reminds us of His motive for enduring: "And the world, because of their iniquity, shall judge him to be a thing of naught; wherefore they scourge him, and he suffereth it; and they smite him, and he suffereth it. Yea, they spit upon him, and he suffereth it, because of his loving kindness and his long-suffering towards the children of men" (1 Ne. 19:9).

With mercy and tender loving kindness as His motive, He set His face forward in strength and, trusting in His Heavenly Father, went forward with His mission: "For the Lord God will help me; therefore shall I not be confounded: therefore have I set my face like a flint, and I know that I shall not be ashamed" (Isa. 50:7). Elder Bruce R. McConkie taught, "The course of his life was toward the cross, and he was steadfast and immovable in his determination to follow this very course, one laid out for him by his Father. He had said of himself through the mouth of Isaiah, 'I set my face like a flint, and I know that I shall not be ashamed.' (Isa. 50:7.) Clearly, there was to be no turning back."[81]

What is our role with humanity—particularly with those who may have strayed from the gospel path? To any who have wandered far away, we seek to help them return that they may again feel of His nearness—to feel, "He is near that justifieth me; who will contend with me? let us stand together: who is mine adversary? let him come near to me. Behold, the Lord God will help me; who is he that shall condemn me? lo, they all shall wax old as a garment; the moth shall eat them up" (Isa. 50:8–9).

Walk in the Light of Your Fire

In our collective and individual struggles with the universal sin of pride, we may tend to try to generate our own light and knowledge as we wander our strange and darkened paths. We know better: "Who is among you that feareth the Lord, that obeyeth the voice of his servant, that walketh in darkness, and hath no light? let him trust in the name of the Lord, and stay upon his God" (Isa. 50:10).

Deep down, we know that we *should* trust the Lord, but pride sometimes darkens our minds and shades our pathways: "Behold, all ye that kindle a fire, that compass yourselves about with sparks: walk in the light of your fire, and in the sparks that ye have kindled. This shall ye have of mine hand; ye shall lie down in sorrow" (Isa. 50:11). The Lord, in His constant concern for our welfare, allows us our agency and the natural consequences of its misuse. He lets us wander in the darkness of our own making that we might weary thereof and seek light.

The tiny sparks that *we* may kindle quickly burn out and become dark and inconsequential in contrast to the Light of the World. Christ declared, "Behold, I am the law, and *the* light." He then taught His disciples, "Ye are my disciples; and ye are *a* light unto this people" (3 Ne. 15:9, 12; emphasis added). He goes on to teach, "Therefore, hold up your light that it may shine unto the world. Behold, I am the light which ye shall hold up—that which ye have seen me do" (3 Ne. 18:24).

As we grow tired of groping in darkness and come to our senses, we may be assured that the Light of the World stands firm and steadfast, where He has always been, "with open arms to receive" (Morm. 6:17). What reassuring peace is ours when we once again realize that "He is near that justifieth me" (Isa. 50:8).

CHAPTER FIFTY-ONE
LOOK UNTO THE ROCK WHENCE YE ARE HEWN

ISAIAH HERE INVITES US TO consider our heritage as children of the Abrahamic covenant: "Hearken to me, ye that follow after righteousness, ye that seek the Lord: look unto the rock whence ye are hewn, and to the hole of the pit whence ye are digged. Look unto Abraham your father, and unto Sarah that bare you: for I called him alone, and blessed him, and increased him" (Isa. 51:1–2).

In illustration of a part representing a greater whole, in my office I have a small wooden plaque with a piece of a reddish brick attached to it. A metal engraving on it reads, "Granite Seminary, 1912, First Seminary in the Church: 'Shall we not go on in so great a cause' D&C 128:22." The plaque was given a few decades ago to those of us who attended a conference. At that time, the historic Granite seminary building was being demolished, and a few of the bricks were salvaged to use in making the plaques. Each brick piece was a significant part of the whole and had an exact fit in the overall structure.

Of course, the physical structure is not what matters. The Granite seminary building and all other seminary meeting places simply housed the inspired seminary program and facilitated the spiritual influence it had for good in the lives of thousands of students through the years. The objective of the seminary and institute program is stated as, "Our purpose is to help youth and young adults understand and rely on the teachings and Atonement of Jesus Christ, qualify for the blessings of the temple, and prepare themselves, their families, and others for eternal life with their Father in Heaven."[82] My plaque, like so many things, is a symbolic reminder of Heavenly Father's work and mission to invite all of His children to return to Him and receive immortality and eternal life. We each have a place and an exact fit in the family of God.

Look unto Abraham, Your Father

We are part and portion of Abraham's eternal family, and as such, we each have an important place and destiny therein. In his ministry to Israel, Isaiah invites us to remember our heritage and the important symbols of our faith. As we carefully consider how we fit into the family of God, our sense of belonging, our sense of our divine nature, and our sense of our eternal progression help motivate us to go forward. As we better understand our divine destiny, we are motivated to repent and live Christlike lives. We come to yearn for the blessings of the temple, which guide us to eternal life for ourselves and our loved ones.

Our father Abraham stands as a grand role model in exemplifying the way we should live to enable us to return to our Heavenly Father. Abraham was not content with the wicked traditions of his fathers. He acted with courage to change the environment of his home and sought eternal blessings for himself and for his family: "I, Abraham, saw that it was needful for me to obtain another place of residence; And, finding there was greater happiness and peace and rest for me, I sought for the blessings of the fathers, and the right whereunto I should be ordained to administer the same; having been myself a follower of righteousness, desiring also to be one who possessed great knowledge, and to be a greater follower of righteousness, and to possess a greater knowledge, and to be a father of many nations, a prince of peace" (Abr. 1:1–2).

Not only is Abraham our father and our role model, but he is an exemplar in similitude of our Heavenly Father. The story of Abraham and of his son, Isaac, offers us a type, or prefiguring, of Christ. Nephi's brother, Jacob, taught about the ancient prophets: "Behold, they believed in Christ and worshiped the Father in his name, and also we worship the Father in his name. And for this intent we keep the law of Moses, it pointing our souls to him; and for this cause it is sanctified unto us for righteousness, even as it was accounted unto Abraham in the wilderness to be obedient unto the commands of God in offering up his son Isaac, which is a similitude of God and his Only Begotten Son" (Jacob 4:5).

Considering Abraham and Isaac in "similitude of God and his Only Begotten Son," the original name *Abram* means "exalted father." *Abraham* means "father of a great multitude" (see Genesis 17:5).[83] Isaac, like Jesus, experienced a miraculous birth. Paul referred to Isaac as an "only begotten son": "By faith Abraham, when he was tried, offered up Isaac: and he that had received the promises offered up his only begotten son" (Hebrews

11:17). When Abraham was tried with the command to sacrifice his only son, Isaac, the place of the intended sacrifice was Mount Moriah in Jerusalem, not far from Golgotha, where Christ was sacrificed. This was also the location of Solomon's temple, where sacrifices in similitude of Christ were performed. As Christ carried His own cross upon His back, Isaac carried the wood for his sacrifice upon his back (see Genesis 22:6). Isaac, like Christ, was a willing sacrifice. At the time, Abraham was an old man and Isaac was likely in his thirties—the same age as was Jesus at the time of His sacrifice—and could have easily escaped or overpowered his father. But he did not—he submitted to the will and plan of his father, just as Jesus did.

As we look to Abraham and follow his example, we receive the promised reward of our righteous sacrifices. Isaiah taught, "For the Lord shall comfort Zion: he will comfort all her waste places; and he will make her wilderness like Eden, and her desert like the garden of the Lord; joy and gladness shall be found therein, thanksgiving, and the voice of melody" (Isa. 51:3).

Awake, Awake, Put On Strength

The mission of prophets of all ages has been to invite and persuade people to follow the way of happiness. Joseph Smith taught, "Happiness is the object and design of our existence; and will be the end thereof, if we pursue the path that leads to it; and this path is virtue, uprightness, faithfulness, holiness, and keeping all the commandments of God."[84]

I would here like to offer a "Liken unto Us" commentary on some of the principles of happiness as taught by Isaiah in chapter 51 as he discusses how, "in the last days, the Lord shall comfort Zion and gather Israel—The redeemed shall come to Zion amid great joy" (Isa. 51:chapter heading). As we look forward to these blessings, we may certainly find illustration of these principles by looking back to father Abraham and to other prophets as our role models.

"Hearken unto me, my people; and give ear unto me, O my nation: for a law shall proceed from me" (Isa. 51:4). We must exert effort and faith to "hearken," or listen, to the Lord. We live in a noisy and confused world where many voices vie for our attention and loyalty. If we tune our ear to the voice of the Lord, we will hear His message and direction for us. Of the time when the life of Abraham hung in delicate balance, Abraham said, "I lifted up my voice unto the Lord my God, and the Lord hearkened and heard" (Abr. 1:15). The Lord told Abraham of a new land and a new life. Abraham then had to muster the courage to follow Him—to "give ear unto" the Lord and do His will.

"My righteousness is near; my salvation is gone forth" (Isa. 51:5). We bask in the glorious light of the restored gospel. The plan of salvation has gone forth in the earth and is within the grasp of anyone who will reach out and accept it. We need not wait for another day and time—the Lord has blessed us with all we need. As we embrace the truth, it prompts and guides us to the holy temple, where we may gain more light and truth. With each passing year, more temples dot the land and the ordinances of salvation come ever nearer to all of God's children throughout the earth.

"The heavens shall vanish . . . the earth shall wax old . . . but my salvation shall be for ever, and my righteousness shall not be abolished" (Isa. 51:6). As we have learned through the recurring and constant theme of the teachings of Isaiah—if we put our trust in anything or anyone except the Lord, it will vanish. But as we embrace the truth and light of the Lord, we can be assured that we have acquired a treasure that endures for time and all eternity.

"Fear ye not the reproach of men, neither be afraid of their revilings" (Isa. 51:7). As we place our trust in the Lord, He places His protection upon us. He will give us courage to stand bold in the face of persecution, or the strength and wisdom to flee to safe havens when necessary. To Abraham, the Lord directed, "Abraham, get thee out of thy country, and from thy kindred, and from thy father's house, unto a land that I will show thee" (Abr. 2:3). Abraham had endured the reviling of his people—even their attempt to kill him. Now he courageously left them, trusting in the Lord's promised blessings for him and his family.

"Awake, awake, put on thy strength. . . . Awake, awake, stand up, O Jerusalem" (Isa. 51:9, 17). The nature of our fallen world is that we are all subject to binding and damning chains of such things as lust, addiction, laziness, indifference, pride, overzealousness, and false doctrines that weigh us down and bind us from living "after the manner of happiness" (2 Ne. 5:27). Father Lehi's plea for his family is the same as that of all righteous parents who desire true and lasting happiness for their children. He said, "O that ye would awake; awake from a deep sleep, yea, even from the sleep of hell, and shake off the awful chains by which ye are bound, which are the chains which bind the children of men, that they are carried away captive down to the eternal gulf of misery and woe" (2 Ne. 1:13).

"Therefore the redeemed of the Lord shall return, and come with singing unto Zion; and everlasting joy shall be upon their head: they shall obtain gladness and joy; and sorrow and mourning shall flee away" (Isa. 51:11). Consider how, during your greatest times of trial, you have been buoyed up and encouraged by the truths of the restored gospel. Now consider how much harder your trials would have been without these truths. The descendants of Abraham, who have long been scattered, are being gathered to gospel light and truth so that all may experience gospel peace and joy. They are being gathered so that they may be "crowned with glory, even in Zion, by the hands of the servants of the Lord, even the children of Ephraim. And they shall be filled with songs of everlasting joy" (D&C 133:32–33). We are being prepared to receive the crown of glory through the ordinances of the gospel, including those of the temple. This glory bequeaths "everlasting joy" upon our heads.

"The Lord thy maker . . . hath stretched forth the heavens, and laid the foundations of the earth" (Isa. 51:13). In the temple, we come to understand the purpose of the Lord's creation and the eternal worth of His greatest creation: mankind! We begin to comprehend the relationship between the "stretched forth heavens" and the "foundations of the earth." We are taught in the Pearl of Great Price that Abraham learned the purpose of our time on earth: "And we will prove them herewith, to see if they will do all things whatsoever the Lord their God shall command them." As we successfully navigate mortality and pass the tests thereof, we "shall have glory added upon [our] heads for ever and ever" (Abr. 3:25–26).

"I am the Lord thy God, that divided the sea. . . . And I have put my words in thy mouth, and I have covered thee in the shadow of mine hand, that I may plant the heavens, and lay the foundations of the earth, and say unto Zion, Thou art my people" (Isa. 51:15–16). The Lord, who showed forth His power to divide the sea, can also divide and move seas of evil and unbelief. He "puts words in [the] mouth" of those who prepare to receive His revelations. The shadow of His hand is a protective covering upon those who follow Him. We become His people by following Him, keeping His commandments, and receiving the saving ordinances of the gospel, including the temple endowment, wherein His name is put upon us and we are sealed up to enjoy the type of life that He now enjoys. Abraham desired "to receive instructions, and to keep the commandments of God." Because of this righteous desire, he "became a rightful heir, a High Priest, holding the right belonging to the fathers" (Abr. 1:2).

Just as my piece of brick from the Granite seminary is a representative part and portion of the whole, we as children of God are part of His eternal family. Isaiah did well to point us to Abraham our father. Through the covenants and promises reaffirmed by the Lord through him, we may gain eternal life and thereby have a fullness of joy.

CHAPTER FIFTY-TWO
HOW BEAUTIFUL UPON THE MOUNTAINS

AT THE TIME OF THE fall of Adam and Eve, the Lord cursed the devil and spoke these words: "And I will put enmity between thee and the woman, between thy seed and her seed; and he shall bruise thy head, and thou shalt bruise his heel" (Moses 4:21). A respected teacher of mine once gave what I felt was a great definition of enmity. He said, "There is a bar, or divider, between good and evil. The righteous hate the things of Satan. The wicked hate the things of God."[85]

He That Publisheth Peace

In light of Isaiah 52, let us consider three prophets and how the enmity of others cost them their lives. The first is Abinadi, who went boldly on his mission to cry repentance to wicked King Noah and his people. After Abinadi was imprisoned, Noah brought him before his wicked priests who, except for one, were steeped in pride and refused to listen to Abinadi. They chided Abinadi, perhaps being sarcastic, as they quoted the words of Isaiah: "How beautiful upon the mountains are the feet of him that bringeth good tidings; that publisheth peace; that bringeth good tidings of good" (Mosiah 12:21). Perhaps they were demanding that Abinadi tell them only happy things.

Abinadi did not cower to their intimidation. He said, "Are you priests, and pretend to teach this people? . . . wo be unto you for perverting the ways of the Lord!" (Mosiah 12:25–26). He later quoted back to them the words from Isaiah, putting them in proper context: "For O how beautiful upon the mountains are the feet of him that bringeth good tidings, that is the founder of peace, yea, even the Lord, who has redeemed his people; yea, him who has granted salvation unto his people." He taught them of eternal life and how we gain such through Christ: "They are raised to dwell with God who has redeemed them; thus they have eternal life through

Christ, who has broken the bands of death." Then he continued with a rebuke for the wicked priests: "But behold, and fear, and tremble before God, for ye ought to tremble; for the Lord redeemeth none such that rebel against him and die in their sins" (Mosiah 15:18, 23, 26). Noah and his priests could not stand the truth. They killed Abinadi.

Our second prophet is Joseph Smith. One of his life passions was to lead the Saints to the temple. In all of his persecutions and trials, he kept his heart and mind focused on the ordinances of salvation and worked diligently to prepare the people and the place for the receiving of these ordinances. He loved the writings of Isaiah and particularly loved the words "How beautiful upon the mountains are the feet of him that bringeth good tidings, that publisheth peace; that bringeth good tidings of good, that publisheth salvation; that saith unto Zion, Thy God reigneth!" (Isa. 52:7). This passage may have inspired Joseph to select the name *Nauvoo*, a Hebrew word meaning "to be beautiful," for the Saints' beloved city. The temple—the center place of Zion—would be the center place of Nauvoo.

Joseph Smith diligently proclaimed the plan of salvation and the purpose of the temple—to give us the opportunity for the type of life enjoyed by Heavenly Father. The wicked apostates could not stand this doctrine and the other glorious truths of the restored gospel. Finally they converged on the Lord's Prophet and martyred him at Carthage Jail.

Put On Thy Beautiful Garments

The third prophet we will consider is Isaiah himself. He dedicated his life to teaching the eternal truths of the gospel of repentance and tried diligently to persuade the children of Israel to seek and follow the path to eternal life. He taught, "Awake, awake; put on thy strength, O Zion; put on thy beautiful garments, O Jerusalem, the holy city: for henceforth there shall no more come into thee the uncircumcised and the unclean" (Isa. 52:1). The charge to "awake; put on thy strength" is an imperative to rise up and receive the full power of the priesthood our Heavenly Father desires to bestow upon us. Elias Higbee, one of Joseph Smith's contemporaries, posed a question about verse 1: "What is meant by the command in Isaiah, 52d chapter, 1st verse, which saith: Put on thy strength, O Zion—and what people had Isaiah reference to?" The Prophet answered him, saying, "He had reference to those whom God should call in the last days, who should hold the power of priesthood to bring again Zion, and the redemption of Israel; and to put on her strength is to put on the authority of the priesthood, which she, Zion, has a right to by lineage; also to return to that power which she had lost" (D&C 113:7–8).

One way we put on "beautiful garments" is by receiving temple covenants. We wear the sacred clothing of the temple to remind us of the covenants we make therein. Our covenants prepare us to join with Christ in receiving the glory of the Father. We prepare for our joining, or "marriage," to Christ by being "arrayed in fine linen, clean and white: for the fine linen is the righteousness of the saints" (Rev. 19:8). Emphasizing the importance of being clean and white, Isaiah taught, "Depart ye, depart ye, go ye out from thence, touch no unclean thing; go ye out of the midst of her; be ye clean, that bear the vessels of the Lord" (Isa. 52:11). We receive the blessing of assessment of our cleanliness or worthiness for temple blessings from our authorized priesthood leaders through our temple recommend interviews.

To be deemed worthy for temple blessings, we must have the courage to shake off the things of the world. As Isaiah said, "Shake thyself from the dust; arise, and sit down, O Jerusalem: loose thyself from the bands of thy neck, O captive daughter of Zion" (Isa. 52:2). Concerning this verse, the Lord revealed through Joseph Smith, "What are we to understand by Zion loosing herself from the bands of her neck; 2d verse? We are to understand that the scattered remnants are exhorted to return to the Lord from whence they have fallen; which if they do, the promise of the Lord is that he will speak to them, or give them revelation. See the 6th, 7th, and 8th verses. The bands of her neck are the curses of God upon her, or the remnants of Israel in their scattered condition among the Gentiles" (D&C 113:9–10).

There is always a steep price to pay for sin. Addictions cost us our health, time, money, relationships, and self-worth. Greed may temporarily fill our bank account, but it sets us on a course to spiritual bankruptcy. The toys and trinkets of the world often detract us from our commitments to help the Lord in the building of His kingdom.

The things of God are available to all and cost nothing, whereas the things of the world come at a hefty price. The Lord said to John the Revelator, "I will give unto him that is athirst of the fountain of the water of life freely" (Rev. 21:6). Isaiah said, "For thus saith the Lord, Ye have sold yourselves for nought; and ye shall be redeemed without money" (Isa. 52:3). Isaiah's mission was to help bring all people to Christ and acquaint them with Him that they may freely partake of His plan of redemption: "Therefore my people shall know my name: therefore they shall know in that day that I am he that doth speak: behold, it is I" (Isa. 52:6). Unfortunately, the enmity of the devil finally prevailed in the hearts of those who refused to listen to Isaiah's teachings—tradition has it that he was "sawn asunder."[86] Nothing, however, could prevail over the triumph of his spiritual life and mission. As with Abinadi and the Prophet Joseph Smith, he went on to receive his crown of glory.

How Beautiful upon the Mountains

Hopefully, we all have beautiful places etched indelibly into our minds and hearts. For example, the Grand Canyon of the Yellowstone, in summer and winter, is one of my personal favorites. I also have pleasant memories of outings in mountains and fields, in lakes and rivers, on beaches, and in canyons and forests. However, the most enduring beauties of my mind and heart are the spiritual vistas of my life—my temple marriage, the births of my children and grandchildren, and my imaginings of our heavenly abode with our Heavenly parents and loved ones.

For Alma, who heeded the call of Abinadi, fled wicked king Noah, and converted to gospel truth, the waters of Mormon became beautiful. This was also true for those he loved and served: "Yea, the place of Mormon, the waters of Mormon, the forest of Mormon, how beautiful are they to the eyes of them who there came to the knowledge of their Redeemer; yea, and how blessed are they, for they shall sing to his praise forever" (Mosiah 18:30).

As the Prophet Joseph Smith and his brother Hyrum beheld their beloved Nauvoo for the last time as they left on horseback for Carthage, they paused at the temple. Joseph looked at this magnificent house of the Lord, likely pondered the purpose thereof, surveyed the beautiful city, and declared, "This is the loveliest place and the best people under the heavens."[87]

Isaiah, in one of the most poignant poetic expressions of his ministry, declared:

> How beautiful upon the mountains are the feet of him that bringeth good tidings, that publisheth peace; that bringeth good tidings of good, that publisheth salvation; that saith unto Zion, Thy God reigneth!
>
> Thy watchmen shall lift up the voice; with the voice together shall they sing: for they shall see eye to eye, when the Lord shall bring again Zion.

Break forth into joy, sing together, ye waste places of Jerusalem: for the Lord hath comforted his people, he hath redeemed Jerusalem.

The Lord hath made bare his holy arm in the eyes of all the nations; and all the ends of the earth shall see the salvation of our God. (Isa. 52:7–10)

The beautiful message of the restored gospel and the marvelous privilege of being endowed with power and potential for eternal life all center in the atoning mission of Jesus Christ. Beautiful are the feet of those who carry this message to the ends of the earth.

CHAPTER FIFTY-THREE
SURELY HE HATH BORNE OUR GRIEFS

AT THE CONCLUSION OF THE previous chapter, in praise of Christ, Isaiah introduced his final servant song: "Behold, my servant shall deal prudently, he shall be exalted and extolled, and be very high" (Isa. 52:13).

A classic Christmas film, *Nora's Christmas Gift*, helps teach us the true spiritual foundation of Christ-centered service. Nora is a valiant soul who dedicates her life to the service and well-being of others. She exudes an aura of enthusiasm. She is fun-loving, bright, and positive. The organizing of an annual town Christmas pageant is one of her many contributions to her community. Through her life of service, she endures her own sorrows, including the death of her beloved husband and the great personal trial of physical blindness. In the midst of her darkness she withdraws into a shell of self-pity. As her friends rally to support her, one of them helps her rediscover her spiritual bearings and even convinces her to come out of her self-imposed exile to attend the annual Christmas pageant. To the surprise of all, she presents herself on stage just at the moment when the man portraying the Savior is healing the deaf and the blind. At the moment of her "healing" in the pageant, she speaks to the audience:

> It's a miracle. I can see. It's a miracle. I can see. I can see,
> you know. I guess everybody doesn't have to go blind in
> order to see, but I'm so stubborn, I guess I did. When
> George and I first moved here fifty-five years ago, I said
> to myself, "Nora, don't you rest until you belong in this
> town." Oh, I was so smart; I thought I knew just how to
> do it. When Henrietta Johnson's husband died, I milked
> her cows every morning for a year. There were some morn-
> ings when I wasn't sure I wanted to be that nice, but I did
> it. See, in my mind, I was always the star of the show.

I made you laugh. I helped you out. I cheered you up when you felt down, and as long as I was giving, I felt real good. Then everything changed. I became like these [referencing the blind and lame in the pageant]. Of course, it wasn't true—I wasn't really like these—until tonight. But now I see. This Christmas story isn't about giving. It's about all the things we can't possibly give. You can't make these eyes work again or bring my George back to me. I could never hope to cure the secret ills of your hearts. But Someone was born into this world to do all those things, and He has been trying to tell me, "Nora, let go. Let me do it. Let go of that pride that makes you think you gotta run the show. Now listen, because this is what's been making you blind. Let earth receive her King." I never heard the words before. Let earth receive her King. Let Me. Let Me.[88]

We will now see more of this theme of trusting in the Lord in this the fourth and final of Isaiah's servant songs, comprising the last three verses of chapter 52 and all of chapter 53. As is often the case with Isaiah's prophecies, there may be dual applications, but we will again focus our discussion on the servant song as it applies to our Savior.

He Shall Be Exalted and Extolled, and Be Very High

I have heard discussions doubting the omniscience of God and Christ and suggesting that there is a realm that is simply "unknowable." Such intellectual bantering mostly amuses me—of course the things of God are unknowable to mortal man. That is why we need God! If I have a secret ill in my heart, and I am appealing to my Heavenly Father and my Savior for help, I must trust that They will know how to help me in all things. Of Christ, Isaiah proclaimed, "Behold, my servant shall deal prudently, he shall be exalted and extolled, and be very high" (Isa. 52:13). Christ is always prudent and wise because He is omniscient. There is no problem He cannot help us with. Of God's knowledge, Lehi taught, "But behold, all things have been done in the wisdom of him who knoweth all things" (2 Ne. 2:24). Jesus taught us not to pray with pretension like the hypocrites but to pray privately with humility, "for your Father knoweth what things ye have need of, before ye ask him" (Matt. 6:8).

Isaiah continues, "As many were astonied at thee; his visage was so marred more than any man, and his form more than the sons of men: So shall he sprinkle many nations; the kings shall shut their mouths at him: for that which had not been told them they shall see; and that which they had not heard shall they consider" (Isa. 52:14–15). Of this passage, Elder Bruce R. McConkie taught:

> Isaiah's prophecy about the marred servant is clearly Messianic and applies to Jesus who was crucified and rose from the dead to sprinkle the saving power of his blood in all nations. It is of him that kings shall shut their mouths as they ponder the marvel of his resurrection and all that he did. . . . All of the Lord's servants who are marred or hurt or persecuted in this life—and who remain faithful—shall have all their sorrows made up to them in manifold measure in the resurrection.[89]

A Man of Sorrows and Acquainted with Grief

A few years ago, I watched a debate between an atheist and a man defending Christianity. During the debate, the atheist made a blasphemous and profane statement about the Atonement that undoubtedly grated on the sensibilities of all believing Christians—it did on mine. And yet, I felt a sense of sadness and sorrow for this misguided man who had become so darkened. Nora's physical blindness seemed mild compared to this man's spiritual blindness.

Those who reject the gospel and become darkened by sin and rebellion do not receive the blessing of sweet healing. Wondering at man's inability to see the Savior for what He was, Isaiah questioned, "Who hath believed our report? and to whom is the arm of the Lord revealed? (Isa. 53:1). Reiterating Isaiah, John later taught, "But though he had done so many miracles before them, yet they believed not on him: That the saying of Esaias the prophet might be fulfilled, which he spake, Lord, who hath believed our report? and to whom hath the arm of the Lord been revealed? Therefore they could not believe, because that Esaias said again, He hath blinded their eyes, and hardened their heart; that they should not see with their eyes, nor understand with their heart, and be converted, and I should heal them" (John 12:37–40). If all, like Nora, would feel after humility, their blindness could be healed.

Further, Isaiah saw how the Savior of the world would be viewed as a mere mortal, even one to be scorned, by those whose hearts were hardened against Him: "For he shall grow up before him as a tender plant, and as a root out of a dry ground: he hath no form nor comeliness; and when we shall see him, there is no beauty that we should desire him. He is despised and rejected of men; a man of sorrows, and acquainted with grief: and we hid as it were our faces from him; he was despised, and we esteemed him not" (Isa. 53:2–3).

Christ was nurtured by His heavenly and earthly parents as a tender plant. He "received not of the fulness at the first, but received grace for grace" (D&C 93:12). Undoubtedly, He had the tender feelings of youth and needed the comforting assurance and guidance of His parents as He "increased in wisdom and stature, and in favour with God and man" (Luke 2:52). He progressed from being a tender plant to a strong root, as He declared to His disciples, "I am the vine, ye are the branches: He that abideth in me, and I in him, the same bringeth forth much fruit: for without me ye can do nothing" (John 15:5).

As mentioned in verses 2 and 3 of Isaiah chapter 53, the Savior appeared quite normal by the standards of the day. Physically, He had no particular form, comeliness, or beauty that would make Him stand out in the crowd. The Jews missed the message of the Messiah as they looked for a more powerful and assertive deliverer. Even Nathaniel, in whom there was "no guile," was underwhelmed by the humble origins of the Lord: "Can there any good thing come out of Nazareth?" (John 1:46–47).

Like the deceived atheist, many rejected Christ and His healing mission. When He declared His divine Sonship in the Nazareth synagogue, His hearers "rose up, and thrust him out of the city, and led him unto the brow of the hill whereon their city was built, that they might cast him down headlong" (Luke 4:29). They kept their spiritual eyes firmly closed. When He taught that He was "that bread of life" and that in Him they would have eternal life, many found it "an hard saying," and "from that time many of his disciples went back, and walked no more with him" (John 6:48, 60, 66).

Surely He Hath Borne Our Griefs

Life is full of irony. The atheist who blasphemed Christ and His Atonement—in the Lord's own due time, manner, and extent—will be redeemed and healed by the very man he profaned. Evil King Noah in the Book of Mormon and his wicked priests killed righteous Abinadi, who had come to deliver a message that would have saved them had they the courage to follow the example of Alma. Righteous Nephi killed wicked Laban that righteousness might be preserved: "Behold the Lord slayeth the wicked to bring forth his righteous purposes. It is better that one man perish than that a nation should dwindle and perish in unbelief" (1 Ne. 4:13). Wicked Caiaphas and his cohorts killed righteous Jesus that their wickedness might be preserved: "Consider that it is expedient for us, that one man should die for the people, and that the whole nation perish not" (John 11:50).

Our sinless Savior died that we, as sinners, might live. Abinadi delivered this message of Isaiah to Noah and the priests, even though it cost him his life:

> Surely he hath borne our griefs, and carried our sorrows: yet we did esteem him stricken, smitten of God, and afflicted.
>
> But he was wounded for our transgressions, he was bruised for our iniquities: the chastisement of our peace was upon him; and with his stripes we are healed.
>
> All we, like sheep, have gone astray; we have turned every one to his own way; and the Lord hath laid on him the iniquities of us all.
>
> He was oppressed, and he was afflicted, yet he opened not his mouth; he is brought as a lamb to the slaughter, and as a sheep before her shearers is dumb so he opened not his mouth.
>
> He was taken from prison and from judgment; and who shall declare his generation? For he was cut off out of the land of the living; for the transgressions of my people was he stricken.
>
> And he made his grave with the wicked, and with the rich in his death; *because he had done no evil, neither was any deceit in his mouth.*
>
> Yet it pleased the Lord to bruise him; he hath put him to grief; when thou shalt make his soul an offering for sin he shall see his seed, he shall prolong his days, and the pleasure of the Lord shall prosper in his hand. (Mosiah 14:4–10; emphasis added)

The phrase "Yet it pleased the Lord to bruise him" instructs us that Christ was a willing sacrifice. "Him" and "Lord" refer to the same person. "Him" in this context is referring to the Messiah, the servant. "Lord," written in small capital letters in the Old Testament, refers to Jehovah. In other words, we might say, "It pleased Jehovah to bruise Messiah—or it pleased Christ to offer Himself as a sacrifice." He willed His own death. Although the agony of His Atonement would be so great that He would cry out, "O my Father, if it be possible, let this cup pass from me," the potential of salvation for the family of God was His greater desire, causing Him to say, "Nevertheless, not as I will, but as thou wilt" (Matt. 26:39).

Heirs of the Kingdom of God

We ask the question, "Who are the Lord's seed?" as referenced above in verse 10 of Isaiah 53. Abinadi offers some interpretative commentary of the Isaiah prophecy and helps us understand the concept of the Lord's seed:

> And now I say unto you, who shall declare his generation? Behold, I say unto you, that when his soul has been made an offering for sin he shall see his seed. And now what say ye? And who shall be his seed?
>
> Behold I say unto you, that whosoever has heard the words of the prophets, yea, all the holy prophets who have prophesied concerning the coming of the Lord—I say unto you, that all those who have hearkened unto their words, and believed that the Lord would redeem his people, and have looked forward to that day for a remission of their sins, I say unto you, that these are his seed, or they are the heirs of the kingdom of God.
>
> For these are they whose sins he has borne; these are they for whom he has died, to redeem them from their transgressions. And now, are they not his seed? (Mosiah 15:10–12)

We become "heirs of the kingdom of God" by coming unto Christ, accepting His gospel, and partaking of the ordinances of salvation. As we progress along the gospel path, we also make covenants in the temple that prepare us to inherit eternal life.

Through His perfect Atonement, Christ the servant would "bear [our] iniquities" and make "intercession for the transgressors" (Isa. 53:11–12). He was the Only Begotten Son of God. He was the only person capable of making a sinless sacrifice for sin. If all people of the world only knew the truth about the mission and divine nature of the Suffering Servant, they would rejoice and sing out as did Nora: "Let earth receive her King!"

CHAPTER FIFTY-FOUR
ENLARGE THE PLACE OF THY TENT

I FIND IT PARTICULARLY SIGNIFICANT that Jesus, during His ministry to the Nephites, recited Isaiah chapter 54. Immediately following this recitation, we have His commendation to study the words of Isaiah: "And now, behold, I say unto you, that ye ought to search these things. Yea, a commandment I give unto you that ye search these things diligently; for great are the words of Isaiah" (3 Ne. 23:1–2).

Why is chapter 54 so significant as to be quoted by the Savior in this important context? This chapter is a beautiful expression of the tender mercy of the Lord in gathering and saving His dispersed children. It is the plea of the Bridegroom in seeking after the wandering bride to bring her home to the hearthstone of His holy house and kingdom.

I would like to offer a sampling of phrases from the chapter that evoke temple inspiration for me, and I will share a few thoughts about each to hopefully prompt further contemplation and study.

For Thy Maker Is Thine Husband

"Sing, O barren, thou that didst not bear . . . for more are the children of the desolate than the children of the married wife, saith the Lord" (Isa. 54:1) Eternal truth plucks at our heartstrings and resonates with our souls. An innate desire of Heavenly Father's children is to return to Him. Scattered Israel has been "barren"—has not yet received the promised blessings of the Lord's covenant. They are now being gathered to Christ and to the temples, and they come with song and rejoicing for the goodness of the Lord unto them.

"Enlarge the place of thy tent, and let them stretch forth the curtains of thine habitations: spare not, lengthen thy cords, and strengthen thy stakes" (Isa. 54:2) Our modern Church organizational word *stake* comes from this image. At the time of the initial gathering of scattered Israel in the last days, the Saints were to gather to a particular stake of the Church, such as to Kirtland, Nauvoo, or Salt Lake City. The central purpose of gathering to these stakes was to prepare to be endowed from on high in the temple. We have now enlarged and are continuing to enlarge the tent with stakes throughout the world. Commensurate with the organization of stakes is the establishment of temples. Temple worship has become reasonably available to the majority of the Saints worldwide. The Lord will generously apply the resources of the Church in strengthening its stakes and in providing temples. The tent is growing larger day by day.

The Lord is seeking for the scattered and bringing them under the protective covering of that tent: "For thou shalt forget the shame of thy youth, and shalt not remember the reproach of thy widowhood any more. For thy Maker is thine husband; the Lord of hosts is his name; and thy Redeemer the Holy One of Israel; The God of the whole earth shall he be called" (Isa. 54:4–5). Just as a young man and woman meet, fall in love, and seek eternal sealing in the temple, Israel is repenting, gathering, learning to love the Lord, and desiring unity with Him. As they come unto Him, He tenderly husbands and nurtures them into His care and keeping. He guides them to the temple, where they are sealed to Him for all eternity.

But My Kindness Shall Not Depart from Thee

"In a little wrath I hid my face from thee for a moment; but with everlasting kindness will I have mercy on thee, saith the Lord thy Redeemer" (Isa. 54:8). As Israel rebels, the Lord allows them the consequence of their rebellion, but He does not lose sight of them or forget them. For example, the suffering Saints in Missouri were told: "Zion cannot be built up unless it is by the principles of the law of the celestial kingdom. . . . And my people must needs be chastened until they learn obedience, if it must needs be, by the things which they suffer. . . . Therefore, in consequence of the transgressions of my people, it is expedient in me that mine elders should wait for a little season for the redemption of Zion." The Lord then instructed them that they needed to "be taught more perfectly . . . concerning their duty" and that this could not happen "until mine elders are endowed with power from on high. For behold, I have prepared a great endowment and blessing to be poured out upon them, inasmuch as they are faithful and continue in humility before me" (D&C 105:5–12). True, the Lord may hide His face "for a moment" as we learn obedience, but He stands always ready to gather us with tender mercy as we are ready.

Isaiah emphasizes the Lord's tender mercy for His children in this verse: "For the mountains shall depart, and the hills be removed; but my kindness shall not depart from thee, neither shall the covenant of my peace be removed, saith the Lord that hath mercy on thee" (Isa. 54:10). One way the Lord's kindness and peace has manifestation is in the offering of His protective covenants and promises in temples throughout the world. When President Brigham Young said that the Salt Lake Temple must stand through the Millennium, he was certainly not thinking about only the Salt Lake Temple and certainly not about just the physical structure. He was referencing temples and temple work throughout the earth during the millennial day, as evidenced in this quote: "When the temple is built I want it to stand through the millennium, in connection with many others that will yet be built, that the Elders may go in and labor for their dead who have died without the gospel, back to the days of Adam."[90] In our latter day, when mountains will fall and wickedness will be swept from the earth, what will remain is the Lord's kingdom wherein His gospel may be preached and His endowment may be bestowed upon the righteous in myriad temples throughout the earth. The blessings from the covenants we make in the temple will endure into the Millennium and on through eternity.

No Weapon That Is Formed against Thee Shall Prosper

"No weapon that is formed against thee shall prosper; and every tongue that shall rise against thee in judgment thou shalt condemn. This is the heritage of the servants of the Lord, and their righteousness is of me, saith the Lord" (Isa. 54:17). The Kirtland Saints built their temple "through great tribulation; and out of our poverty we have given of our substance to build a house to thy name, that the Son of Man might have a place to manifest himself to his people." In the dedication of that temple, the Prophet Joseph, calling on the imagery of Isaiah, declared, "No weapon formed against them shall prosper; that he who diggeth a pit for them shall fall into the same himself; . . . no combination of wickedness shall have power to rise up and prevail over thy people upon whom thy name shall be put in this house" (D&C 109:5, 25–26).

Once the temple was dedicated, the Lord proceeded with His purpose of gathering Israel to endow them with His power, protection, and blessing. Just one week after the dedication, He appeared to Joseph and Oliver in the temple and declared, "For behold, I have accepted this house, and my name shall be here; and I will manifest myself to my people in mercy in this house. . . . Yea, the hearts of thousands and tens of thousands shall greatly rejoice in consequence of the blessings which shall be poured out, and the endowment with which my servants have been endowed in this house." Under the Lord's direction, Moses then appeared and committed to Joseph and Oliver "the keys of the gathering of Israel from the four parts of the earth, and the leading of the ten tribes from the land of the north" (D&C 110:7, 9, 11).

The great latter-day gathering to Zion and its temple commenced and has continued until this day and will continue through the Millennium. No wonder the Savior pronounced the words of Isaiah to be "great!" They testify of God and Christ and of Their ever-abounding love and mercy for Their children: "For since the beginning of the world men have not heard, nor perceived by the ear, neither hath the eye seen, O God, beside thee, what he hath prepared for him that waiteth for him" (Isa. 64:4).

CHAPTER FIFTY-FIVE
LET YOUR SOUL DELIGHT ITSELF IN FATNESS

THE THINGS OF GOD ARE not always rational and comprehendible to the mind of fallen, mortal man: "For my thoughts are not your thoughts, neither are your ways my ways, saith the Lord. For as the heavens are higher than the earth, so are my ways higher than your ways, and my thoughts than your thoughts" (Isa. 55:8–9). Paul also testified, "O the depth of the riches both of the wisdom and knowledge of God! how unsearchable are his judgments, and his ways past finding out!" (Romans 11:33).

The only way to learn of Him is to have His ways *revealed* to us—we will never understand by searching solely on our own, even with the most advanced study and science. Jacob taught, "Behold, great and marvelous are the works of the Lord. How unsearchable are the depths of the mysteries of him; and it is impossible that man should find out all his ways. And no man knoweth of his ways save it be revealed unto him; wherefore, brethren, despise not the revelations of God" (Jacob 4:8).

The key to eternal truth lies in having faith and humility enough to recognize the ways of God and to trust in His word, even when it seems irrational. We would not expect an eye doctor to prescribe the application of mud to the eyes to cure blindness, yet that is what the Savior did (see John 9:6–7). (Of course, faith in Christ was the true healing agent, as symbolically made manifest by the washing away of the mud in the Pool of Siloam). We would think that a skin doctor would counsel a leprous man to avoid bathing in a murky river, but Naaman was cured only after humbling himself and doing that very thing at the command of Elisha (see 2 Kings 5:10–14). A financial advisor would likely not counsel a donation of ten percent of one's income as the faithful do in paying tithing.

An Everlasting Covenant

While the world speaks of things relative to money, "Strive for the corner office, the bursting portfolio, the membership in the exclusive country club," the Lord invites, "Ho, every one that thirsteth, come ye to the waters, and he that hath no money; come ye, buy, and eat; yea, come, buy wine and milk without money and without price" (Isa. 55:1). (Money, of course, is not inherently evil—but "the love of money is the root of all evil" [1 Tim. 6:10]. The Lord delights in blessing his people with riches if they will but use them for His purposes [see Jacob 2:18–19]). To receive the free gift of the Lord's "waters" and "wine and milk" is to come unto the source of living water—or to come unto Christ, accept of His Atonement, and receive eternal life.

Although eternal life, "the greatest of all the gifts of God" (D&C 14:7), does not carry a physical price measured in gold or silver, there is a spiritual price to be paid. The price is faith, humility, and obedience. Jacob taught, "Wherefore, redemption cometh in and through the Holy Messiah; for he is full of grace and truth. Behold, he offereth himself a sacrifice for sin, to answer the ends of the law, unto all those who have a broken heart and a contrite spirit; and unto none else can the ends of the law be answered" (2 Ne. 2:6–7).

Why, Isaiah asks, would you expend your precious resources for something un-nourishing? "Wherefore do ye spend money for that which is not bread? and your labour for that which satisfieth not? hearken diligently unto me, and eat ye that which is good, and let your soul delight itself in fatness" (Isa. 55:2). While "fatness" may have a negative connotation in our modern world, fatness was perhaps a desired condition in Isaiah's day because so many experienced scarcity and famine so often.

Today, we "delight in fatness" by diligently and consistently delighting in spiritual things: prayer, fasting, gospel study, charitable service, and temple worship. Isaiah counseled, "Incline your ear, and come unto me: hear, and your soul shall live; and I will make an everlasting covenant with you, even the sure mercies of David" (Isa. 55:3). Striving for a fattened soul, as taught by Isaiah, implies constant, sustained effort in daily gospel living.

The Lord appoints His servants to help His children receive needed spiritual nourishment for their souls. The reasoning of man may suggest that a preacher of the gospel would need a college degree or a particular mastery of texts and languages. Of course, ongoing study is an important key to progression and enlightenment, but the Lord's endowment of wisdom and power does not stem from academic study. It is a spiritual gift bestowed in such things as the whisperings of the Holy Ghost, the proclamations of prophets, insights gained from scripture study, and endowments in the temple. With this power, missionaries young and old are sent to "call a nation that thou knowest not, and nations that knew not thee shall run unto thee because of the Lord thy God, and for the Holy One of Israel; for he hath glorified thee" (Isa. 55:5).

Seek Ye the Lord While He May Be Found

While the world says, "Indulge your lusts, take what you can, ignore your guilt, and gratify yourself without thought for tomorrow," the Lord invites, "Seek ye the Lord while he may be found, call ye upon him while he is near: Let the wicked forsake his way, and the unrighteous man his thoughts: and let him return unto the Lord, and he will have mercy upon him; and to our God, for he will abundantly pardon" (Isa. 55:6–7).

As missionaries go forth, following the Lord's higher way of service and teaching and endowed with His power, their words, although not always eloquent, achieve the desired effect: "For as the rain cometh down, and the snow from heaven, and returneth not thither, but watereth the earth, and maketh it bring forth and bud, that it may give seed to the sower, and bread to the eater: So shall my word be that goeth forth out of my mouth: it shall not return unto me void, but it shall accomplish that which I please, and it shall prosper in the thing whereto I sent it" (Isa. 55:10–11).

One way we can understand this verse is to consider that the "thing" that the Lord desires is to offer opportunity to all to share eternal life with Him. In the fleeting economy of the world, popularity wanes, notoriety withers, structures age and crumble, beauty fades, and bodies decline and die. In the eternal glory of God, His "everlasting covenant," when accepted and kept by those who enter it, becomes "a name, for an everlasting sign that shall not be cut off." The reward of seeking and accepting the higher way of Heavenly Father's plan results in an eternity of peaceful joy: "For ye shall go out with joy, and be led forth with peace: the mountains and the hills shall break forth before you into singing, and all the trees of the field shall clap their hands. Instead of the thorn shall come up the fir tree, and instead of the brier shall come up the myrtle tree; and it shall be to the Lord for a name, for an everlasting sign that shall not be cut off" (Isa. 55:12–13).

How grateful we are for the food we eat and the air we breathe. How grateful we are for the word of the Lord offered in His "higher ways," to nurture and fatten our souls.

CHAPTER FIFTY-SIX
AN EVERLASTING NAME, THAT SHALL NOT BE CUT OFF

A EUNUCH WAS AN EMASCULATED man. Having been deprived of his power of procreation, probably against his will as a young man, he was sometimes assigned to serve in the harem of a king. Often eunuchs were given respected positions of great trust. However, because of this physical impairment, the word *eunuch* became a term of derision. Consider the sad lament of the eunuch—imagine him in one of our modern congregations where so much of the teaching focuses on marriage and family. No wonder he might cry out, "Behold, I am a dry tree" (Isa. 56:3), or in other words, "I have lost my potential for family."

Because of my family, I understand better this definition of exaltation given us in modern revelation: "They shall pass by the angels, and the gods, which are set there, to their exaltation and glory in all things, as hath been sealed upon their heads, which glory shall be a fulness and a continuation of the seeds forever and ever" (D&C 132:19). The "continuation of the seeds forever and ever" means that our families will continue forever. That is the sublime joy of eternal life!

When our oldest son was born, I had a break from school for a few days and remember just sitting and holding him for hours. I remember feeling how dependent he was on us for his care, nourishment, and protection, and how humbled I felt, wondering if I could measure up in my role of providing for our growing family. I also remember how connected he made me feel to eternity, considering that he had just arrived from the premortal realm. As I have had a repeat of this experience with the births of our other children and, in more recent years, our grandchildren, I have experienced many glimpses of the sweet connection of mortality to the eternal world. My greatest joys in life have come from my family.

So how do we respond to the heartache of those we may know and love personally who so desperately long for the blessings of eternal life and family but seem to have been cheated of this joy? Think of a young soldier killed in battle or a young woman who has not been invited to marry. Or how about a young couple shattered by broken covenants, who wonder if all is now lost? What of the man or woman plagued by mental illness or physical impairment to a degree that it prevents them from entering marriage commitments? How does one with same-sex attraction process the prospect of posterity in mortality and in eternity? We could go on to consider countless scenarios wherein people seem to be deprived of the blessing of "immortality and eternal life" (Moses 1:39) with families. Where is comfort? What is the eternal perspective? We may learn answers to these questions from the Lord's message to us in the example of the eunuch as found in this chapter of Isaiah.

My Holy Mountain

The Lord's message, through Isaiah, is an eternal message of hope and peace to the eunuch and to any and all that may be temporarily saddened by the supposed loss of eternal blessings. Through the power of the Atonement, anything that goes wrong in mortality may be put right. That is the perspective that we must all gain to see us through this veiled mortality. No one in any circumstance need lose hope of eternal life if they are willing to come unto the Savior and follow His path and admonition. Through the ordinances of the temple, eternal blessings may be secured to all who worthily seek them.

The Lord reminds that He can and will save and that no one need lament loss of blessings—we just need to see things in eternal perspective: "Thus saith the Lord, Keep ye judgment, and do justice: for my salvation is near to come, and my righteousness to be revealed. Blessed is the man that doeth this, and the son of man that layeth hold on it; that keepeth the sabbath from polluting it, and keepeth his hand from doing any evil. Neither let the son of the stranger, that hath joined himself to the Lord, speak, saying, The Lord hath utterly separated me from his people: neither let the eunuch say, Behold, I am a dry tree" (Isa. 56:1–3).

What must we do to procure the blessings of eternal life? Isaiah neatly summarizes the answer in three parts: "For thus saith the Lord unto the eunuchs that keep my sabbaths, and choose the things that please me, and take hold of my covenant" (Isa. 56:4).

Why Sabbaths? Once when I served as bishop, I needed to counsel personally and privately with another bishop about a matter of mutual concern. The only time we could seem to arrange for our meeting was during my ward Sunday School time. It was an interesting experience for me to travel to my appointment by driving through my own ward boundaries during our scheduled time of worship. I saw people who were in pursuit of recreation or working on home and yard projects. From this experience, and with the perspective as bishop, I was reminded that the keeping of the Sabbath is a benchmark activity—people who consistently keep the Sabbath day holy usually keep other things holy.[91]

To "choose the things that please" the Lord is to keep His commandments. To "take hold of my covenant" occurs as we place our faith in Christ, repent of our sins, accept baptism, and seek to follow the guidance of the Holy Ghost. As we do so, we prepare ourselves for temple worship where we receive our temple endowment with all of the related covenants, obligations and promised blessings.

Often, as I have enjoyed my children and grandchildren, I have wondered, "What could possibly be better than this?" My first response would be, "Nothing!" My second response would be, "Well, it would sure be great if I could have all of this forever, minus all of the trouble and evil of the fallen world our loved ones are growing up in." To all who are willing to accept the Lord's gospel and obey His will, He offers a profound eternal promise of things better than this world: "Even unto them will I give in mine house and within my walls a place and a name better than of sons and of daughters: I will give them an everlasting name, that shall not be cut off" (Isa. 56:5). When God places His name upon His children, He fulfills His promise to give them all that He has. He does so permanently, for all eternity. His gift of eternal life—to include eternal posterity—shall never be revoked or cut off.

Those of us who are blessed with sons and daughters in mortality, *and* those who are not so blessed, will have all the promised blessings of eternity if we are faithful. In the eternal, post-mortal realm, I believe that we will look back and realize that we each experienced all we needed to experience to prepare us for eternal life. We will also look around at our eternal families and realize that no one who accepted and lived the gospel will have lost any good thing or blessing promised by the Lord. We will have our eternal families with us forever and may well exclaim, "Wow, this is far better than we ever imagined while we were but mere mortals!"

Isaiah connects the promised blessings of eternity with the holy temple, or the holy mountain, and reminds that these blessings are available to everyone who will accept them: "Every one that keepeth the sabbath from polluting it, and taketh hold of my covenant; Even them will I bring to my holy mountain, and make them joyful in my house of prayer: their burnt offerings and their sacrifices shall be accepted upon mine altar; for mine house shall be called an house of prayer for all people" (Isa. 56:6–7).

They Are Greedy Dogs

Sometimes when I acted selfishly as a young boy, my mother admonished me, "Don't be a dog in a manger." A dog in a manger cannot eat the hay but snaps at the ox or the horse so they cannot eat it either. Satan is as a dog in a manger. He will never have a body, a wife, or a family. He will never hold an infant in his arms. So in his dark misery, he does all he can to destroy families and prevent others from having what he cannot have.

In his diabolical mission, Satan perverts the purposes of the temple by enticing nonbelievers to build their own counterfeit temples. He lured the ancients into strange idolatry, even to include the deranged practice of "sacred" prostitution in their defiled temples. In our modern society, he uses the same old tricks but repackages them in pornographic print and video and lures people away from their temple covenants and into adulterous and damning relationships. He does anything he can do to destroy the family.

Isaiah rebuked the evil leaders who should have been true shepherds of the Lord's flock but were rather following their own lusts: "His watchmen are blind: they are all ignorant, they are all dumb dogs, they cannot bark; sleeping, lying down, loving to slumber. Yea, they are greedy dogs which can never have enough, and they are shepherds that cannot understand: they all look to their own way, every one for his gain, from his quarter" (Isa. 56:10–11).

It takes real courage to choose the right course of life. Sincere and abiding faith is required to trust in the Lord and in His purposes for all people. But the rewards of righteousness are indeed great: "An everlasting name, that shall not be cut off" (Isa. 56:5).

CHAPTER FIFTY-SEVEN
INHERIT MY HOLY MOUNTAIN

ISAIAH TAUGHT, "THE RIGHTEOUS PERISHETH. . . . and . . . He shall enter into peace" (Isa. 57:1–2).

At the time of this writing, I am thinking of two recent deaths—one bitter and one sweet. A few days ago, a tyrannical dictator of one of the world's most oppressed and backward countries died of a heart attack, apparently in relative peace. His demise was headline news around the world and had analysts wondering what changes would now come to the people he had ruled.

The day following the death of this tyrant, the father of a friend of mine passed away after a long and painful battle with cancer. He was a humble man and remained true to his gospel covenants. He was a faithful husband, father, and grandfather, and spent his life in service to others. His passing was relatively quiet with not much media attention. Although the family was saddened to say good-bye to their beloved father, the sweetness of his life and service will buoy them up until they reunite in the eternal realm.

Of death, the Lord taught, "Thou shalt live together in love, insomuch that thou shalt weep for the loss of them that die, and more especially for those that have not hope of a glorious resurrection. And it shall come to pass that those that die in me shall not taste of death, for it shall be sweet unto them; And they that die not in me, wo unto them, for their death is bitter" (D&C 42:45–47).

The sweet death the Lord speaks of must refer to spiritual matters. One of the sweetest aspects of the death of the righteous is the blessing of reunion that awaits them and their loved ones through fulfillment of the Lord's promises to them.

I can't help but wonder what death is like for the wicked—particularly the tyrant I have here spoken of. We know that the wicked are "brought before the tribunal of God with your souls filled with guilt and remorse, having a remembrance of all your guilt, yea, a perfect remembrance of all your wickedness, yea, a remembrance that ye have set at defiance the commandments of God" (Alma 5:18).

There Is No Peace to the Wicked

In speaking against the sins of apostate Israel, Isaiah again invokes the imagery of the marriage metaphor and portrays how the wicked polluted their marriage covenant with the Lamb. Through their idolatry, they committed spiritual adultery. Their spiritual adultery was also inclusive of the wickedness of physical adultery, practiced in their evil fertility rites in worship of their pagan gods: "But draw near hither, ye sons of the sorceress, the seed of the adulterer and the whore. Against whom do ye sport yourselves? against whom make ye a wide mouth, and draw out the tongue? are ye not children of transgression, a seed of falsehood . . .?" (Isa. 57:3–4).

What does it mean to be "children of transgression"? To a group of the more wicked Pharisees, Jesus said, "Ye are of your father the devil" (John 8:44). The Israelites of Isaiah's day were in outright apostasy and had, in essence, made the devil their father—they were children of transgression. Children of the devil seem to have no bounds to their wickedness. It was one thing for mature and consenting adults to mingle in perverse idolatry but quite another for them to make their children party to the evil through the pernicious practice of child sacrifice: "Enflaming yourselves with idols under every green tree, slaying the children in the valleys under the clifts of the rocks" (Isa. 57:5).

Not only did the idolaters defile righteous principles of marriage and family, but they also defiled the purpose of the sacred temple by associating their false worship with false temples, constructed in counterfeit to the Lord's holy house: "Upon a lofty and high mountain hast thou set thy bed: even thither wentest thou up to offer sacrifice. Behind the doors also and the posts hast thou set up thy remembrance: for thou hast discovered thyself to another than me, and art gone up; thou hast enlarged thy bed, and made thee a covenant with them; thou lovedst their bed where thou sawest it" (Isa. 57:7–9).

In their trusting of false gods, apostate Israel lost the trust and protection of the true God: "And of whom hast thou been afraid or feared, that thou hast lied, and hast not remembered me, nor laid it to thy heart? have not I held my peace even of old, and thou fearest me not?" The Lord would judge their pretended righteousness and find them wanting: "I will declare thy righteousness, and thy works; for they shall not profit thee." Since they have not trusted in Him nor sought His protection, in their day of trouble, he commends them to their idol gods for peace and protection: "When thou criest, let thy companies deliver thee; but the wind shall carry them all away" (Isa. 57:11–13). An idol god so weak as to blow away in the wind is hardly able to protect his followers from the winds of adversity, temptation, and destruction that come their way.

Some time ago, a portion of the eastern coast of Japan was annihilated by a terrible tsunami. We watched in sadness as this mighty wall of water unmercifully churned up everything in its path and destroyed the lives and homes of thousands. The practice of ancient and modern idolatry carves a destructive course through our society, polluting our world with the mire and muck of evil. Those who commit spiritual adultery and despise the invitation to enter the sacred marriage covenant with our Savior will reap the sorrow of their choices and actions: "But the wicked are like the troubled sea, when it cannot rest, whose waters cast up mire and dirt. There is no peace, saith my God, to the wicked" (Isa. 57:20–21).

Trust in the Lord—Inherit the Holy Mountain

There is peace and hope to all who choose the path of righteousness and worthily accept the marriage invitation of the Lamb. They have the happy assurance that they can "look forward with an eye of faith, and view this mortal body raised in immortality," and can joyfully anticipate the Lord saying unto them, "Come unto me ye blessed, for behold, your works have been the works of righteousness upon the face of the earth" (Alma 5:15–16).

Let us consider the death of the father of my friend and the deaths of all who die in the Lord. Isaiah said, "The righteous perisheth, and no man layeth it to heart: and merciful men are taken away, none considering that the righteous is taken away from the evil to come. He shall enter into peace: they shall rest in their beds, each one walking in his uprightness" (Isa. 57:1–2). When a righteous person dies, it is often without fanfare and noise. He is quietly set free from the "evil to come" to the world. He is given rest from the trials of mortality and also begins a new phase of preparing to receive the rest of what Heavenly Father has prepared for those who serve Him. Alma taught, "And then shall it come to pass, that the spirits of those who are righteous are received into a state of happiness, which is called paradise, a state of rest, a state of peace, where they shall rest from all their troubles and from all care, and sorrow" (Alma 40:12).

The destiny of the righteous who die in the Lord is to inherit the celestial kingdom of God and to live the life He lives. The Lord declared, "But he that putteth his trust in me shall possess the land, and shall inherit my holy mountain" (Isa. 57:13). To inherit the holy mountain is to inherit celestial glory. Our worshipful journey through the temple takes us, symbolically, into the celestial kingdom. Our worshipful journey through premortal, mortal, and postmortal life takes us, in reality, into the celestial kingdom. When John the Revelator saw the celestial kingdom of God in vision, he said: "And I saw no temple therein: for the Lord God Almighty and the Lamb are the temple of it. And the city had no need of the sun, neither of the moon, to shine in it: for the glory of God did lighten it, and the Lamb is the light thereof" (Rev. 21:22–23). To receive our endowment in the holy temple prepares us to receive the endowment, or gift, of the celestial kingdom.

Our life quest takes us to the temple. The gathering of Israel is about gathering them to Jesus Christ. Those who gather to Christ and prepare for and receive their temple endowments are, by so doing, standing on the higher ground necessary to reach out and help others come up to the mountain of the Lord's house: "Cast ye up, cast ye up, prepare the way, take up the stumblingblock out of the way of my people. For thus saith the high and lofty One that inhabiteth eternity, whose name is Holy; I dwell in the high and holy place, with him also that is of a contrite and humble spirit, to revive the spirit of the humble, and to revive the heart of the contrite ones" (Isa. 57:14–15).

The imagery of the temple compared to a high mountain is inspiring and, as mentioned previously, is a repeated theme throughout Isaiah. As we climb a mountain, we rise above the noise and pollutions of the valley floor. We gain an expanded vision of eternity. We are able to look back at our journey and see more clearly the path for others to follow. From our higher view, we better see the pitfalls that may distract others. One way to understand what it means to "prepare the way" is to help others find and travel the highway of righteousness, of faith, repentance, baptism, and receiving the Holy Ghost (see Isaiah 40:3). We may "take up the stumblingblock out of the way of my people" by loving them and serving them and by teaching them of the joy and peace the gospel brings and helping them avoid sin and evil along their life journey. If we are humble and contrite and if those we love and teach are humble and contrite, we will all join with Heavenly Father in eternal peace and joy.

For those who may have stumbled or fallen, there is hope in Christ through faith and repentance. As we help lift and succor, the Lord redeems and heals: "I have seen his ways, and will heal him: I will lead him also, and restore comforts unto him and to his mourners. I create the fruit of the lips; Peace, peace to him that is far off, and to him that is near, saith the Lord; and I will heal him" (Isa. 57:18–19).

Sweet is the life, death, and postmortal life of those who walk the path of the righteous!

CHAPTER FIFTY-EIGHT
LIKE A SPRING . . . WHOSE WATERS FAIL NOT

MANY YEARS AGO, AS I served as executive secretary to my stake president, I learned a fascinating principle from him as I observed how he would consider the issuance of callings. Often, when a name would be considered for the position of bishop or quorum president, for example, he would reach for a loose-leaf binder containing a five-year tithing record for all members of the stake. His review of this record would play a big part in whether or not the person was called to serve. I learned that the payment of tithes and offerings is a pretty good benchmark of a person's overall faithfulness. People generally do not pay tithing consistently over extended time if they are not committed to the principles of the gospel.

Fasting is another great benchmark of genuine spiritual conversion. One who sincerely and properly fasts as taught by the Lord is able to draw from deep wells of knowledge, wisdom, inspiration, and spiritual guidance. The interesting thing about these spiritual benchmarks is that they are inward, personal worship activities. When done properly, only the authorized priesthood leaders would know of a person's tithing status. A proper fast would hardly be known to anyone.

Isaiah now offers some of the most profound teaching in all the scriptures concerning the laws of the fast and of Sabbath observance. In so doing, he uses an effective teaching method. He reveals the problem—what they are doing wrong—then expounds true doctrine and explains how to apply it. Finally, he unfolds the beautiful blessings that come to those who properly fast and keep the Sabbath.

Ye Fast for Strife and Debate

Isaiah's charge from the Lord to teach these important matters was to "cry aloud, spare not, lift up thy voice like a trumpet, and shew my people their transgression, and the house of Jacob their sins." The Lord said of their hypocrisy, "Yet they seek me daily, and delight to know my ways, as a nation that did righteousness, and forsook not the ordinance of their God: they ask of me the ordinances of justice; they take delight in approaching to God" (Isa. 58:1–2). In other words, they were performing the rituals but were lacking sincerity and purpose (see footnote 2a).

They go on as if to say, "Look at us. We have been fasting. See how humble and famished we are!" Or, in the words of Isaiah, "Wherefore have we fasted, say they, and thou seest not? wherefore have we afflicted our soul, and thou takest no knowledge? Behold, in the day of your fast ye find pleasure and exact all your labours" (Isa. 58:3). "Exact all your labors" means to "inflict travail on others," (footnote 3d) as if to say, "Oh poor me! I am so weak from fasting I don't think I can help you today."

Isaiah continues, "Behold, ye fast for strife and debate, and to smite with the fist of wickedness: ye shall not fast as ye do this day, to make your voice to be heard on high" (Isa. 58:4). Israel's fasting was void of spirituality. They were merely going through the motions and becoming disagreeable. "Fasting without spiritual motivation only engenders discomfort and irritability" (see footnote 4b).

The Lord condemns their shallow and pretentious rituals: "Is this such a fast that I have chosen? a day for a man to afflict his soul? is it to bow down his head as a bulrush, and to spread sackcloth and ashes under him? wilt thou call this a fast, and an acceptable day to the Lord?" (Isa. 58:5).

Call the Sabbath a Delight

Isaiah now proclaims the Lord's true law of the fast: "Is not this the fast that I have chosen? to loose the bands of wickedness, to undo the heavy burdens, and to let the oppressed go free, and that ye break every yoke? Is it not to deal thy bread to the hungry, and that thou bring the poor that are cast out to thy house? when thou seest the naked, that thou cover him; and that thou hide not thyself from thine own flesh? (Isa. 58:6–7).

Fasting helps us personally, and helps us in blessing others. Disciplining ourselves by putting our body in subjection to our spirit gives us power over temptation and evil. We may be personally oppressed by some grinding temptation or addiction. As we fast, we not only gain the physical power needed to overcome, but the Lord multiplies our spiritual strength and helps us strive upward and onward. One blessing of fasting may be the inspiration given to help us with our personal struggles.

The fast offerings we make to the Lord are used to bless those who need help with the necessities of life. These offerings go to the general Church fund, and then local leaders, under inspiration, draw upon these funds to help and bless those in their stewardship as needed. But the fast offering is not just about money—it is also about time and caring and service. We can receive strength and inspiration to bring someone into our home or to use our talents to provide service for someone in need. The bishop holds the keys to the Lord's storehouse. This storehouse is not just a source of food and clothing but includes all of the talents of all ward members. The bishop may call on us to use these talents to help those in need. From the inspiration we gain through our fasting, we may ask him what we can do even before he may ask us. Such free-will service is a bishop's dream come true.

We now hear the Lord's true law of the Sabbath: "If thou turn away thy foot from the sabbath, from doing thy pleasure on my holy day; and call the sabbath a delight, the holy of the Lord, honourable; and shalt honour him, not doing thine own ways, nor finding thine own pleasure, nor speaking thine own words" (Isa. 58:13). The law of the Sabbath is to seek to do the will of the Lord and yield our own will to His will. As we persist in seeking the Lord's will, it soon becomes our will and pleasure. At times we tend to focus on what we *should not* do on the Sabbath. I have personally found that if I focus on the things I *should* be doing and strive to do them, the day pretty much takes care of itself. On such days, the Sabbath really becomes a delight.

Like a Spring of Water, Whose Waters Fail Not

Now that Isaiah has identified the problem and taught the true law of fasting and Sabbath observance, he expounds many joyous and hopeful promises to those who choose to live these divine truths. Here are some of my thoughts about the principles found in this chapter:

"Then shall thy light break forth as the morning" (Isa. 58:8). Spiritual darkness covers our world and grows more intense each day. Spiritual light disperses darkness. Christ is *the* light of the world! As we keep the Sabbath and fast and pray with sincerity and diligence, we learn more of Christ and come closer to Him. As we do so, our spiritual light increases as the morning light increases with each passing moment: "That which is of God is light; and he that receiveth light, and continueth in God, receiveth more light; and that light groweth brighter and brighter until the perfect day" (D&C 50:24). Spiritual light ultimately guides us into the presence of God.

"Thine health shall spring forth speedily" (Isa. 58:8). Many health experts recommend fasting as a healing process. Certainly periodic fasting helps us learn to control our appetites, cleanse our body of toxins, and thus achieve better health. Of even greater miracle and significance is spiritual health. *Health* and *healing* stem from the same root. Health is healing. As we fast and pray, the Lord, in His own way and time, heals us of our physical and spiritual ills. Our soul—our body and our spirit—is of great worth to Him. To the faithless scribes who thought Him blasphemous, He asked, "Whether is it easier to say to the sick of the palsy, Thy sins be forgiven thee; or to say, Arise, and take up thy bed, and walk?" (Mark 2:9). The Lord cares about our body and our spirit and has power to heal both.

"Thy righteousness shall go before thee; the glory of the Lord shall be thy rearward" (Isa. 58:8). In my military training years ago, we learned to "cover" one another—to protect someone as best we could from all angles as they went forward. We sometimes used a phrase now popular across society: "I've got your back," meaning, "I have you covered." As we go forward in life, we wear "the breastplate of righteousness," (D&C 27:16) which shields and protects us from spiritual harm. Even a soldier with a breastplate is still vulnerable from other angles, just as we are spiritually vulnerable from all angles. "Rearward" refers to the rear guard of an army. As we fast, pray, and strive to do our best, the Lord becomes our "rearward." He covers us with His Atonement. He knows the path and the terrain. He shields us from all angles as we go forward.

"Then shalt thou call, and the Lord shall answer; thou shalt cry, and he shall say, Here I am" (Isa. 58:9). The Lord hears and answers our prayers. Through fasting and prayer, we may gain inspiration to know what is best for us and what help we need. The Lord will answer if we ask in righteousness. We may gain the knowledge and blessing of Nephi, who taught, "Yea, I know that God will give liberally to him that asketh. Yea, my God will give me, if I ask not amiss; therefore I will lift up my voice unto thee; yea, I will cry unto thee, my God, the rock of my righteousness. Behold, my voice shall forever ascend up unto thee, my rock and mine everlasting God. Amen" (2 Ne. 4:35).

"And the Lord shall guide thee continually, and satisfy thy soul in drought, and make fat thy bones: and thou shalt be like a watered garden, and like a spring of water, whose waters fail not" (Isa. 58:11). The promise of this verse helps us understand the particularly sweet connection between seeking the Lord's guidance and receiving living waters, or partaking of the Atonement. We often fast and pray diligently as we attend the temple, seeking special guidance and blessings. As we seek the Lord's guidance through prayer and fasting, He becomes to us as "a spring of water, whose waters fail not." The water He gives us is "living water." This living water is eternal, or everlasting, life—"The water that I shall give him shall be in him a well of water springing up into everlasting life" (John 4:10, 14).

"And they that shall be of thee shall build the old waste places: thou shalt raise up the foundations of many generations. . . . Then shalt thou delight thyself in the Lord; and I will cause thee to ride upon the high places of the earth, and feed thee with the heritage of Jacob thy father: for the mouth of the Lord hath spoken it" (Isa. 58:12, 14). "They that shall be of thee" can refer to our descendants—to our family. Here again we may connect this thought to the power of the Atonement and to the temple wherein we may have our families sealed to us for time and all eternity. In seeking this blessing during our mortal trials, we and our families will encounter "opposition in all things" (2 Ne. 2:11) and will have need of inspired guidance. Through fasting, prayer, and proper Sabbath observance, we may receive the revelation we need to help our loved ones rise up from darkness and "ride upon the high places of the earth," or receive the promised blessings of the temple. We may then ride with them into eternal life—traveling with the Lord as our rearward.

There is a lot more to fasting than just going hungry and a lot more to keeping the Sabbath than just going to church. As we rise to the level of understanding and worship that the Lord asks of us, He blesses us with more than we could ever, of ourselves, imagine. He grants us the blessing of letting our "soul delight itself in fatness" (Isa. 55:2).

CHAPTER FIFTY-NINE
THE REDEEMER SHALL COME TO ZION

THERE IS A LEGEND OF a young Indian boy who, according to his tribal custom, climbed a mountain in search of his life's vision. As he was descending, he discovered a rattlesnake that said to him, "I am very cold. Please warm me and carry me down to the valley." The boy replied, "Oh no, I know what you are. If I carry you, you will bite me." The snake persisted and finally convinced the boy that he would not be harmed, so the boy nestled the shivering snake inside his shirt and carried him to the valley. As the boy took the snake out of his shirt to set it on the ground, the snake bit him. The boy protested, "You promised that I would not be harmed!" As the snake slithered away, it said to the boy, "You knew what I was when you picked me up." To the rational mind, this seems like such a strange story—who in their right mind would even approach a poisonous snake, let alone pick it up? Yet this seems to be the sad saga of Israel, then and now, as we sometimes give in to the allure and seduction of vanity, even when warned of the danger.

We gain instruction and warning as we study how Israel continued through their cycles of apostasy and redemption. Gospel scholar Victor Ludlow offers a helpful outline of the progression of Israel: "In chapters 59 and 60, Isaiah describes a complete transformation of Israel as she moves from wickedness to righteousness through a sequence of changes: sin (59:1–8), repentance (59:9–15a), deliverance (59:15b–21), gathering (60:1–9), rebuilding (60:10–13), prosperity (60:14–18), and the presence of the Lord (60:19–22). Combining poetry and prophecy, Isaiah portrays a pattern of progression as Israel rises from the depths of spiritual death to eternal life in God's presence."[92] I follow this outline to organize my subheadings for chapters 59 and 60 and will identify the divisions with underlined bold italics.

Sin: They Hatch Cockatrice' Eggs

The Lord always warns us and pleads with us to avoid the evil serpent and his damning allures—but He allows us our agency and does not go with us into darkness. It is of our own doing when we grow distant from Him: "But your iniquities have separated between you and your God, and your sins have hid his face from you, that he will not hear" (Isa. 59:2).

One of the saddest commentaries of all scripture is the Lord's assessment of the people of the earth in the days of Noah: "And God saw that the wickedness of men had become great in the earth; and every man was lifted up in the imagination of the thoughts of his heart, being only evil continually" (Moses 8:22). Isaiah similarly spoke to Israel: "For your hands are defiled with blood, and your fingers with iniquity; your lips have spoken lies, your tongue hath muttered perverseness. None calleth for justice, nor any pleadeth for truth: they trust in vanity, and speak lies; they conceive mischief, and bring forth iniquity" (Isa. 59:3–4).

They should have known better. They were, in a sense, picking up a poisonous snake. Isaiah said, "They hatch cockatrice' eggs, and weave the spider's web: he that eateth of their eggs dieth, and that which is crushed breaketh out into a viper" (Isa. 59:5). The cockatrice, a legendary serpent, is often translated "adder"—a very real and very deadly poisonous snake. Many snakes must grow into their venom, but the adder is venomous from the hatch. The children of Israel were, in a symbolic sense, hatching, or taking from the hatch, or breaking open cockatrice eggs to eat them, knowing full well that they were deadly. This seems such a silly notion, but it continues today as some seek out and ingest harmful substances and philosophies.

The spider's webs woven by the rebellious bind them as do the chains of hell: "Their webs shall not become garments, neither shall they cover themselves with their works: their works are works of iniquity, and the act of violence is in their hands." Their webs of wickedness do not protect or cover them as do the robes of righteousness that provide the covering of the Atonement to those so vested. "Their feet run to evil, and they make haste to shed innocent blood: their thoughts are thoughts of iniquity; wasting and destruction are in their paths" (Isa. 59:6–7).

Shalom or _Shalom Aleichem_ is a common greeting among the Jews. It translates, "Peace be upon you." The greeted returns the salutation with _Aleicham Shalom_, or, "And upon you be peace." I occasionally attend Catholic mass with family, and as part of the worship, we shake hands with those around us and offer the greeting "Peace," and receive the reply, "And peace unto you." These expressions are greetings of personal peace—as if to say, "How are you personally?" or "May you have personal peace." To the wicked and rebellious, there is no personal peace: "The way of peace they know not; and there is no judgment in their goings: they have made them crooked paths: whosoever goeth therein shall not know peace" (Isa. 59:8).

Repentance: We Roar All Like Bears, and Mourn Sore Like Doves

A former student of mine has spent his adult lifetime suffering a heavy price in prison for a serious crime he committed. Many years ago, he wrote me and told of being transferred from one part of the prison to another and the exhilaration he felt at glimpsing the light of the moon and stars for the first time in many months. We who are free may take the light and beauty of the world for granted. Hopefully, we do not take for granted the spiritual light provided us by our Savior.

Often, those in bondage of sin long for light in the darkness of their circumstance: "Therefore is judgment far from us, neither doth justice overtake us: we wait for light, but behold obscurity; for brightness, but we walk in darkness. We grope for the wall like the blind, and we grope as if we had no eyes: we stumble at noonday as in the night; we are in desolate places as dead men" (Isa. 59:9–10).

Suffering for sin is inherent—there is no escape, although there may be some delay to the full portion of the suffering. Repentance relieves suffering. Our Savior taught, "For behold, I, God, have suffered these things for all, that they might not suffer if they would repent; But if they would not repent they must suffer even as I" (D&C 19:16–17). There is a difference between our suffering and Christ's suffering. We suffer to prompt us to repent—Christ suffered to atone for our sins.

During the repentance process, suffering can be rather intense. Suffering Israel exclaimed, "We roar all like bears, and mourn sore like doves: we look for judgment, but there is none; for salvation, but it is far off from us. For our transgressions are multiplied before thee, and our sins testify against us: for our transgressions are with us; and as for our iniquities, we know them" (Isa. 59:11–12).

Covenant Israel had the gospel light and truth and should have been holding it up for all to see and proclaiming it for all to hear: "Lifting up your voices as with the sound of a trump, proclaiming the truth according to the revelations and commandments which I have given you" (D&C 75:4). Rather, they had trampled the truth and, by so doing, distanced themselves from the Lord's sweet justice and mercy: "And judgment is turned away backward, and justice standeth afar off: for truth is fallen in the street, and equity cannot enter" (Isa. 59:14).

By trampling the truth, they failed to receive the Lord's full protection and placed themselves as prey, subject to the whims of their pursuing enemies: "Yea, truth faileth; and he that departeth from evil maketh himself a prey" (Isa. 59:15).

Deliverance: The Redeemer Shall Come to Zion

During the suffering and repentance process, the Lord does not forsake us. He stands ready to deliver us and has the knowledge and power to do so. He hears our cries and steps in to save us as soon as we are ready to come unto Him and accept His outstretched hand: "Behold, the Lord's hand is not shortened, that it cannot save; neither his ear heavy, that it cannot hear" (Isa. 59:1).

Satan, that lying and vile snake, wields great power. But one of the most reassuring doctrines of the gospel is that Christ holds "the keys of hell and of death" (Rev. 1:18). Satan only operates under limited permission, and that permission will be revoked in a future day. John the Revelator saw that Christ "laid hold on the dragon, that old serpent, which is the Devil, and Satan, and bound him a thousand years" (Rev. 20:2).

Christ will deliver Israel with great power: "For he put on righteousness as a breastplate, and an helmet of salvation upon his head; and he put on the garments of vengeance for clothing, and was clad with zeal as a cloke." He will "repay" and bring "fury to his adversaries, recompense to his enemies." Although Satan will flood the earth with wickedness, the Lord will stand steadfast. He, who created all the waters of the earth by His command and controls the waters as with the parting of the Red Sea, will counter the flood of evil: "When the enemy shall come in like a flood, the Spirit of the Lord shall lift up a standard against him" (Isa. 59:17–19).

Satan's fury is terrible, and his venom is deadly. But Christ can fix all that goes wrong. He has established His covenant with Israel and has made provision for the salvation of all who will repent and come unto Him: "And the Redeemer shall come to Zion, and unto them that turn from transgression in Jacob, saith the Lord. As for me, this is my covenant with them, saith the Lord; My spirit that is upon thee, and my words which I have put in thy mouth, shall not depart out of thy mouth, nor out of the mouth of thy seed, nor out of the mouth of thy seed's seed, saith the Lord from henceforth and for ever" (Isa. 59:20–21).

CHAPTER SIXTY
ARISE, SHINE: FOR THY LIGHT IS COME

WHILE RECENTLY VISITING THE UPPER peninsula of Michigan, I toured the historic Quincy copper mine near Lake Superior. It was a fascinating experience to learn of the history of this enterprise that had its beginning just before the Civil War and continued until after World War II. The mine operated the world's largest steam-powered ore-and-man hoist that transported the miners through ninety-two levels, descending nearly two miles below ground.

It is hard for me to imagine the courage and grit of the miners who descended into this eerie abyss each day as they worked to support their families. I came away with a reverence for them. I also came away with a greater appreciation for light, warmth, and fresh air. I am a bit claustrophobic and had an uneasy feeling about being so far underground. The tunnels were not well lighted, and at one point, our tour guide turned off all the lights so we could experience the complete natural darkness of the place. As we mounted our tractor-pulled trailer to begin our exit from the mine, I felt a growing sense of relief. As we rounded a bend, we could see the welcoming light of the mine entrance in the distance. When we exited, we were refreshed by the beautiful scenery of the area and the brilliant light and comforting warmth of the sun.

Gathering: And the Gentiles Shall Come to the Light

We may liken the end of the Great Apostasy to emerging from a darkened mine. After many stifling and oppressive years of spiritual darkness, the glorious gospel light has been restored to the earth. The Lord has organized His Church and missionary forces to take the gospel's good news to the world. All people are being invited to gather to the brilliant light and the comforting warmth of the Son of God, the Savior of the world.

Isaiah beckoned, "Arise, shine; for thy light is come, and the glory of the Lord is risen upon thee. For, behold, the darkness shall cover the earth, and gross darkness the people: but the Lord shall arise upon thee, and his glory shall be seen upon thee. And the Gentiles shall come to thy light, and kings to the brightness of thy rising" (Isa. 60:1–3).

We all likely know people—perhaps ourselves or those we love dearly—who have groped in spiritual darkness but have now come to the light. We experience joy at seeing the great plan of redemption make real changes in eternal souls. We rejoice in gospel conversion. Alma expressed his feelings of his repentance: "And oh, what joy, and what marvelous light I did behold; yea, my soul was filled with joy as exceeding as was my pain!" (Alma 36:20). We rejoice in those who are being gathered into the fold from all parts of the world through repentance.

These verses of Isaiah are replete with words of gathering: "Shall come to thy light. . . . they gather themselves together . . . sons shall come from far. . . . and flow together . . . because the abundance of the sea shall be converted unto thee, the forces of the Gentiles shall come unto thee. . . . all they from Sheba shall come" (Isa. 60:3–6).

We recall the words of the Prophet Joseph Smith about the reason for gathering Israel: "The main object was to build unto the Lord a house whereby He could reveal unto His people the ordinances of His house and the glories of His kingdom, and teach the people the way of salvation; for there are certain ordinances and principles that, when they are taught and practiced, must be done in a place or house built for that purpose."[93]

As people gather to Zion, they bring many treasures with them. These treasures are physical and spiritual: "The multitude of camels shall cover thee . . . they shall bring gold and incense. . . . All the flocks of Kedar shall be gathered together unto thee . . . they shall come up with acceptance on mine altar, and I will glorify the house of my glory" (Isa. 60:6–7). *Gold, incense, altar,* and *house of my glory* all relate to the temple and worship therein. Treasures of gold may not only represent physical resources but also spiritual gifts or talents bestowed by Heavenly Father upon His children to be used in the building of the kingdom and the gathering of the Saints.

Charles Allen, a resident of modern Nauvoo, is an example of how the Lord prepares His people with gifts so that they may play a part in the gathering of Israel and in the purpose of building temples. Brother Allen's life story is an inspiring and fascinating account of a humble man who was blessed in developing his woodworking talents and led by the Lord to reside in modern Nauvoo where he was commissioned to use his skills in constructing the windows and doors for the rebuilding of the Nauvoo Temple. He accomplished this great work during years of regular priesthood service and trials of illness and even the deaths of some of the members of his family. His physical and spiritual gifts were put to the task in building the Lord's temple.[94]

As the gathering of Israel goes forward, people will feel an innate desire to come home to the gospel light. Homing pigeons are trained to carry messages and return, through hardship and danger, to their designated nests or homes. Once people experience gospel conversion, they are instinctively drawn home to the temple and to the glory of the Lord in His holy house. Isaiah said, "Who are these that fly as a cloud, and as the doves to their windows? Surely the isles shall wait for me, and the ships of Tarshish first, to bring thy sons from far, their silver and their gold with them, unto the name of the Lord thy God, and to the Holy One of Israel, because he hath glorified thee" (Isa. 60:8–9).

Rebuilding: In My Favor Have I Had Mercy upon Thee

Israel will gather to Zion and bring forth their talents and resources in preparation to help others to gather, even until the day when the ten lost tribes will be brought back to the gospel light: "And the sons of strangers shall build up thy walls, and their kings shall minister unto thee: for in my wrath I smote thee, but in my favour have I had mercy on thee. Therefore thy gates shall be open continually; they shall not be shut day nor night; that men may bring unto thee the forces of the Gentiles, and that their kings may be brought" (Isa. 60:10–11).

The temple is a great visual reminder of the principle of the Lord's blessing of abundance. Temples are made from the finest of fixtures, carpeting, furniture, mechanical equipment, draperies, glass, wood, etc. Adequate resources of time and money are expended to keep temples clean and perfect in appearance. When we go to the temple, we sense the physical manifestation of the Lord's abundance. And yet the greatest comfort we receive is from things spiritual: guidance from the Holy Ghost, direction and protection through eternal covenants, and the enduring peace that comes from participating in sacred ordinances.

Imagine life on earth in the millennial day once all wickedness has been swept away. Then we will more clearly see the Lord's physical and spiritual abundance as opposed to the desolation of the nations of the wicked: "For the nation and kingdom that will not serve thee shall perish; yea, those nations shall be utterly wasted" (Isa. 60:12). With wickedness gone, the earth renewed, and resources generously provided, missionary and temple work will leap forward: "The glory of Lebanon shall come unto thee, the fir tree, the pine tree, and the box together, to beautify the place of my sanctuary; and I will make the place of my feet glorious" (Isa. 60:13). The Lord provides glorious physical temples to match the glorious spiritual blessings He bestows therein.

Prosperity: **For Brass I Will Bring Gold**

The Lord prospers righteous societies with spiritual and physical abundance. In the pride cycle, societies fall from the condition of prosperity because of their own vanity—not by the desire of the Lord. Of the Zion society of the Nephites after the ministry of Christ to them we are told: "And they had all things common among them; therefore there were not rich and poor, bond and free, but they were all made free, and partakers of the heavenly gift. . . . And the Lord did prosper them exceedingly in the land." They were undoubtedly comfortable with their prosperity, but they were happy because of their true conversion: "And it came to pass that there was no contention in the land, because of the love of God which did dwell in the hearts of the people. . . . and surely there could not be a happier people among all the people who had been created by the hand of God" (4 Ne. 1:3, 7, 15–16).

The Lord expects us to increase our gifts, and He helps us as we strive to do so. Whatever we bring, the Lord will make it better and richer—He multiplies the harvest: "For brass I will bring gold, and for iron I will bring silver, and for wood brass, and for stones iron: I will also make thy officers peace, and thine exactors righteousness" (Isa. 60:17).

As wickedness disappears, righteousness reigns. Israel's former enemies, now converted, become friends and protectors: "The sons also of them that afflicted thee shall come bending unto thee; and they that despised thee shall bow themselves down at the soles of thy feet; and they shall call thee, The city of the Lord, The Zion of the Holy One of Israel" (Isa. 60:14).

We may find an example of this principle of modern-day "sons" reverencing latter-day Israel by contrasting the vicious Extermination Order of Governor Boggs of Missouri in 1838 with the dual proclamations from the modern governors of Missouri and Kansas. Governor Boggs declared that the Mormons were enemies and were to be driven out of the state or killed. On occasion of the open house of the newly constructed Kansas City Missouri Temple in April of 2012, Governor Nixon of

Missouri and Governor Brownback of Kansas each issued proclamations of commendation to the Church. From Governor Nixon's proclamation, we read:

> Whereas the Church of Jesus Christ of Latter-day Saints maintains an important and historic place in the state of Missouri. . . .
>
> The Kansas City Missouri Temple stands as a shadow by day and a pillar by night to all who are defenders of religious liberty and tolerance, and further witnesses that the rights of faith and conviction are alive in the great State of Missouri. . . .
>
> I, Jeremiah W. (Jay) Nixon, Governor of the State of Missouri, do hereby recognize The Church of Jesus Christ of Latter-day Saints for their dedication to their religious convictions and positive contribution to their individual communities and to the State of Missouri.[95]

Once persecuted and rejected, the Lord's children are now protected and respected. Israel is compared to a nursing child: "Thou shalt also suck the milk of the Gentiles, and shalt suck the breast of kings: and thou shalt know that I the Lord am thy Saviour and thy Redeemer, the mighty One of Jacob" (Isa. 60:16). The Lord, as any righteous parent, loves His children and seeks only the best care and nourishment for them. The mighty of the earth that once oppressed them are now converted and assume a mothering role in gathering Israel. In our society, mothers are typically the most loving and nurturing caretakers. Even greater than the love of a mother is the love of our Heavenly Father and our Savior. They will tenderly guide, nourish, lead, and protect gathering Israel.

For protection, ancient Israel depended on city walls of stone and mortar with guards posted on watchtowers. We of modern Israel look to such things as law enforcement, military, electronic security, and monitoring systems to warn and protect us. When Zion is fully established in the Millennium, we can recycle our security devices, retool our weapons of war, and retrain our policemen and soldiers: "Violence shall no more be heard in thy land, wasting nor destruction within thy borders; but thou shalt call thy walls Salvation, and thy gates Praise" (Isa. 60:18). Our protection is, and will be, our Savior, in whom we have salvation. Our gratitude to Him for His protection will be our praise of Him.

Presence of the Lord: **An Everlasting Light**

We recall how John the Revelator saw the celestial kingdom in vision and how there was "no temple therein. . . . And the city had no need of the sun . . . for the glory of God did lighten it" (Rev. 21:22–23). Isaiah teaches the same message: "The sun shall be no more thy light by day; neither for brightness shall the moon give light unto thee: but the Lord shall be unto thee an everlasting light, and thy God thy glory. Thy sun shall no more go down; neither shall thy moon withdraw itself: for the Lord shall be thine everlasting light, and the days of thy mourning shall be ended" (Isa. 60:19–20).

The crowning purpose of the temple is to prepare us to be brought into the presence of the Lord in the celestial kingdom. Once we attain this glory, the temple will have fulfilled its purpose. Life in the celestial kingdom is a temple-like life. The Church also will have served its purpose—rather than bishops, stake presidents, and other leaders, our organizational structure in the eternal realm will continue with mothers and fathers, grandmothers and grandfathers. This patriarchal order will be the eternal governing order of the celestial kingdom.

John the Revelator also saw the end of mourning and sorrow: "They shall hunger no more, neither thirst any more; neither shall the sun light on them, nor any heat. For the Lamb which is in the midst of the throne shall feed them, and shall lead them unto living fountains of waters: and God shall wipe away all tears from their eyes" (Rev. 7:16–17).

Mourning will have an end because death, sin, and evil become extinct: "Thy people also shall be all righteous: they shall inherit the land for ever, the branch of my planting, the work of my hands, that I may be glorified" (Isa. 60:21). The land that we are to inherit forever is this earth. We know that this earth, like the people who inhabit it, is going through eternal progression from Eden to telestial to paradisiacal (terrestrial) to celestial.

As I contemplate eternal glory, the sweetest thought of all is of my eternal family when all heartache, mourning, and trial is passed. As I consider the greatest joys of my life, my thoughts center on my family: my wife, my children, and my grandchildren—my little ones. Isaiah proclaimed, "A little one shall become a thousand, and a small one a strong nation: I the Lord will hasten it in his time" (Isa. 60:22).

My own family is a part and portion of the greater covenant family of Abraham, whose family began small—as "a little one"—and then multiplied into the vast family of Israel it is today. "The *little one* is the gathered house of Israel, which started very small but will grow until it becomes very powerful in the strength of the Lord. This promise to Israel is an extension of the Lord's promise to Abraham, the father of the house of Israel, wherein a little one (Abraham) became a strong nation (Gen. 12:2; 18:18; see D&C 133:57–58)."[96]

The true Church and its holy temples serve to instruct, prepare, and offer us glimpses of eternal life, but nothing can compare to actually living with our families in the presence of the Lord forever in celestial light and glory!

CHAPTER SIXTY-ONE
BEAUTY FOR ASHES

At the beginning of our Savior's mortal ministry, He entered the synagogue in His hometown of Nazareth and "stood up for to read." He was given the book of Isaiah, from which He quoted, "The Spirit of the Lord is upon me, because he hath anointed me to preach the gospel to the poor; he hath sent me to heal the brokenhearted, to preach deliverance to the captives, and recovering of sight to the blind, to set at liberty them that are bruised, To preach the acceptable year of the Lord." After reading this passage, "he closed the book, and he gave it again to the minister, and sat down. And the eyes of all them that were in the synagogue were fastened on him. And he began to say unto them, This day is this scripture fulfilled in your ears" (Luke 4:16–21; see Isaiah 61:1–2). He thus declared Himself the divine Son of God—the promised Messiah who would come to deliver the people.

Tragically, the hearers in the synagogue that day could not recognize or stand gospel truth: "And all they in the synagogue, when they heard these things, were filled with wrath, And rose up, and thrust him out of the city, and led him unto the brow of the hill whereon their city was built, that they might cast him down headlong." As His mission was not yet complete, "he passing through the midst of them went his way" (Luke 4:28–30).

The Oil of Joy for Mourning

A sad irony is how people allow themselves to become so angry as to reject the very gospel truths that would, if embraced, bring them everlasting joy. Let us who believe the messages of truth come to understand the joy of Christ's mission from a review of this chapter of Isaiah.

"The Spirit of the Lord God is upon me; because the Lord hath anointed me to preach good tidings unto the meek; he hath sent me to bind up the brokenhearted, to proclaim liberty to the captives,

and the opening of the prison to them that are bound" (Isa. 61:1).
The meek and humble shepherds of Bethlehem were visited with good
tidings of Christ's birth. These were not ordinary shepherds—they kept the
temple flock to be offered in similitude of the coming sacrifice of the Good
Shepherd.[97] For generations, their work of shepherding had prepared them
for the advent of Christ into the world. What joy they must have felt as the
"angel of the Lord" appeared unto them and said, "Fear not: for, behold, I
bring you good tidings of great joy, which shall be to all people, For unto
you is born this day in the city of David a Saviour, which is Christ the
Lord" (Luke 2:9–11).

The message and mission of the Messiah was for all people—both those
in the trials of mortality and those patiently waiting in spirit prison. The
joy of the gospel does not end at death. Christ opened the prison doors of
death and hell and made provision for the dead to be taught the gospel.

**"To proclaim the acceptable year of the Lord, and the day of
vengeance of our God; to comfort all that mourn"** (Isa. 61:2). We
see an interesting ratio between the "year" of the Lord and the "day" of
His vengeance. The day of the Lord's vengeance refers us to His Second
Coming when wickedness will be quickly swept from the face of the earth,
as if in a day. The Lord will comfort all that mourn and humbly come
unto Him. The righteous will enjoy the "acceptable year of the Lord," or
His extended and eternal blessing of peace and joy upon those who serve
Him.

**"To appoint unto them that mourn in Zion, to give unto them
beauty for ashes, the oil of joy for mourning, the garment of praise for
the spirit of heaviness; that they might be called trees of righteousness,
the planting of the Lord, that he might be glorified"** (Isa. 61:3). In the
mythology of the phoenix, we learn that this majestic bird lives a long life
and then builds a nest of twigs that ignites, consuming both nest and bird.
From this rubble, new life springs forth in a new, young bird that then
goes on to live the life cycle once again.

In biblical times, mourners would sprinkle ashes over themselves and
wear rough clothing as figurative manifestation of humility and sorrow.
Out of the "ashes" of their humility would arise new commitment to truth
and principle.

Christ suffered in Gethsemane, the location's name meaning "oil
press." In Gethsemane, He was "pressed" for the sins of the world, causing
Him to give up His precious blood. The very names *Christ* and *Messiah*
mean "Anointed One." Anointing oil symbolizes healing through Christ,

the Anointed One. As we are humble and repentant, He heals our broken hearts and replaces our sorrow with joy. Because of His victory over death and hell, we may arise from the ashes of trial and mourning and gain everlasting glory.

I Will Make an Everlasting Covenant with Them

"And they shall build the old wastes, they shall raise up the former desolations, and they shall repair the waste cities, the desolations of many generations" (Isa. 61:4). Jerusalem is an example of an "old waste" city. It has been wasted or destroyed countless times. *Jerusalem* means "to be holy," "to be pure," "the foundation of peace," or "possession of peace."98 Ironically, Jerusalem has experienced much of unholiness, impurity, and war through many centuries. At the Second Coming of Christ, Jerusalem will "rise up" from its former desolations and will stand with New Jerusalem as a significant capital of righteousness. Not only will the place be repaired, but the heartache, mourning, sorrow, and desolation of the people through the millennia will be healed through the Messiah they have so long awaited.

"And strangers shall stand and feed your flocks, and the sons of the alien shall be your plowmen and your vinedressers" (Isa. 61:5). In the gospel sense, we usually think of strangers as noncovenant Israel—those who have not accepted the gospel of Christ. Paul taught the Ephesians that although they "sometimes were far off," through conversion to the gospel they "are made nigh" and Christ "hath broken down the middle wall of partition between us. . . . Now therefore ye are no more strangers and foreigners, but fellow citizens with the Saints, and of the household of God" (Ephesians 2:13–14, 19). As the gospel goes to the world, the former oppressors of Israel will join with them and even assist them in our Savior's work of breaking down all walls of partition.

"But ye shall be named the Priests of the Lord: men shall call you the Ministers of our God: ye shall eat the riches of the Gentiles, and in their glory shall ye boast yourselves" (Isa. 61:6). Jesus taught Peter, "Feed my sheep" (John 21:17). The power and authority for feeding the sheep, or preaching the gospel to the nations, is granted from the Lord to ministers ordained with His priesthood. With the priesthood, we take the gospel to the Gentiles and bring them unto the fold, where we "eat their riches," or receive and enjoy their talents and fellowship, in our efforts to continue the spread of the gospel.

"For your shame ye shall have double; and for confusion they shall rejoice in their portion: therefore in their land they shall posses the double: everlasting joy shall be unto them" (Isa. 61:7). Israel seemed to receive more than their fair share of trouble and oppression. As they repented and came unto Christ, they would receive "double; everlasting joy" the Lord promised the repentant. To modern Israel, the Lord declared, "For since the beginning of the world have not men heard nor perceived by the ear, neither hath any eye seen, O God, besides thee, how great things thou hast prepared for him that waiteth for thee" (D&C 133:45). The everlasting joy of the Lord is just that—everlasting! Once the trial of this mortal world is done, there is no going back to the old confusion and shame of wickedness.

"For I the Lord love judgment, I hate robbery for burnt offering; and I will direct their work in truth, and I will make an everlasting covenant with them" (Isa. 61:8). God loves righteousness and hates wickedness and "robbery." We rob Him if we withhold His portion of our responsibilities, such as when we neglect to serve others or withhold our tithes and offerings. He hates false, incomplete, and pretentious sacrifices. But when we follow the course of truth and worship Him with our all, He offers us an everlasting covenant. In mortality, this everlasting covenant has fulfillment in the principles and ordinances of the gospel, including the ordinances of the temple, where we receive needed direction and make covenants that will carry us forward to eternal life. In eternity, these covenants have fulfillment in everlasting family, peace, and joy.

"And their seed shall be known among the Gentiles, and their offspring among the people: all that see them shall acknowledge them, that they are the seed which the Lord hath blessed" (Isa. 61:9). The seed of the Lord are his covenant children, of whom He is the Father of their salvation. Abinadi taught of the repentant, "For these are they whose sins he has borne; these are they for whom he has died, to redeem them from their transgressions. And now, are they not his seed?" (Mosiah 15:12). The Lord explained this great blessing to Abraham: "And I will bless them that bless thee, and curse them that curse thee; and in thee (that is, in thy Priesthood) and in thy seed . . . shall all the families of the earth be blessed, even with the blessings of the Gospel, which are the blessings salvation, even of life eternal" (Abr. 2:11).

My Soul Shall Be Joyful in My God

"I will greatly rejoice in the Lord, my soul shall be joyful in my God; for he hath clothed me with the garments of salvation, he hath covered me with the robe of righteousness, as a bridegroom decketh himself with ornaments, and as a bride adorneth herself with her

jewels" (Isa. 61:10). We need only ponder our temple worship and the symbolism thereof to drink of the deep doctrinal significance of this verse. In the temple, we are covered by the Atonement. We are symbolically clothed with "the garments of salvation." "These garments . . . suggest the garments and robes of the priesthood, as found in the temple. These earthly garments and robes, when one is purified, will be exchanged for eternal robes of glory. Jacob compared the robe of righteousness to 'being clothed with purity' (2 Ne. 9:14; Ps. 132:16; Isa. 22:21)"[99]

"For as the earth bringeth forth her bud, and as the garden causeth the things that are sown in it to spring forth; so the Lord God will cause righteousness and praise to spring forth before all the nations" (Isa. 61:11). From the seemingly small seed of a young boy's prayer in a sacred grove, the Lord has brought forth the bounteous harvest of a global Church and a message that is spreading to the entire world. If hearers of this message will be humble and obedient, the seed of the gospel will grow in their hearts until it brings them into God's presence. Alma taught the poor Zoramites, "But if ye will nourish the word . . . by your faith with great diligence, and with patience, looking forward to the fruit thereof, it shall take root; and behold it shall be a tree springing up unto everlasting life" (Alma 32:41).

It seems unfathomable that anyone would take offense at the pure gospel message. Anyone who will receive the message with joy will receive the anointing of the "oil of joy" and "be glorified" (Isa. 61:3) forever!

CHAPTER SIXTY-TWO
A CROWN OF GLORY

Isaiah continues to teach of Heavenly Father's desire to bestow eternal life, or a crown of glory, upon His children: "Thou shalt also be a crown of glory in the hand of the Lord, and a royal diadem in the hand of thy God" (Isa. 62:3).

My daughter once requested a special bracelet for Christmas. After struggling with my dismay over the price, I relented and ordered it for her. A few days later, I saw an "exact replica" for about one-sixth of the cost and ordered that one also. To me, they looked the same. In my deliberating of which to give her, I put the matter to the ultimate test—I presented both the real and the replica, side by side, to my wife. She immediately chose the real over the replica and recommended that I give the real one to my daughter. Now that many years have passed and I have seen how much this bracelet has meant to my daughter, I am grateful that I chose the real one. It was well worth the cost.

In the scriptures, we are often taught the contrast between replica and real. John the Revelator saw the throne of God in celestial glory: "And round about the throne were four and twenty seats: and upon the seats I saw four and twenty elders sitting, clothed in white raiment; and they had on their heads crowns of gold" (Rev. 4:4). When Joseph Smith inquired of the Lord as to the meaning of the twenty-four elders, he received this answer, which he then related: "We are to understand that these elders whom John saw, were elders who had been faithful in the work of the ministry and were dead; who belonged to the seven churches, and were then in the paradise of God" (D&C 77:5).

John later saw "the four and twenty elders fall down before him that sat on the throne, and worship him that liveth for ever and ever, and cast their crowns before the throne, saying, Thou art worthy, O Lord, to receive glory and honour and power: for thou hast created all things, and for thy pleasure they are and were created" (Rev. 4:10–11). The Lord's "pleasure" is to provide eternal life for His children. The crowns of gold represent eternal life in celestial glory. God's glory is expanded as more people receive His gift of eternal life.

John later saw Lucifer and his followers: "On their heads were as it were crowns *like* gold" (Rev. 9:7; emphasis added). Satan always counterfeits the things of God and tries to persuade us to choose replica crowns that merely look like gold, crowns that are not enduring. He would have us choose pride for humility, vanity for selflessness, and damnation for exaltation.

A Royal Diadem in the Hand of Thy God

Isaiah continues his valiant mission to declare the love and salvation of the Lord to Israel and His desire to grant them exaltation: "For Zion's sake will I not hold my peace, and for Jerusalem's sake I will not rest, until the righteousness thereof go forth as brightness, and the salvation thereof as a lamp that burneth" (Isa. 62:1).

As we hold up the gospel light to the nations and proclaim the message of salvation to all who will hear, many will come forward to receive the ordinances of salvation necessary to prepare them for their crowns of glory and for receiving a new name: "And the Gentiles shall see thy righteousness, and all kings thy glory: and thou shalt be called by a new name, which the mouth of the Lord shall name. Thou shalt also be a crown of glory in the hand of the Lord, and a royal diadem in the hand of thy God" (Isa. 62:2–3).

Often the Lord has given new names to individuals to signify a new level of commitment: Saul to Paul, Abram to Abraham, Jacob to Israel, and Simon Barjona to Peter. All who overcome the world, seek out the temple, and make and keep gospel covenants are to be called by a new name. John saw that he "that overcometh will I make a pillar in the temple of my God . . . and I will write upon him the name of my God, and the name of the city of my God, which is new Jerusalem . . . and I will write upon him my new name" (Rev. 3:12). Elder Bruce R. McConkie helps us understand the significance of this new name: "God's name is God. To have his name written on a person is to identify that person as a god. How can it be said more plainly? Those who gain eternal life become gods."[100]

Isaiah next invokes the marriage metaphor to teach the blessings and joy awaiting those who accept the gospel message and seek out their crown of glory: "Thou shalt no more be termed Forsaken; neither shall thy land any more be termed Desolate: but thou shalt be called Hephzi-bah, and thy land Beulah: for the Lord delighteth in thee, and thy land shall be married. For as a young man marrieth a virgin, so shall thy sons marry thee: and as the bridegroom rejoiceth over the bride, so shall thy God rejoice over thee" (Isa. 62:4–5). *Hephzibah* means "my desire is in her," and *Beulah* means "married wife" (footnotes 4c and d). The Lord desires to nurture us, the married wife, and to share eternal glory with us.

As is customary in marriage, the bride takes the name of the bridegroom. Christ's desire is to "marry" us—to bestow His name upon us and bind us to Him by covenant in eternal glory. He delights in our faith, repentance, and enduring valiance in keeping our covenants. He rejoices as we receive our crowns of gold and present them at the throne of our Heavenly Father.

Cast Up the Highway

Using further imagery to illustrate Christ's bringing His loved ones to Him, Isaiah speaks of the highway built for returning Israel and how we are to help the gatherers best travel in their return: "Go through, go through the gates; prepare ye the way of the people; cast up, cast up the highway; gather out the stones; lift up a standard for the people" (Isa. 62:10).

There is a legend of a king who constructed a great highway and designed a contest open to all comers. His only description of the challenge was to see who could best travel the highway. On the day of the event, there were many entrants—some drove chariots, some rode horses, some walked, and some ran. As each contestant came to a certain point in the highway, they were met by a huge pile of rocks and debris blocking the road. Upon their return, they complained to the king that their progress had been slowed by this annoyance.

In the late evening, a weary traveler came to the king with a bag of gold and reported that he had encountered a roadblock and had stopped to clear the path so that others could more freely pass. At the bottom of the pile of debris, he had found the bag of gold and was bringing it to the king so the rightful owner could be sought out. The king replied to the man, "You are the rightful owner. He who travels the road best is he who makes the road more passable for those who follow."

The Lord's path to eternal life is not a highway designed for luxury and convenience, whereupon we cruise along in total oblivion to those who may need assistance. It is the highway of righteousness. We, as covenant Israel, are to do all within our capacity and power to assist all who desire to make the journey. We first mark the path—we "lift up a standard." This standard is the standard of truth. Once the highway is marked, we invite all to travel. As they travel, we do all we can to remove the stumbling stones of fear, doubt, and misinformation.

In preparing the highway, our church leaders have counseled us to not keep silent but to open our mouths and proclaim gospel truth. We need not fear what our opponents may say—if they are critical of our beliefs, they may be so out of insecurity or false tradition. They too may choose to travel the path if we will sincerely invite them to come along. Isaiah said, "I have set watchmen upon thy walls, O Jerusalem, which shall never hold their peace day nor night: ye that make mention of the Lord, keep not silence. And give him no rest, till he establish, and till he make Jerusalem a praise in the earth" (Isa. 62:6–7). Just as the watchmen upon the walls were constantly alert to danger, we are to be alert and reach out to help all who are traveling the highway of holiness. We show them the way by holding up the gospel of Jesus Christ.

As we leave the world by traveling this highway of holiness, we are invited to the Lord's feast. The Lord provides "corn" and "wine" to be eaten by those who have produced it. It is not to be usurped by another: "But they that have gathered it shall eat it, and praise the Lord; and they that have brought it together shall drink it in the courts of my holiness" (Isa. 62:8–9). The feast of corn and wine reminds us of how we should be grateful for the Lord's sustenance, and while it talks about a physical feast, it also refers to a feast of spiritual things. As in ancient Israel, we eat this spiritual feast in the place of holiness designated by the Lord and not in our "own gates." "Thou mayest not eat within thy gates the tithe of thy corn, or of thy wine. . . . But thou must eat them before the Lord thy God in the place which the Lord thy God shall choose" (Deuteronomy 12:17–18). We feast spiritually through such things as prayer, scripture study, fasting, and through temple worship in the Lord's holy house.

In ancient Israel, temple worship included eating "before the Lord" a meal to include the sacrificial offering. Families often ate this meal together. This sacred mealtime was to be a time of peace, joy, and common purpose. In seeking to eat the spiritual feast of the temple, in the "courts" of His "holiness," we seek to take our families to the temple and there unite together in joy, peace, and common purpose as we seek eternal sealings and eternal life.

As we fully partake of the Lord's feast, we become His people. We attend this feast by coming out of the world, or Babylon. As we leave the world, we enter the highway of righteousness that leads us through the first principles and ordinances of the gospel, on to the higher ordinances of the temple, and then on to eternal life, the crown of glory: "Behold, the Lord hath proclaimed unto the end of the world, Say ye to the daughter of Zion, Behold, thy salvation cometh; behold, his reward is with him, and his work before him. And they shall call them, The holy people, The redeemed of the Lord: and thou shalt be called, Sought out, A city not forsaken" (Isa. 62:11–12).

CHAPTER SIXTY-THREE
THE DAY OF VENGEANCE—THE YEAR OF REDEMPTION

THE WICKED FIND THEMSELVES ON the wrong side of history and prophecy. For example, the evil Jewish leaders of Jesus's day may have imagined a majestic Messiah who would ride into their world as if on a mighty warhorse, with acclamation of royal trumpets and at the command of a terrible army that would deliver vengeance to the oppressive Romans. Christ came in triumph, of course—but in a different way. Many missed the meaning of the prophecy of Zechariah that their Savior would come proclaiming peace and salvation and riding on a lowly donkey: "Rejoice greatly, O daughter of Zion; shout, O daughter of Jerusalem: behold, thy King cometh unto thee: he is just, and having salvation; lowly, and riding upon an ass, and upon a colt the foal of an ass" (Zechariah 9:9). Christ, in fulfillment of this prophecy, entered Jerusalem riding on a donkey to shouts of hosanna from His faithful disciples at the beginning of the week in which he would triumph over the enemies of death and hell. Of this event Matthew related, "Tell ye the daughter of Sion, Behold, thy King cometh unto thee, meek, and sitting upon an ass, and a colt the foal of an ass" (Matt. 21:5).

In our latter day as we anticipate the Second Coming of Christ, some doubters seem to expect that, if He comes at all, He will come in lowliness and meekness with hardly a notice and not much more than a wink at their sins. But Christ will come at His Second Coming in majestic triumph, riding as if on a great horse, commanding a great army, and executing vengeance as He sweeps evil completely out of the world. Of the Second Coming, John the Revelator recorded, "And I saw heaven opened, and beheld a white horse; and he that sat upon him was called Faithful and True. . . . And he was clothed with a vesture dipped in blood. . . . And out of his mouth goeth a sharp sword, that with it he should smite the nations:

and he shall rule them with a rod of iron: and he treadeth the winepress of the fierceness and wrath of Almighty God. And he had on his vesture and on his thigh a name written, KING OF KINGS, AND LORD OF LORDS" (Rev. 19:11–16).

I Will Tread Them in Mine Anger

Isaiah poses two questions about the Second Coming: Who is this wearing red? And why is He wearing red? "Who is this that cometh from Edom, with dyed garments from Bozrah? this that is glorious in his apparel, travelling in the greatness of his strength? I that speak in righteousness, mighty to save. Wherefore art thou red in thine apparel, and thy garments like him that treadeth in the winefat" (Isa. 63:1–2)?

Joseph Smith was privileged to see as Isaiah saw and speak as Isaiah spoke in proclaiming the goodness of the Lord: "For since the beginning of the world have not men heard nor perceived by the ear, neither hath any eye seen, O God, besides thee, how great things thou hast prepared for him that waiteth for thee. And it shall be said: Who is this that cometh down from God in heaven with dyed garments. . . . And he will say: I am he who spake in righteousness, mighty to save. And the Lord shall be red in his apparel, and his garments like him that treadeth in the wine-vat" (D&C 133:45–48).

Isaiah refers to Edom in the opening verses of chapter 63. *Edom*, or *Esau*, means "red." When Esau was born, he "came out red, all over like an hairy garment; and they called his name Esau." Esau wickedly despised his birthright and rejected the gospel covenant: "And Esau said to Jacob, Feed me, I pray thee, with that same red pottage; for I am faint: therefore was his name called Edom. . . . Esau despised his birthright" (Gen. 25:25, 30, 34). Edom was also the name of the land where Esau dwelt: "And Jacob sent messengers before him to Esau his brother unto the land of Seir, the country of Edom" (Gen. 32:3). Edom, from the time of the Maccabees, became known as Idumea.[101]

In modern revelation, the Lord associates Idumea with the world: "The Lord shall have power over his saints, and shall reign in their midst, and shall come down in judgment upon Idumea, or the world" (D&C 1:36). Christ, therefore, "cometh from Edom," having overcome the world through the shedding of His blood.

Within the week of the Savior's triumphal entry into Jerusalem, His garments were stained red from within—from His own blood in Gethsemane. At His Second Coming, His garments will be symbolically stained red from without—from the blood of the wicked of the world upon whom He will take vengeance: "I have trodden the winepress alone; and of the people there was none with me: for I will tread them in mine anger, and trample them in my fury; and their blood shall be sprinkled upon my garments, and I will stain all my raiment. For the day of vengeance is in mine heart, and the year of my redeemed is come" (Isa. 63:3–4).

In destroying the wicked, Christ is cleansing and preparing the earth to receive its greater glory when it shall become the millennial kingdom of God. In a glorious vision Joseph Smith and Sidney Rigdon experienced, they learned of the fate of the wicked at the Second Coming: "These are they who suffer the wrath of God on earth. These are they who suffer the vengeance of eternal fire. These are they who are cast down to hell and suffer the wrath of Almighty God, until the fulness of times, when Christ shall have subdued all enemies under his feet, and shall have perfected his work; When he shall deliver up the kingdom, and present it unto the Father, spotless, saying: I have overcome and have trodden the wine-press alone, even the wine-press of the fierceness of the wrath of Almighty God" (D&C 76:104–107).

The coming of Christ is truly "the great and the terrible day" (Joel 2:31). Here again we may find hope in the ratio of the time of destruction to the time of redemption: a day to a year. "For the day of vengeance is in mine heart, and the year of my redeemed is come" (Isa. 63:4). The destruction of the wicked will be sad and terrible, but it will not take long. The salvation of the redeemed will be happy and glorious, and it will endure forever. "The cleansing will be accomplished quickly, as in a day, when the deliverance will be complete and the time of favor will begin. *The acceptable year of the Lord* subtly emphasizes his mission of saving grace. It is a long period in which the righteous enjoy the 'favor' of the Lord (NIV)."[102]

The Lovingkindnesses of the Lord

The day of redemption will bring innumerable "lovingkindnesses" to those who follow the Lord and keep His commandments. Isaiah said, "I will mention the lovingkindnesses of the Lord, and the praises of the Lord, according to all that the Lord hath bestowed on us, and the great goodness toward the house of Israel, which he hath bestowed on them according to his mercies, and according to the multitude of his lovingkindnesses. For he said, Surely they are my people, children that will not lie: so he was their Saviour" (Isa. 63:7–8).

Christ was a willing sacrifice, submitting His own desire to the will of the Father. Through His Atonement—through the staining of His garments with the blood of His suffering—He demonstrated perfect empathy and love for all of Father's children: "In all their affliction he was afflicted, and the angel of his presence saved them: in his love and in his pity he redeemed them; and he bare them, and carried them all the days of old" (Isa. 63:9). To the Nephites, Christ said, "And behold, I am the light and the life of the world; and I have drunk out of that bitter cup which the Father hath given me, and have glorified the Father in taking upon me the sins of the world, in the which I have suffered the will of the Father in all things from the beginning" (3 Ne. 11:11).

Isaiah recalls the lovingkindnesses of the Lord in delivering Israel from the pursuing pharoah: "Then he remembered the days of old, Moses, and his people, saying, Where is he that brought them up out of the sea with the shepherd of his flock? . . . That led them by the right hand of Moses with his glorious arm, dividing the water before them to make himself an everlasting name?" (Isa. 63:11–12). He that brought them safely out of Egypt is Christ, who brings all who trust in Him safely out of the world.

The Habitation of Thy Holiness

Isaiah now begins his great Intercessory Prayer, which continues through the next chapter. (After a brief introduction here, we will address it more in depth in chapter 64.)

"Look down from heaven, and behold from the habitation of thy holiness and of thy glory: where is thy zeal and thy strength, the sounding of thy bowels and of thy mercies toward me? are they restrained?" (Isa. 63:15). Where is the habitation of God's holiness? "The earthly temple is God's dwelling place on earth; the heavenly temple is his habitation in heaven."[103] The Atonement connects heaven and earth. We make this connection through living and keeping the principles and ordinances of the gospel and through the receipt of our temple endowment.

Isaiah's plea to know if the Lord's mercy had been restrained is similar to the earlier plea of Israel to know if the Lord had forsaken them. The answer is an emphatic "No!" and is evidenced by His providing the perfect Atonement. We may trust Jehovah in all things. He will always remember us. He is our Savior and our Intercessor.

CHAPTER SIXTY-FOUR
WE ARE THE CLAY, AND THOU OUR POTTER

IN HIS FIRST GENERAL CONFERENCE as the fourteenth president of the Church, President Howard W. Hunter reiterated the message he had delivered at the press conference at the time of his call: "I invite the Latter-day Saints to look to the temple of the Lord as the great symbol of your membership. It is the deepest desire of my heart to have every member of the Church worthy to enter the temple. It would please the Lord if every adult member would be worthy of—and carry—a current temple recommend. The things that we must do and not do to be worthy of a temple recommend are the very things that ensure we will be happy as individuals and as families."[104]

The temple was also the great symbol of the ancient Israelites. Each year, the presiding high priest would enter the holy of holies, the most sacred place in the temple. He would perform certain rites in connection with the Day of Atonement. He would offer animal sacrifices in similitude of the coming Atonement of Christ. The high priest performed his duties in the symbolic role of mediator—intercessor with the Lord in behalf of the children of Israel. Today, rather than the performing of animal sacrifices, we partake of the sacrament in remembrance of the Atonement.

After instituting the sacrament at His final Passover feast and before His prayer and suffering in Gethsemane, Christ, as the Great High Priest and Intercessor, offered what has become known as His Intercessory Prayer in behalf of His Apostles and all who would believe on Him through them. A helpful outline of this marvelous prayer is as follows:

> In the first part (see John 17:1–3), Jesus offered himself as the great sacrifice. His hour had come.
>
> The next part of the prayer (see John 17:4–19) was a reverent report to the Father of his mortal mission.

In the last part (see John 17:20–26) of his prayer, Jesus interceded not only for the eleven apostles present, but for all who shall believe on Jesus "through their word," in order that all would come to a perfect unity, which unity invested Christ in them as Christ is in the Father. Thus all would be perfect in unity, and the world would believe that the Father had sent his Son.[105]

O Lord, Thou Art Our Father

As Isaiah now approaches the end of his ministry and testimony, he offers what has become known as his intercessory prayer. In this prayer, he speaks directly to the Lord for himself and for all of Israel. Isaiah's intercessory prayer is found in chapters 63:15 through 64:12. The Lord's response to the prayer is the context of chapters 65 and 66, the two concluding chapters of the book. In this prayer, Isaiah becomes, in a sense, a type for Christ, who intercedes with the Father in our behalf.

Isaiah begins by pleading with the Lord to look down from heaven and "sound" His feelings about Israel. "Look down from heaven, and behold from the habitation of thy holiness and of thy glory: where is thy zeal and thy strength, the sounding of thy bowels and of thy mercies toward me? are they restrained?" (Isa. 63:15). *To sound*, as a verb, is to measure or ascertain the depth of water by means of a line or pole to detect sound waves. Isaiah is petitioning the Lord to sound the depths of His bowels—of His inner feelings of mercy and compassion, as if to say, "Lord, hast thou forgotten us? Dost thou feel mercy for us? Wilt thou please use thy strength to help us?"

Isaiah continues: "O Lord, why hast thou made us to err from thy ways, and hardened our heart from thy fear? Return for thy servants' sake, the tribes of thine inheritance" (Isa. 63:17). Joseph Smith offered helpful correction to this verse: "O Lord, why hast thou suffered us to err from thy ways, and to harden our heart from thy fear" (JST, Isa. 63:17). The Lord does not harden hearts. He pleads for softened hearts and waits upon His people until they return to Him in humility and repentance.

Isaiah, in prophetic power, then laments the destruction of the temple, an event yet future to him by more than one hundred years at the hands of the Babylonians—the temple was destroyed in 587 B.C.: "The people of thy holiness have possessed it but a little while: our adversaries have trodden down thy sanctuary" (Isa. 63:18).

To lose the temple would be to lose a great symbol of Israel's connection to Heavenly Father. Christ, in His role as our intercessor and mediator, becomes the father of our salvation: "For these are they whose sins he has borne; these are they for whom he has died, to redeem them from their transgressions. And now, are they not his seed?" (Mosiah 15:12). God the Father is the father of our spirits. Christ the Son is the father of our salvation. We, through repentance and baptism, become the seed, or children, of Christ.

This doctrine of the role of Christ as redeemer and father of our salvation has been taught throughout Isaiah's writings and now becomes part of the petition of his intercessory prayer: "Doubtless, thou art our father, though Abraham be ignorant of us, and Israel acknowledge us not: thou, O Lord, art our father, our redeemer; thy name is from everlasting. . . . We are thine: thou never barest rule over them; they were not called by thy name. . . . But now, O Lord, thou art our father; we are the clay, and thou our potter; and we all are the work of thy hand" (Isa. 63:16, 19; 64:8). Our Heavenly Father desires to grant unto us the type of life He has. His Son, like a potter with clay, molds and shapes our lives so that we will be worthy of this eternal life.

Our Savior, in His Intercessory Prayer, taught these same doctrines:

> And this is life eternal, that they might know thee the only true God, and Jesus Christ, whom thou hast sent. . . . I have manifested thy name unto the men which thou gavest me out of the world: thine they were, and thou gavest them me. . . . Holy Father, keep through thine own name those whom thou hast given me, that they may be one, as we are. . . . That they all may be one; as thou, Father, art in me, and I in thee, that they also may be one in us. . . . that they may be made perfect. (John 17:3, 6, 11, 21, 23)

Heavenly Father desires to bless us with all that He has and provides a Savior for us to bring us unto Him. Isaiah acknowledges the goodness of the Lord and the greatness of His bounty in blessing us with eternal life: "For since the beginning of the world men have not heard, nor perceived by the ear, neither hath the eye seen, O God, beside thee, what he hath prepared for him that waiteth for him" (Isa. 64:4). In our times of struggle and sorrow, we may often return to these simple truths of the scriptures to find strength and encouragement to go forward and to keep life in proper perspective.

That the Mountains Might Flow Down at Thy Presence

How do we feel about the Second Coming of Christ? Are we anxious for Him to come? Are we nervous about His Coming? Are we prepared? I suppose like many, I think, *Well, there are things I would like to do yet.* But on the other hand, sometimes I think the world can't get much worse, and then some new atrocity comes along to prompt my wish, *Please come now and put the world right!*

Isaiah, in his prayer, offers a plea for Christ to come and make things right: "Oh that thou wouldest rend the heavens, that thou wouldest come down, that the mountains might flow down at thy presence, As when the melting fire burneth, the fire causeth the waters to boil, to make thy name known to thine adversaries, that the nations may tremble at thy presence! When thou didst terrible things which we looked not for, thou camest down, the mountains flowed down at thy presence" (Isa. 64:1–3). Gratefully, the Lord will come and put the world right. He will destroy the mountains of man: the pride of the world, the idolatry, the false worship, the war, the terror, and all that is evil.

Toward the end of the vision recorded by John the Revelator, the Lord repeatedly told him, "Behold, I come quickly. . . . And, behold, I come quickly. . . . Surely I come quickly." John, who has continued his work on the earth since the mortal ministry of the Savior and who has had the heavens opened and has seen as God sees, certainly has proper perspective about the Second Coming. He responded simply, "Even so, come, Lord Jesus" (Rev. 22:7, 12, 20).

Isaiah and John—these two great and powerful witnesses of Christ—certainly qualify to offer us hope and joy in anticipating the Second Coming. To their offering we also add the protective promise of Nephi: "Wherefore, he will preserve the righteous by his power, even if it so be that the fulness of his wrath must come, and the righteous be preserved, even unto the destruction of their enemies by fire. Wherefore, the righteous need not fear; for thus saith the prophet, they shall be saved, even if it so be by fire" (1 Ne. 22:17).

Our Holy and Beautiful House

Isaiah continues his plea for Israel to acknowledge their sins and declares that there is hope for redemption: "Thou meetest him that rejoiceth and worketh righteousness, those that remember thee in thy ways: behold, thou art wroth; for we have sinned: in those is continuance, and we shall be saved. But we are all as an unclean thing, and all our righteousnesses are as filthy rags; and we all do fade as a leaf; and our iniquities, like the wind, have taken us away" (Isa. 64:5–6).

From the dark depths of the Liberty Jail, Joseph Smith petitioned the Lord, "Remember thy suffering saints, O our God; and thy servants will rejoice in thy name forever" (D&C 121:6). Of course, Joseph and Isaiah understood, as oft repeated in scripture, that the forgetting of loved ones and of covenants made is not of the Lord but rather a character trait of His wayward children. He always remembers and ever waits for the requisite humility and repentance of the wanderers that He might bring them into the full covering shadow of His Atonement.

Isaiah continues by speaking of Israel's sorrow for their sins and for the pending loss of their temple: "Be not wroth very sore, O Lord, neither remember iniquity for ever: behold, see, we beseech thee, we are all thy people. . . . Our holy and beautiful house, where our fathers praised thee, is burned up with fire: and all our pleasant things are laid waste" (Isa. 64:9, 11).

Isaiah concludes his prayer of intercession with some sincere and yearning questions: "Wilt thou refrain thyself for these things, O Lord? wilt thou hold thy peace, and afflict us very sore?" (Isa. 64:12). The Lord, in sweet and tender mercy, now answers His prophet's questions in the concluding two chapters of the book.

CHAPTER SIXTY-FIVE
AN INHERITOR OF MY MOUNTAINS

ONE OF THE GREAT DOCTRINES of the gospel is what we call the oath and covenant of the priesthood. If we receive the priesthood of God, magnify our callings therein, and obey the commandments, God will give us the type of life that He enjoys. Our Savior said, "He that receiveth my Father, receiveth my Father's kingdom; therefore all that my Father hath shall be given unto him" (D&C 84:38).

When I was called to serve as our stake executive secretary, Elder Carlos E. Asay visited our stake conference on the first Saturday of my service. In our stake presidency meeting, he asked us to introduce ourselves. Since I had not yet been sustained or set apart, I replied, "I am the acting executive secretary," to which he replied, "Well, when are you going to stop acting and go to work?" I think he was joking—somewhat.

Elder Asay taught us about the oath and covenant of the priesthood. He illustrated the doctrine with a story that captured my heart and has stayed with me these many years. A few years later, he shared the story in general conference. He told of a missionary who was the only son of a very wealthy man. The work was difficult, and the young man grew discouraged and wavered in his faith and commitment. He announced to his mission president that he was terminating his mission and going home. After the president failed to persuade him to stay and recommit, he notified the boy's father. The father requested a personal session with his son and flew directly to the mission. The father told the son, "My son, I have lived for the day when you would serve a full-time mission. I did so because I love you and I love God. And I know that there is no work more essential than that of teaching truth to the peoples of the world." The son was humbled and replied, "Dad, I didn't realize that a mission meant so much to you." The father answered, "It means everything to me. All my life I have worked and saved with one person in mind: you. And my goal has been to provide you a decent inheritance. . . . My son, my only heir, if you will be faithful in this calling and prove yourself worthy in every respect, all that I possess will be yours." After some emotion and deliberation, the son replied, "I will stay."[106] He did stay and completed a successful mission.

To gain eternal life, we need to drink deeply of the doctrines of salvation and go forward with faith and determination in living and teaching the gospel. We need to stop acting below our potential and go to work.

They That Forget My Holy Mountain

In response to Isaiah's pleading questions—"Wilt thou refrain thyself for these things, O Lord? wilt thou hold thy peace, and afflict us very sore?" (Isa. 64:12)—the Lord offers a review of how Israel had rejected Him and His efforts to get them to step up to their full potential. He then recounts to them their great promise as potential heirs of eternal life if they will but repent, accept His gospel, and go to work in His kingdom.

Israel, in their time of distress and sorrow, turned to the Lord. He replied, "I am sought of them that asked not for me; I am found of them that sought me not: I said, Behold me, behold me, unto a nation that was not called by my name." It is as if He is saying, "So now you seek me!—why not sooner?" Israel had been called to take upon them the name of Christ but had refused to be embraced by His outstretched arms: "I have spread out my hands all the day unto a rebellious people, which walketh in a way that was not good, after their own thoughts" (Isa. 65:1–2).

Israel had followed the idolatry of their neighbors: "A people that provoketh me to anger continually to my face; that sacrificeth in gardens, and burneth incense upon altars of brick. . . . which eat swine's flesh, and broth of abominable things is in their vessels" (Isa. 65:3–4). In their pride, they had concocted their own false religion and false moral standards. Like the Zoramites of the Book of Mormon who had deluded themselves into thinking that God had "elected us to be thy holy children" (Alma 31:16), Israel also declared, "For I am holier than thou" (Isa. 65:5).

The Lord answered their false worship: "These are a smoke in my nose, a fire that burneth all the day. Behold, it is written before me: I will not keep silence, but will recompense, even recompense into their bosom, Your iniquities, and the iniquities of your fathers together, saith the Lord, which have burned incense upon the mountains, and blasphemed me upon the hills: therefore will I measure their former work into their bosom" (Isa. 65:5–7).

In a figurative sense, by burning "incense upon the mountains," Israel had climbed the wrong mountain—they had sought the mountains of idolatry rather than the mountain of the Lord. Those who mistake one for the other suffer the Lord's justice: "But ye are they that forsake the Lord, that forget my holy mountain. . . . Therefore will I number you to the sword, and ye shall all bow down to the slaughter: because when I called, ye did not answer; when I spake, ye did not hear; but did evil before mine eyes, and did choose that wherein I delighted not. Therefore thus saith the Lord God, Behold, my servants shall eat, but ye shall be hungry: behold, my servants shall drink, but ye shall be thirsty: behold, my servants shall rejoice, but ye shall be ashamed: Behold, my servants shall sing for joy of heart, but ye shall cry for sorrow of heart, and shall howl for vexation of spirit" (Isa. 65:11–14).

A friend of mine had a thoughtful saying: "We can never seem to get enough of what we do not need." That is how addiction works. A person does not *need* illegal, harmful drugs, but once he partakes, he soon can't seem to get enough and will trade all in his power to get his fix. Even good things like wholesome food and drink, when overindulged, become detrimental to the natural processes and functions of the body. Idolatry and all of its attendant perversions and addictions is the same—it harms and does not nourish. The partaker remains hungry and thirsty for more.

An Inheritor of My Mountains

The Lord now declares the joyous blessings He has prepared for those who will come unto Him, repent of their sins, and follow His ways: "As the new wine is found in the cluster" or as wheat among tares, He gleans and gathers and brings all who will come to His mountain: "And I will bring forth a seed out of Jacob, and out of Judah an inheritor of my mountains: and mine elect shall inherit it, and my servants shall dwell there" (Isa. 65:8–9). To inherit His mountain is to come unto Him and receive the blessings of His atoning sacrifice. As we do so, we may inherit the blessings of the temple, where we are given an endowment to prepare us to become potential heirs of all that the Father has.

In contemplation of the joy and promise of eternal life, consider a difficult time of your life that is now long past. For example, I recall the rigors of my military boot camp—the spiritual and physical demands. As I look back now, the unpleasant has mostly taken back stage to the positive, life-disciplining lessons I learned. As we endure the trials of our fallen world and come faithfully to the Lord through our covenant keeping, "the former troubles are forgotten. . . . For, behold, I create new heavens and a new earth: and the former shall not be remembered, nor come to mind. But be ye glad and rejoice for ever in that which I create: for, behold, I create Jerusalem a rejoicing, and her people a joy. And I will rejoice in Jerusalem, and joy in my people: and the voice of weeping shall be no more heard in her, nor the voice of crying" (Isa. 65:16–19).

For the repentant, past sins are forgotten: "Behold, he who has repented of his sins, the same is forgiven, and I, the Lord, remember them no more" (D&C 58:42). For the abused and the oppressed, all past sorrows will be healed, "and God shall wipe away all tears from their eyes" (Rev. 7:17). The old heartaches from physical and spiritual death will be gone forever: "And in that day Satan shall not have power to tempt any man. And there shall be no sorrow because there is no death" (D&C 101:28–29).

In the coming millennial and celestial days, the heirs of God will enjoy a fullness of life and a completeness of joy. The frustrations and limitations of aging will be no more. The foibles of youth and the sorrow of untimely death will vanish: "There shall be no more thence an infant of days, nor an old man that hath not filled his days: for the child shall die an hundred years old" (Isa. 65:20). This is confirmed in modern revelation: "In that day an infant shall not die until he is old; and his life shall be as the age of a tree; And when he dies he shall not sleep, that is to say in the earth, but shall be changed in the twinkling of an eye, and shall be caught up, and his rest shall be glorious" (D&C 101:30–31).

The blessings of a godlike life include complete fulfillment in the labors of our minds and hands. No longer will greedy warlords usurp the freedoms and resources of the poor. Oppressive governments wielding unjust laws will never again be able to rob the productivity of the diligent for their own unholy causes. Excessive taxes to pay for the evils of society will no longer be required: "And they shall build houses, and inhabit them; and they shall plant vineyards, and eat the fruit of them. They shall not build, and another inhabit; they shall not plant, and another eat: for as the days of a tree are the days of my people, and mine elect shall long enjoy the work of their hands. They shall not labour in vain nor bring forth for trouble; for they are the seed of the blessed of the Lord, and their offspring with them" (Isa. 65:21–23).

In exalted life, we will find that our every desire will be granted—for we will desire, as taught by Nephi, only the good: "Yea, my God will give me, if I ask not amiss" (2 Ne. 4:35). Joseph Smith learned, "And in that day whatsoever any man shall ask, it shall be given unto him" (D&C 101:27). The Lord said to Isaiah, "And it shall come to pass, that before they call, I will answer; and while they are yet speaking, I will hear" (Isa. 65:24).

In the millennial day and the celestial life, all creatures will dwell in perfect harmony and peace. The enmity and violence of man against man, beast against man, man against beast, and beast against beast will be no more: "And in that day the enmity of man, and the enmity of beasts, yea, the enmity of all flesh, shall cease from before my face" (D&C 101:26). Of this time, Isaiah said, "The wolf and the lamb shall feed together, and the lion shall eat straw like the bullock: and dust shall be the serpent's meat. They shall not hurt nor destroy in all my holy mountain, saith the Lord" (Isa. 65:25).

As I remember and consider Elder Asay's question to me of so long ago, I realize how profound it was. To find true happiness, we need to stop acting and go to work. If we are plagued by pride or by the temptation to play a role that is not the role of true sons and daughters of God, we need to change and come unto Him in humble repentance. As we do so, He will gather us to His home—to His holy mountain—to His temple. Eternal life is a templelike life, only more grand than we mere mortals can imagine, for the complete sphere of our eternal habitation becomes as the temple.

CHAPTER SIXTY-SIX
AN OFFERING UNTO THE LORD IN MY HOLY MOUNTAIN

As we tune in to our daily news, we mourn at reports of exiles and refugees from the "wars and rumors of wars" that are occurring around the world in fulfillment of prophecy that "the whole earth shall be in commotion" (D&C 45:26). I will describe two points of exile that I have visited—Masada and the Mississippi River—and will use them as an illustration to help us understand the teachings of this final chapter of Isaiah.

Years ago while visiting Israel, we toured Masada, an isolated rock plateau in the Judean desert overlooking the Dead Sea. Long ago, a group of about a thousand Jewish rebels barricaded themselves on top of Masada, where they employed an elaborate system of granaries and water cisterns in provision against the pending Roman invasion of A.D. 70. When the Romans came, they built a rampart to access the fortress. (There is historic disagreement about the fate of the Jews with the invasion of the Romans—some accounts suggest a suicide pact wherein most died). On our visit, our guide told us that modern soldiers of the Israeli army go to Masada and swear an oath of allegiance that "Masada will not fall again." The oath implies that, unlike with the holocaust and the siege of Masada, the Jews will never again be backed into a corner with no place to go for refuge and safety.

The story of Masada gives us an understanding of the zeal with which the Jews have struggled to secure a free state. We are also reminded that our Heavenly Father loves all of His children. He desires that the Israelis, the Palestinians, and all people have freedom and live in peace and harmony—a condition that continues to escape the nations of our world but will come in the millennial day during the reign of Christ: "He inviteth them all to come unto him and partake of his goodness; and he denieth none that come unto him, black and white, bond and free, male and female; and he remembereth the heathen; and all are alike unto God, both Jew and Gentile" (2 Ne. 26:33).

Many times, I have stood at the edge of the Mississippi River in Nauvoo and tried to imagine the plight and faith of the oppressed refugees who were fleeing their beautiful temple and community for a place in the great unknown. Their desire had been to worship their God in peace and security and to bless the world by the message of the restored gospel. Satan, sensing the grandeur of their mission, had stirred up the hearts of conspiring souls to oppose them and to drive them out. But they would not be defeated. Although they had been driven from Nauvoo, they eventually succeeded in establishing a base for the proclamation of the gospel throughout the world. They battled mud, cold, heat, hunger, sickness, and death to win a free land where they could worship according to their conscience and build a new temple to their God. From this new land and new temple in the West, the gospel would go to the world. Many temples would be built. Scattered Israel would continue to be gathered, including the Jews, who would someday come to the knowledge of their true Redeemer.

I Will Choose Their Delusions

Isaiah concludes his message with one of the themes evident in all of his writing: God will put down idolatry and slay the wicked. He will invite Israel to repent and return to their Savior, the foundation of their faith, and receive the blessings of eternal life through the ordinances of the gospel.

The Lord condemns those who perform false temple worship and sacrifice. This apostate sacrifice does them about as much good as if they were to kill a dog or a man or a forbidden swine, offerings that were not acceptable to the Lord: "He that killeth an ox is as if he slew a man; he that sacrificeth a lamb, as if he cut off a dog's neck; he that offereth an oblation, as if he offered swine's blood; he that burneth incense, as if he blessed an idol. Yea, they have chosen their own ways, and their soul delighteth in their abominations" (Isa. 66:3). For their false offerings, the Lord would "respond to their evils and punish them": "I will choose their delusions, and will bring fears upon them; because when I called, none did answer; when I spake, they did not hear" (Isa. 66:4; footnote 4a).

With the Second Coming will come the final destruction of the wicked. Those who change the laws of God to match their own lusts and perversions and attempt to "sanctify themselves" with their own apostate worship will suffer death: "For, behold, the Lord will come with fire, and with his chariots like a whirlwind, to render his anger with fury, and his rebuke with flames of fire. For by fire and by his sword will the Lord plead with all flesh: and the slain of the Lord shall be many. They that sanctify themselves, and purify themselves in the gardens behind one tree in the midst, eating swine's flesh, and the abomination, and the mouse, shall be consumed together, saith the Lord" (Isa. 66:15–17).

What a shocking and horrible thought it is to our mortal minds to imagine hordes of the dead piled up in a sweeping purge of the earth. Our peace and understanding come in remembering the plan of God. He loves all. Even in death, all people remain under His plan and keeping. Death comes to all, and the manner of our death does not determine the manner of our afterlife. All souls who have ever lived will receive a full and complete opportunity to hear and accept gospel truth—some here and some in the world of spirits. So, we go forward, trusting in the Lord and His methods and await the day when we will have a full understanding of all things.

Where is the House That Ye Build unto Me?

The Lord asks questions central to the plan and purpose of mortal life: "Thus saith the Lord, The heaven is my throne, and the earth is my footstool: where is the house that ye build unto me? and where is the place of my rest?" (Isa. 66:1). God rules from heaven and is always mindful of earth. All things on earth are subject to Him and His governance. He has directed prophets of the ages to build temples on the earth that he may dwell therein. King Solomon said, "But will God indeed dwell on the earth? behold, the heaven and heaven of heavens cannot contain thee; how much less this house that I have builded?" (1 Kgs. 8:27). The Lord's purposes are made manifest in earthly temples—but His work spans heaven and earth and time and eternity and is not confined to a physical structure. The purpose of the temple is to bring us beyond the temple—to the eternal life offered us through our Heavenly Father and our Savior.

The blessings of eternity are not offered to a select few but are available to all who will humbly seek them. Earthly riches, prestige, and power are not the qualifiers for the Lord's blessings. He seeks after those who are humble and provides chastisement when we need to be humbled: "For all those things hath mine hand made, and all those things have been, saith the Lord: but to this man will I look, even to him that is poor and of a contrite spirit, and trembleth at my word" (Isa. 66:2).

The temple is, in a sense, the Lord's command post. From the temple, He speaks His messages of sorrow to the proud and joy to the repentant: "Hear the word of the Lord, ye that tremble at his word; Your brethren that hated you, that cast you out for my name's sake, said, Let the Lord be glorified: but he shall appear to your joy, and they shall be ashamed. A voice of noise from the city, a voice from the temple, a voice of the Lord that rendereth recompense to his enemies" (Isa. 66:5–6).

Shall a Nation Be Born at Once?

It will be fascinating to someday see as God sees and understand how the physical movement of nations and peoples relates to their spiritual movement and conversion to the gospel. The nation of Israel, for example, has struggled to build a free country as a refuge from persecution and oppression. However, their spiritual gathering is yet future. The chapter heading of Isaiah 66 states, "At the Second Coming, Israel, as a nation, shall be born in a day."

The Book of Mormon teaches, "Nevertheless, the Lord will be merciful unto them, that when they shall come to the knowledge of their Redeemer, they shall be gathered together again to the lands of their inheritance" (2 Ne. 6:11). Again from the Book of Mormon we read, "And now, my beloved brethren, I have read these things that ye might know concerning the covenants of the Lord that he has covenanted with all the house of Israel—That he has spoken unto the Jews, by the mouth of his holy prophets, even from the beginning down, from generation to generation, until the time comes that they shall be restored to the true church and fold of God; when they shall be gathered home to the lands of their inheritance, and shall be established in all their lands of promise" (2 Ne. 9:1–2).

Isaiah said, "Before she travailed, she brought forth; before her pain came, she was delivered of a man child. Who hath heard such a thing? who hath seen such things? Shall the earth be made to bring forth in one day? or shall a nation be born at once? For as soon as Zion travailed, she brought forth her children" (Isa. 66:7–8). Zion is travailing to be born. When Christ comes, the birth of Zion will be quickly completed, and the spiritual gathering will go forward with haste.

We who are the children of the exiles who crossed the Mississippi are to gather the relatives of the exiles who sought safety at Masada, as well as all scattered people of the earth, to the gospel and to the temple. In this happy day of gathering, those who were scattered are to be tenderly nourished and comforted and will receive the joy and peace of the restored gospel: "Rejoice ye with Jerusalem, and be glad with her, all ye that love her: rejoice for joy with her, all ye that mourn for her: That ye may suck, and be satisfied with the breasts of her consolations; that ye may milk out, and be delighted with the abundance of her glory. For thus saith the Lord, Behold, I will extend peace to her like a river, and the glory of the Gentiles like a flowing stream: then shall she suck, ye shall be borne upon her sides, and be dandled upon her knees" (Isa. 66:10–12).

To My Holy Mountain

Isaiah continues his prophetic vision of all nations gathering to the Lord. Our study now ends where it began—with the Lord gathering the nations of the earth to Him and to His temple, to His holy mountain: "For I know their works and their thoughts: it shall come, that I will gather all nations and tongues; and they shall come, and see my glory. . . . and they shall declare my glory among the Gentiles. And they shall bring all your brethren for an offering unto the Lord out of all nations upon horses, and in chariots, and in litters, and upon mules, and upon swift beasts, to my holy mountain Jerusalem, saith the Lord, as the children of Israel bring an offering in a clean vessel into the house of the Lord" (Isa. 66:18–20).

With all wickedness swept from the earth, and with the righteous gathering to Zion, we enter the promised paradise. "We believe . . . that Christ will reign personally upon the earth; and, that the earth will be renewed and receive its paradisiacal glory" (A of F 1:10). During this millennial reign of the Savior, the temples throughout the world will be ablaze with the work and glory of the Lord. This millennial day will be a preparatory day for the time when this earth and its righteous inhabitants will go forward, sealed as families, to receive the celestial glory so long promised: "For as the new heavens and the new earth, which I will make, shall remain before me, saith the Lord, so shall your seed and your name remain. And it shall come to pass, that from one new moon to another, and from one sabbath to another, shall all flesh come to worship before me, saith the Lord" (Isa. 66:22–23).

What a glorious future for those who accept and follow the Lord!

EPILOGUE

As I was finishing my thoughts and writings on the book of Isaiah, I ran across an old term paper I wrote about three decades ago in an inservice class one of my most respected teachers taught. I had entitled the paper "Covenant People in Modern Times: What It Means to Be a Recipient of the Abrahamic Covenant." I had written it in the format of what I called a "spiritual will" to my children—the things I would wish for them as they live out their lives as children of the covenant.

I was fascinated to discover that I had not cited a single verse from Isaiah. I think I was perhaps intimidated by his writings back then. This seems so strange in light of the fact that I now have so much love for his writings. Now I can hardly imagine writing or speaking about the Lord's everlasting covenant with Israel without thinking of Isaiah. I love the writings of Isaiah! I look forward to a continued lifetime of pondering his inspired testimony.

In conclusion, I desire to share with you my testimony that I know that Jesus Christ is the divine Son of God and that He has restored His gospel and Church on the earth today. I testify that in this the last dispensation, we have been and are guided by living prophets who, like Isaiah, will keep us on the right path to happiness and eternal life.

Although I did not cite Isaiah in my term paper of long ago, the themes I developed and the truths I have taught to my children then and now are consistent with the words and teachings of Isaiah. Eternal truth is just that—eternal. It is not diminished but is only enhanced by time and experience. Truth resonates with the soul. I encourage you, my readers, to continue to seek truth. I hope and pray that the writings of Isaiah will be a part of your lifetime search for truth. I hope and pray that what I have written here will enhance your understanding of truth and assist you in your forward quest.

My sincere desire for my children, my grandchildren, and for you, my readers, is that you will live to receive the Lord's gift of eternal life. I pray that we may keep the temple firmly in our hearts and minds as the great symbol of our faith and that we will worship there often so we can focus our lives on our Savior and on the great plan of our Heavenly Father. I pray that we may all press forward on the gospel path and someday be united in faith and fellowship in the "new heavens and the new earth" (Isa. 66:22) and that we may enjoy the eternal felicity provided us by the gospel of Jesus Christ.

May you continue to love and learn the words of Isaiah and of all prophets!

"For great are the words of Isaiah" (3 Ne. 23:1).

APPENDIX A
ISAIAH IN THE BOOK OF MORMON

SINCE THE BOOK OF MORMON is positioned as such a mainstay of our personal lifelong gospel study, and since it contains such a large portion of the writings of Isaiah, I feel that a few observations about Isaiah and the Book of Mormon are in order.

This book follows the chapter-by-chapter text of Isaiah in the King James Bible while making reference to the Book of Mormon. About one-third of the biblical record of Isaiah is quoted in the Book of Mormon. Although some of the Book of Mormon quotations are verbatim, many, perhaps one-half of the quotations, contain some changes. Many of the changes are quite significant. It is helpful to consider that the Isaiah quotations in the Book of Mormon came from the brass plates of Laban and thus offer us an even more pure record than does the King James version since "many plain and precious things [were] taken away from the book" (1 Ne. 13:28) after the time of Christ's ministry.

It is significant to note that three major Book of Mormon prophets— Nephi, Jacob, and Abinadi—plus the Savior Himself, quoted extensively from Isaiah. Also of important consideration is that the Savior and each of these prophets offer significant doctrinal commentary on the Isaiah writings they quote. The Isaiah quotations found in the Book of Mormon all center on Christ: His mortal ministry and Second Coming, His gathering of Israel, and His dealings with Israel in the making and keeping of gospel covenants.

As an example of the importance of the Isaiah quotations in the Book of Mormon, we look to the Savior's ministry among the Nephites wherein He quotes to them Isaiah chapter 54. In this quotation, He is teaching the significance of the gathering of Israel to the stakes of Zion in the latter days. As we assist in the gathering, we are counseled, "Enlarge the place of thy tent, and let them stretch forth the curtains of thy habitations; spare not, lengthen thy cords and strengthen thy stakes. . . . with everlasting kindness will I have mercy on thee. . . . For the mountains shall depart and the hills be removed, but my kindness shall not depart from thee, neither shall the covenant of my peace be removed" (3 Ne. 22:2, 8, 10).

In His commentary on these Isaiah verses, the Savior further expounds on the gathering of Israel: "And behold, this is the thing which I will give unto you for a sign—for verily I say unto you that when these things which I declare unto you . . . shall be made known unto the Gentiles. . . . that they may repent and come unto me and be baptized in my name and know of the true points of my doctrine, that they may be numbered among my people, O House of Israel" (3 Ne. 21:2, 6). (The phrase "these things which I declare unto you" refers to the Book of Mormon [see 3 Nephi 21:chapter heading].)

We are to enlarge the stakes of Zion in accommodation of the gathering of Israel. To gather Israel, we must be able to teach them the true points of the doctrine of Christ. We find such true points of doctrine in the Book of Mormon: Another Testament of Jesus Christ. The Book of Mormon is the keystone of our religion and an important key to the gathering of Israel. It is significant that immediately after the Savior quoted and interpreted Isaiah, He gave the command, "And now, behold, I say unto you, that ye ought to search these things. Yea, a commandment I give unto you that ye search these things diligently; for great are the words of Isaiah" (3 Ne. 23:1). The writings of Isaiah and the teachings of the Book of Mormon go hand in hand. Both contain the words of Christ pertinent to the gathering of Israel.

APPENDIX B
THE CONTEXT OF ISAIAH—THE HOUSE OF ISRAEL

A BASIC UNDERSTANDING OF THE house of Israel is essential to our understanding the prophecies of Isaiah. Hopefully, a few brief comments about the past, present, and future of the house of Israel will be helpful to our study of Isaiah.

Past: From the Joseph Smith Translation of the Bible, we read, "And it came to pass, that Abram fell on his face, and called upon the name of the Lord. And God talked with him, saying, My people have gone astray from my precepts, and have not kept mine ordinances, which I gave unto their fathers" (JST, Gen. 17:3–4).

In solution to the straying of the people from the Lord's precepts and their breaking of the holy ordinances, the Lord established His plan and covenant with Abraham: "Neither shall thy name any more be called Abram, but thy name shall be Abraham; for a father of many nations have I made thee. And I will make thee exceeding fruitful, and I will make nations of thee, and kings shall come out of thee. And I will establish my covenant between me and thee and thy seed after thee in their generations for an everlasting covenant, to be a God unto thee, and to thy seed after thee" (Gen. 17:5–7).

The establishment of the covenant with Abraham, and the story of how he and his descendants interact with this covenant, has a long and rich history. We recall the passion and drama of the passing of the birthright through Isaac, Jacob (Israel), and Joseph. We revere valiant Joseph as he became a temporal savior for his extended family during their sojourn in Egypt. We recall the miracles of Moses and Aaron as they brought the people out of bondage and into the Lord's tutoring of them in the Sinai. We admire the courage and leadership of Joshua as he led them back into the promised land. We observe the folly of kings and the division of Israel.

We anguish at the pride and rebellion of the Lord's people, particularly as they found themselves in the face of serious threat from Assyria and later from Babylon. We mourn the captivity of the ten northern tribes by Assyria and the captivity of Judah by Babylon. We marvel at the scattering of Israel throughout the world.

The ministry of the prophet Isaiah begins in 740 B.C., when Assyria is threatening Israel. The folly of Israel was that they looked to worldly power for protection from their enemies. Isaiah's challenging mission was to persuade them to look to the Lord and to trust in Him and in His salvation.

Isaiah's mission was bittersweet. Multitudes of the children of Israel continued in their rebellion and thus suffered the foretold fate of being destroyed or scattered to the four winds. At times, some heeded his call to repentance and were spared great destruction. Ultimately, the house of Israel was dispersed throughout the world to wait for the dawning of the new day of the preaching of the gospel.

Much of Isaiah's writing is Messianic prophecy—that Christ would condescend to come to our fallen world to teach of His Father's plan and to atone for the sins of the world. When He came in mortal ministry, Israel continued in their scattered state throughout the world, with some remaining remnants of the Jews centered at Jerusalem and under Roman rule. Even under their Roman oppressors, these Jews had garnered a high degree of religious freedom but had strayed from the pure intent of the law of Moses, which was to point them to Christ. They had missed the point of the law and the intended spiritual legacy of Israel. Paul taught, "For they are not all Israel, which are of Israel" (Rom. 9:6). Those who should have been the true shepherds of Israel had themselves gone wandering.

Nevertheless, the gospel message would go forth, and Christ would glean the honest in heart and secure them into His fold. His ministry would reach out to the Jews who would believe and to scattered Israel throughout the world. At the conclusion of His mortal ministry, He charged His Apostles, "Go ye therefore, and teach all nations, baptizing them in the name of the Father, and of the Son, and of the Holy Ghost" (Matt. 28:19). He Himself visited as promised: "And other sheep I have, which are not of this fold: them also I must bring, and they shall hear my voice; and there shall be one fold, and one shepherd" (John 10:16). After ministering to the Nephites, He then continued His visits to the other scattered tribes of Israel.

Present: We now live in one of the most glorious and adventurous times of all creation: the dispensation of the fullness of times. Since the time of the First Vision, the Lord has been spiritually gathering Israel. John the Revelator "saw another angel fly in the midst of heaven, having the everlasting gospel to preach unto them that dwell on the earth, and to every nation, kindred, and tongue, and people" (Rev. 14:6).

We live in a time of the official gathering of Israel as authorized and directed by God. In the newly dedicated Kirtland Temple, Joseph Smith and Oliver Cowdery experienced glorious visions and the restoration of priesthood keys. They testified, "After this vision closed, the heavens were again opened unto us; and Moses appeared before us, and committed unto us the keys of the gathering of Israel from the four parts of the earth, and the leading of the ten tribes from the land of the north" (D&C 110:11). Ours is a day when the Church has matured and has been organized in such a manner as to meet the challenge of seeking out the honest in heart from the four corners of the globe. We live in times of the literal fulfillment of much of Isaiah's prophetic vision.

Future: The blessed work of gathering will continue into the millennial reign of Christ and on to the time of the celestialization of the earth, all as foreseen by Isaiah and shown to us in his inspired writings. We will yet experience the day when the lost tribes of Israel will return to the gospel fold and once again embrace the covenant—when they will travel the highway of righteousness and renewal and be gathered to Christ: "And they who are in the north countries shall come in remembrance before the Lord; and their prophets shall hear his voice, and shall no longer stay themselves. . . . And the boundaries of the everlasting hills shall tremble at their presence. And there shall they fall down and be crowned with glory, even in Zion, by the hands of the servants of the Lord, even the children of Ephraim. And they shall be filled with songs of everlasting joy" (D&C 133:26, 31–33).

In the book of Isaiah we see his glorious vision of past, present, and future. His prophecies are awe inspiring. His message is the message of all prophets: he invites all people to Christ so that we may enjoy His peace and blessings and fully partake of the provision of His Atonement. That is why Isaiah's words are great—he invites us to renew our faith, repent of our sins, and prepare for eternal life with Heavenly Father.

ENDNOTES

1. Howard W. Hunter, "Fear Not, Little Flock," *1988–89 Devotional and Fireside Speeches* (Provo: Brigham Young University Press, 1989), 112.

2. Author's note: Not only did Isaiah speak "as touching all things," but he spoke of all things many times. There is much repetition in the writings of Isaiah. I invite you to not be troubled by it but to relax and enjoy his diligent and repeated efforts to teach gospel truth. Also, a helpful hint in studying Isaiah is to remember that chapter and verse designations are a modern invention to assist us in our attempts to think sequentially and logically about the myriad principles he teaches us. In Hebrew, Isaiah's writings are rendered basically as one long, continuous poem. In my writing about Isaiah, I am following the chapter and verse designations of the King James Bible to help give order to the text, but we are well served to consider the writings mostly as one long rendition.

3. Donald W. Parry, Jay A Parry, and Tina M. Peterson, *Understanding Isaiah* (Salt Lake City: Deseret Book Company, 1998).

4. Victor L. Ludlow, *Isaiah: Prophet, Seer, and Poet* (Salt Lake City: Deseret Book Company, 1982).

5. Author's note: The title Lord, written in small capital letters in the King James Bible, refers to Jehovah, or Jesus Christ.

6. David B. Guralnik, ed., *Webster's New World Dictionary of the American Language* (Englewood Cliffs, New Jersey: World-Publishing, 1970), 1564.

7. Gordon B. Hinckley, "The Great Millennial Year," *Ensign*, November 2000.

8. Brigham Young, *Discourses of Brigham Young*, comp. by John A. Widstoe (Salt Lake City: Deseret Book Company, 1954), 416.

9. Parry, Parry, Peterson, 29.

10. See the First Presidency and the Council of the Twelve Apostles of the Church of Jesus Christ of Latter-day Saints, "The Family: A Proclamation to the World." This proclamation was read by President Gordon B. Hinckley as part of his message at the general Relief Society meeting held September 23, 1995, in Salt Lake City, Utah.

11. Ibid.

12. Ibid.

13. Parry, Parry, Peterson, 48.

14. Ibid., 49.

15. Author's note: An ensign is a flag or banner, sometimes mounted on a pole and used as a rallying point for soldiers. When the ensign is raised in battle, the soldiers see it above the haze and smoke of war and rally, or gather, to it. An ensign is thus a symbol for gathering.

16. Elaine S. Dalton, "A Return to Virtue," *Ensign*, November, 2008, 78.

17. *Hymns*, no. 249.

18. See Eleanor Knowles, *Howard W. Hunter* (Salt Lake City, Utah: Deseret Book Company, 1994), 147.

19. Parry, Parry, Peterson, 80. "The sign provided to Ahaz was first fulfilled with the union of Isaiah and his wife and the birth of their son Maher-shalal-hash-baz. At least nine months would have passed since the conditions of the sign were given to Ahaz, for the text makes it clear that Isaiah 'went unto the prophetess' after the pronouncement of the sign."

20. Ibid., 80.

21. Ibid., 84.

22. Ibid., 86.

23. Bible Dictionary, s.v., "Lucifer."

24. Guralnik,1055.

25. Parry, Parry, Peterson, 120–21.

26. Joseph Smith Jr., *Teachings of the Prophet Joseph Smith*, comp. Joseph Fielding Smith (Salt Lake City: Deseret Book Company, 1972), 14.

27. Joseph Smith, Jr., *Lectures on Faith* (Salt Lake City: Deseret Book Company, 1835), 7:11.

28. "The Spirit of God," *Hymns*, no. 2.

29. Ludlow, 201.

30. Dallin H. Oaks, "Scripture Reading and Revelation," *Ensign*, January 1995.

31. Spencer W. Kimball, "Why Call Me Lord, Lord, and Do Not the Things Which I Say," *Ensign*, May 1975.

32. Joseph Smith, Jr., *History of the Church of Jesus Christ of Latter-day Saints*, ed. B. H. Roberts (Salt Lake City: The Church of Jesus Christ of Latter-day Saints, 1912) 6:322.

33. James E. Faust, "Eternity Lies before Us," *Ensign*, May 1997. (Also quoted by Heber J. Grant, in Conference Report, Apr. 1921, 211.)

34. Jay M. Todd, "President Howard W. Hunter: Fourteenth President of the Church," *Ensign*, July 1994, 4–5.

35. Author's note: Isaiah's words, in dualistic prophecy, may have application to various time periods. It is interesting to consider the modern effects of the construction of the Aswan dam. This disruption of the natural flow of the Nile has caused tremendous loss of natural silt and fertilizer to the downstream ecosystem, has buried much treasure of Egypt, and has displaced many people from the formerly fertile areas to more dry and arid regions. In a sense, the Egyptians have been against the Egyptians.

36. Parry, Parry, Peterson, 182.

37. Author's note: The word *chiasmus* comes from the Greek letter equivalent to *X*. Chiasmus is a literary form wherein multiple thoughts or clauses are placed parallel to each other in a reversal of structure. Imagine clauses written as A, B, and C and then reversed, with matching thoughts as C, B, A. Generally the more powerful or more intense ideas will appear in the second half of chiastic passages. Chiasmus is found throughout the Bible and the Book of Mormon and was particularly popular in both Greek and Latin literature.

For example:

A. The Lord directs Jonah to preach to the wicked Ninevites (Jonah 1:1–2).

  B. Jonah sins, not wanting Nineveh to be saved (1:3, 9–11).

    C. Jonah repents and the Lord saves him (1:17; 2).

    C. The Ninevites repent and the Lord saves them (3).

  B. Jonah sins, not wanting Nineveh to be saved (4:1–5).

A. The Lord inquires of Jonah: "Should not I spare Ninevah?" (4:9–11).

38. Author's note: There are as many passages *before* Jonah 2:8 as there are *after*. This center point of the chiasmus is the focal point of the message of the book. The story of Jonah is much more than a fish story!

39. Guralnik, 1139 and 1289, respectively.

40. Dennis L. Largey, *Book of Mormon Reference Companion* (Salt Lake City: Deseret Book Company, 2003) 674.

41. Parry, Parry, Peterson, 202. (Citing *Times and Seasons*, Nauvoo, Ill., 5 (1844):7488).

42. In Conference Report, Apr. 1967, 84–85; see also *Improvement Era*, June 1967, 80.

43. Joseph Smith, Jr., *History of the Church*, 5:423.

44. Joseph Smith, Jr., *TPJS*, 348; emphasis removed.

45. Lucile C. Tate, *LeGrand Richards: Beloved Apostle* (Salt Lake City: Bookcraft, Inc., 1982), 134–35.

46. Ibid., 132.

47. Joseph Smith, Jr., *History of the Church*, 1:20.

48. Spencer W. Kimball, "The False Gods We Worship," *Ensign*, June 1976.

49. Gordon B. Hinckley, "The Times in Which We Live," *Ensign*, November 2001.

50. Anne R. McDonald and Gaylen Young, "Descendants Honor Faithful 'Wee Granny,'" *Church News of the Church of Jesus Christ of Latter-day Saints*, Saturday, July 28, 2001.

51. Ibid.

52. Bible Dictionary, s.v., "Repentance."

53. James E. Faust, "Eternity Lies before Us," *Ensign*, May 1997. (Also quoted by Heber J. Grant in Conference Report, Apr. 1921, 211; see also Wilford Woodruff, in the Utah Pioneers (1880), 23.)

54. *Journal of Discourses*, 11:372.

55. Parry, Parry, Peterson, 305–6.

56. Bruce R. McConkie, *A New Witness for the Articles of Faith* (Salt Lake City: Deseret Book Company, 1985), 521.

57. Author's note: I first became aware of this analogy via a teaching-video portrayal of the training of Arabian horses produced by the Church

Educational System for the Old Testament seminary course in July of 1991. (Old Testament Media: *Trust in the Lord*).

58. William W. Hallo and K. Lawson Younger, Jr., eds., *The Context of Scripture, Vol 2: Monumental Inscriptions from the Biblical World* (Boston: Brill, 2000), 302–3.

59. Author's note: The following verse has sometimes tickled my funny bone: "When they arose early in the morning, behold they were all dead corpses." It sounds as though they "woke up dead." I have tried, on occasion, to share this humorous insight with my students, but they always seem to spoil it by pointing out that the antecedent to the first "they" is the remnant of Judah and the second "they" the dead Assyrians, rather than the camp of Judah. Oh well.

60. Lucy Mack Smith, *History of Joseph Smith by His Mother, Lucy Mack Smith*, ed. Preston Nibley (Salt Lake City: Bookcraft, 1958), 309–310.

61. Author's note: The events of the annihilation of the armies of King Sennacherib discussed in chapters 36 and 37 occurred in 701 B.C.—rather late in the administration of Hezekiah. As we see here in chapter 38, the Lord is promising to *yet* "defend this city" against the Assyrians. We therefore conclude that the events of chapters 38 and 39 occurred *before* the events of chapters 36 and 37. Isaiah was likely less concerned about chronology in his writing than we are.

62. Joseph Smith Jr., *TPJS*, 241.

63. Jonathan Keates, *Handel: The Man and His Music* (London: Hamish Hamilton, 1985), 243.

64. Tim Slover, *Messiah: The Little-Known Story of Handel's Beloved Oratorio* (Sandy, Utah: Silverleaf Press, 2007), 39–40.

65. Author's note: Isaiah's prophesies of the latter one-third of his writings are some of his most moving and profound. While the first two-thirds of the book seem weighted with the Lord's justice interspersed with His tender mercy, the latter third seems heavy with tender mercy interspersed with justice. And of course, we acknowledge that our Savior's true character, made manifest through His Atonement, is a constant, perfect blend of His justice and mercy. Only in our limited, mortal view do we sometimes try to unduly separate the two.

66. Bruce C. and Marie K. Hafen, *The Belonging Heart: The Atonement and Relationships with God and Family* (Salt Lake City: Deseret Book Company, 1994), 79.

67. B. H. Roberts, *A Comprehensive History of the Church* (Provo, UT: Brigham Young University Press, 1965), 4:89.

68. Author's note: These four servant songs are found in Isaiah 42:1–4; 49:1–6; 50:4–9; and 52:13–53:12.

69. Ludlow, 360.

70. Edward L. Kimball and Andrew E. Kimball, Jr., *Spencer W. Kimball* (Salt Lake City: Bookcraft, 1977), 334.

71. Gordon B. Hinckley, "Do Ye Even So to Them," *Ensign*, December 1991, 5.

72. The concept of "Israel" can be confusing at times. Victor Ludlow helps us understand the term and some specific application to this chapter: "The name *Israel* has acquired a variety of connotations over the centuries. A brief review of the three major applications of the term *Israelite* will be helpful in understanding its different meanings in Isaiah: 1. *'Blood' Israelite.* Any descendant of the house of Israel (Jacob) now scattered throughout the earth. The most recognizable body of blood Israelites are the Jews. 2. *'Land' Israelite.* Anyone who inhabits the area known as Israel. This area has also been called Canaan, Samaria, Judea, the Holy Land, Palestine, etc. (The modern citizens of this land are identified by modern writers as 'Israelis,' and not 'Israelites.') 3. *'Covenant' Israelite.* Anyone who accepts the God and covenants of Israel. Today this term applies specifically to members of The Church of Jesus Christ of Latter-day Saints. So, when Isaiah addresses 'Israel,' he may be including any one of these categories. Usually, though, he is speaking to either blood or covenant Israel. Given the context of Isaiah 43, it appears that the Lord is addressing covenant Israel, those whom he has called by name as his peculiar people for his own glory." Ludlow, 363–64.

73. See David McCullough, *The Great Bridge: The Epic Story of the Building of the Brooklyn Bridge* (New York: Simon & Schuster, 1972).

74. Wendell Berry, *Sex, Economy, Freedom, & Community* (New York: Pantheon Books, 1993), 103; quoted in Neal A. Maxwell, "Our Creator's Cosmos," CES Conference on Doctrine and Covenants and Church History, Brigham Young University, August 13, 2002.

75. Flavius Josephus, *Josephus, Complete Works: The Antiquities of the Jews*, trans. William Whiston (Grand Rapids, Michigan: Kregel Publications, 1974), 228.

76. C. S. Lewis, *Mere Christianity* (New York: Macmillan, 1960), 61.

77. Author's note: We, of course, have great love for the Bible but recognize that there are some errors in translation. The statement that the Lord "creates evil" is a mistranslation. This thought is repeated in Amos: "Shall there be evil in a city, and the Lord hath not done it" (3:6). This error is corrected by the Joseph Smith Translation of Amos 3:6, where he substitutes *known* for *done*. Also, the Book of Mormon adds clarity: "For I say unto you that whatsoever is good cometh from God, and whatsoever is evil cometh from the devil" (Alma 5:40); "Wherefore, all things which are good cometh of God; and that which is evil cometh of the devil" (Moro. 7:12). How blessed we are by continuing revelation!

78. See "The Family: A Proclamation to the World."

79. Joseph Smith, Jr., *TPJS*, 304.

80. Spencer W. Kimball, *The Miracle of Forgiveness* (Salt Lake City: Bookcraft, 1969), 270.

81. Bruce R. McConkie, *Doctrinal New Testament Commentary* (Salt Lake City: Bookcraft, 1975), 1:439.

82. *Gospel Teaching and Learning: A Handbook for Teachers and Leaders in Seminaries and Institutes of Religion* (Salt Lake City: The Church of Jesus Christ of Latter-day Saints, 2012) section 1.1.

83. See *Old Testament Student Manual, Genesis–2 Samuel* (Salt Lake City: The Church of Jesus Christ of Latter-day Saints, 1980), 74–80.

84. Joseph Smith, Jr., *TPJS*, 255–56.

85. Author's note: This was taught to us by President Ed Pinegar when he served as the president of the Missionary Training Center in Provo, Utah, while I served as a branch president there. At the time, I wrote the statement in the margin of my scriptures.

86. Bible Dictionary, s.v., "Isaiah."

87. *History of the Church*, 6:554.

88. *Nora's Christmas Gift*, directed by Michael McLean (Salt Lake City: Bonneville Media Communications, 1989), film.

89. Bruce R. McConkie, *The Mortal Messiah* (Salt Lake City: Deseret Book Company, 1981), 4:354.

90. *Journal of Discourses*, 11:372.

91. Author's note: I recently learned that the term *benchmark* originated in the cobbler's trade. The cobbler would have his customer place his foot on a bench and then outline it as a pattern for the cut of the shoes.

This seems an appropriate term in discussing how payment of tithes, fasting, and observance of the Sabbath are fairly good patterns or indicators of a person's gospel commitments.

92. Ludlow, 492.

93. Joseph Smith Jr., *TPJS*, 307–8.

94. Author's note: I have much enjoyed reading *The Window Maker*, published by Allyn House Publishing in Nauvoo. It is an inspirational autobiographical account of Brother Allen's preparation and work on the temple. At the time of this writing, visitors to Nauvoo may see a display of the construction of the windows in a corner of the Allyn House gift shop—Brother Allen's family business. Often visitors are blessed by having Brother Allen there personally to tell of his work and experiences.

95. Office of the Governor State of Missouri: Proclamation, Jefferson City, Missouri, April 4, 2012, http://www.mormonnewsroom.org/article/mormons-kansas-city-missouri-temple-governors-proclamations#C1.

96. Parry, Parry, Peterson, 540.

97. See McConkie, *The Mortal Messiah*, 1:347.

98. In James Strong, *The New Strong's Exhaustive Concordance of the Bible* (Nashville, TN: Thomas Nelson Publishers, 1990), 111.

99. Parry, Parry, Peterson, 547.

100. McConkie, *DNTC*, 3:458.

101. Bible Dictionary, s.v., "Idumea."

102. Parry, Parry, Peterson, 543.

103. Ibid., 562.

104. Howard W. Hunter, "Exceeding Great and Precious Promises," *Ensign*, November 1994, 8.

105. *The Life and Teachings of Jesus and His Apostles* (Salt Lake City: The Church of Jesus Christ of Latter-day Saints, 1979), 172.

106. Carlos E. Asay, "The Oath and Covenant of the Priesthood," *Ensign*, November 1985.

ABOUT THE AUTHOR

REG CHRISTENSEN AND HIS WIFE, Carol, live in Waunakee, Wisconsin. They are the parents of seven and grandparents of twelve. Reg recently retired as the Church Educational System coordinator for the Green Bay, Madison, and Wausau, Wisconsin stakes and as director of the institute of religion adjacent to the University of Wisconsin in Madison. He began his CES career in Lehi, Utah, where he taught released-time seminary for twenty-three years. Reg has enjoyed a lifetime of church service as a missionary, Young Men president, bishopric counselor, high councilor, stake executive secretary, branch president, bishop, high priest group leader, ward seminary teacher, and ward clerk. He enjoys reading, traveling, exploring nature, bird watching, and being with family and friends.